MOSCOW UNDER STALINIST RULE, 1931–34

Moscow under Stalinist Rule, 1931–34

Nobuo Shimotomai
*Professor, Hosei University
Tokyo*

St. Martin's Press   New York

© Nobuo Shimotomai 1991

All rights reserved. For information write:
Scholarly and Reference Division,
St. Martin's Press, Inc., 175 Fifth Avenue,
New York, N.Y. 10010

First published in the United States of America in 1991

Printed in Hong Kong

ISBN 0–312–06212–5

Library of Congress Cataloging-in-Publication Data
Shimotomai, Nobuo, 1948–
Moscow under Stalinist rule, 1931–34 / Nobuo Shimotomai.
p.   cm.
Includes bibliographical references and indexes.
ISBN 0–312–06212–5
1. Moscow (R.S.F.S.R.)—Politics and government.   2. Stalin, Joseph, 1879–1953.   3. Moscow Region (R.S.F.S.R.)—Economic conditions.   I. Title.
DK601.S445   1991
947'.3120842—dc20   91–9083
                                                     CIP

Contents

List of Maps, Figures and Tables   vii

Preface   viii

Glossary and Abbreviations   xi

1   Moscow: History, Geography, and Society

    1.1   History   1
    1.2   Geography   4
    1.3   Society   7
    1.4   The June plenum resolution on Moscow   10

2   Moscow Party Organisation and Membership

    2.1   Party Membership   13
    2.2   The party purge (*chistka*)   16
    2.3   The control commission and Party sanctions   21
    2.4   Party education in Moscow   23

3   Decision-Making in the Party

    3.1   Party leadership   27
    3.2   The Party apparatus   36
    3.3   The 1934 reorganisation   42

4   The Party at the District Level

    4.1   Characteristics of different districts   45
    4.2   Control of the district by MK and MGK   45
    4.3   The Frunze and Stalin districts: two case studies   50

5   The Governmental Process in Moscow

    5.1   The soviet as unit of government   55
    5.2   The Oblispolkom Presidium and Mossoviet Presidium   55
    5.3   The sections   59
    5.4   Planning: system and practice   60

6   The Party and Social Problems

    6.1   Law and order   64

6.2	The internal passport system	67
6.3	Education	68
6.4	The problem of waifs and strays	69

7 Industry in Moscow

7.1	Party leadership structure and industry	72
7.2	Heavy industry: problems of growth	75
7.3	The Moscow Party and light industry	78

8 Transport and Energy

8.1	Railway transport	86
8.2	The fuel and energy problem	89

9 Agricultural Policy

9.1	Kolkhoz agriculture	96
9.2	Party leadership of campaigns	100
9.3	*Politotdel* and agricultural control	103

10 Management of the Municipal Economy

10.1	Moscow city planning	109
10.2	Water supply	111
10.3	Housing policy	112
10.4	City transport	118
10.5	Building the Metro	121

11 Supply and Shortage

11.1	The struggle for supplies	125
11.2	Emergency supplies: rabbits, fish and vegetables	127
11.3	The role of the free (*Kolkhoz*) market	132
11.4	Factory supply and rationing	134
11.5	Public catering	137

12 Conclusions — 140

Notes — 145

Bibliography — 172

Name Index — 175

Subject Index — 177

List of Maps, Figures and Tables

Maps

1.1	Moscow Region, 1929–35	6
4.1	Moscow City	46

Figures

1.1	Administrative Subdivision of the Moscow Region in 1931	4
11.1	Price of 1 kg beef in the Bazaar, 1932–33	134
11.2	Price of 1 kg rye bread in the bazaar, 1932–33	135

Tables

1.2	Population Dynamics 1887–1933 of Moscow Region, 1897–1933	7
1.3	Social Composition, City of Moscow	8
2.1	Membership Trends in the Moscow Party Organisation, 1928–35	14
2.2	Occupational Classification of Party Members, 1 January, 1932	15
2.3	Party Members in Moscow according to year of entry, 1 January, 1932	15
2.4	Reasons stated for Expulsion from the Party in Moscow	16
2.5	Party Membership in the Frunzew District, 1931–34	23
2.6	The Trend of Moscow Party Membership, 1933–38	24
3.1	The MK Bureau in 1932–34	28
3.2	The MGK Bureau in 1932–34	30
4.1	District Committee Secretaries in Moscow City, 1931–34	47
5.1	Mossoviet Presidium, March 1933	58

Preface

This study looks at political and social processes in Moscow, at both regional and city level, in a crucial period of Moscow's history, 1931–34. Moscow was one of the world's biggest cities, and since 1918 the seat of Lenin's new government and of a world revolutionary and labour movement. It was the hub not only of Soviet politics but also of the Soviet economy.

Some insight into the Soviet system in general should therefore be obtainable by analysing the Moscow Region as a microcosm. The period of 1931–34 has been chosen because these were years of great transformation in Moscow, and also for the Soviet Union in general. Traditional light industries were being overshadowed by developing heavy industry. Grandiose projects were getting under way, while in the countryside coercive collectivisation was resulting in hardship and even famine. Significant cultural change was accompanied by attrition of much of the older urban structures.

This period was one of severe shortage and crisis, following the industrialisation and collectivisation drives. The First Five-Year Plan officially ended in 1932, but it was not until the 17th party congress in 1934 that the shape of the Second Five-Year Plan was decided. In this confused situation the working class, much of it recently recruited from the countryside, struggled on in acute hardship, taking what comfort it could from official reasssurances. It was from the general turmoil of this period that there emerged the basic outline of the political and social structures that would shape the Soviet system for half a century and constitute the mould in which modern Soviet society has been formed.

Our existing knowledge of Soviet local government under Stalinist rule has been based on Merle Fainsod's classic analysis of Smolensk region (west of the Moscow region), published in 1958, and also on Prof. Taniuchi's work (available only in Japanese). The former, although its totalitarian model is perhaps obsolescent, contained an analysis that has been broadly accepted. The lack of other accessible sources, as well as the neglect of this period by Soviet historians, enhanced the reputation of this study. Nevertheless, Fainsod's 'Smolensk model' may hardly be applicable universally to other regions of the USSR. Smolensk was rather unusual in that it remained predominantly an agricultural area even during the industrialisation drive of the 1930s. Industry was of minor importance and the local leaders faced industrial tasks that were comparatively simple and produced few surprises. It was therefore quite natural that Fainsod paid scant attention to politics and decision-making at the city level.

In the Moscow Region it was different. This was a region where huge heavy and light industries, and administrative, commercial and cultural institutions were concentrated, and its social composition reflected a pattern of development quite at variance with that of rural areas, and even with that of the newly-industrialising cities. This meant that the Moscow party and government faced novel and complex tasks: urban planning, urban transport development, housing and food supply were among the activities that were quite different in Moscow compared to more rural centres like Smolensk. In this respect, Moscow was not perhaps representative, though some elements would become important elsewhere in the future.

Even though urban workers at the time were severely restricted in their rights, they were by no means unfailingly passive. Intellectuals and technical specialists formed distinct social strata, and the political leadership had to take their interests into account even though, as in the case of the Metrovick affair of 1933, coercion was a favoured method of control. Different types of social structure and social interactions produce correspondingly different political cultures and ambience.

This study traces such developments, concentrating mainly on the bureaucratic and political structure of the Moscow region (*oblast'*) and city as they strove to cope with a rapidly-changing situation. It also focuses on the process of creating and implementing policies, interactions between various institutions and elites, and relations between the central power and Moscow. In the different sectors of the economy, the degree of involvement by institutions and authorities varied. In some matters, central authority overruled local leaders, but in others the local leaders could take the initiative. Even in these formative Stalin years, ordinary citizens could create a 'feedback' in the form of unrest, as the textile workers did in 1932. Policy formation in Moscow occurred partly in the various commissions that broke through institutional boundaries by inviting specialist opinions, thereby diminishing the role of the formal power-holders. It is also worth noting that in urban areas such as Moscow the soviets were more active. The influential personal roles of Kaganovich, Khrushchev, Bulganin and Malenkov will be described in this context.

This was a time of great transformations. The destruction of historical legacies like the Sukharev Tower or the Cathedral of Our Saviour was followed by the construction of factories, houses, the Metro, and the Moscow-Volga Canal. Young people, especially those of worker or poor peasant origin, were recruited into the newly-opened higher technical schools. The ruination of rural areas during collectivisation was in stark contrast to the changing face of the city.

Meanwhile, long-running ideological disputes affected the line of development. Moscow had been the powerbase of the 'rightists', led by Uglanov until 1928. His gradualist approach was followed by a sharp turn to the left under Molotov, and, above all, Bauman, who would also be condemned by the party authorities. Kaganovich's appointment as Moscow party leader in April 1930 was closely related to this problem of political reliability in Moscow: significantly, Ryutin, a leading anti-stalinist in 1932, has been a Moscow district committee secretary in the 1920s.

The main sources are published handbooks, statistical reports and local and national newspapers and journals, some of which are available only in Soviet libraries. Use has also been made of some restricted-circulation party documents. Archival materials have been consulted for some sections.

Many people helped in the writing of this book. Thanks are due to the members of CREES (University of Birmingham; Director Prof. Amann), where the author agreeably spent almost two years in 1983–85. Above all, thanks are particularly due to Prof. R. W. Davies, without whose advice and constant encouragement this book would never have been completed, and whose seminar provided the author with a new and knowledgeable approach to this difficult area of research. S. Wheatcroft, J. Barber, J. Haslam, A. Rees, J. Cooper and C. Merridale, all of CREES, were stimulating sources of information and insight. Mrs. B. Bennett and Mrs. C. Trollope in different ways helped in the writing. At the final stages, Professor T. Colton of Toronto (now Harvard) University gave valuable comments. The enormous transformation involved in the conversion of the original text from Tokyo-style to Birmingham-style English was undertaken by J. N. Westwood. Last but not least, thanks are due to Prof. Taniuchi, who provided so much guidance in the study of this field.

Institutional help, much appreciated, came from the Nitobe Fellowship of the International House of Japan, the Japan Foundation, Birmingham University, the Kennan Institute, the Institute of Oriental Studies in Moscow, Seikei University and Hosei University in Tokyo.

NOBUO SHIMOTOMAI

Glossary and Abbreviations

Apparatchiki	Full-time Party officials
APU	Architectural Planning Administration
Arplan	Commission for Architecture and Planning
Avktokachki	Automatic rockers
Chistka	Purge
Domtrest	Housing trust
Gorodskoe khozyaistvo	Municipal economy
Gorkom	City Committee of the Party
Gorispolkom	City Soviet executive committee
Gorono	City education department
Gosplan	State Planning Commission
Ispolkom	Executive committee of Soviet
Kolkhoz	Collective farm
Komispol	Soviet's implementation control agency
KOMVUZ	Communist Higher Education Institute
Knyaz'	Feudal prince
Kustar'	Handicraft or artisan
MGK	Moscow City Committee
MK	Moscow Region Committee
Mosgorzhilsoiuz	Moscow city housing union
Moskanalstroi	Moscow canal construction
Mosnarpit	Moscow public catering
Mosryb	Moscow fish trust
Mosvodoprovod	Moscow water-supply trust
Moszhiltrest	Moscow Housing Trust
MSPO	Moscow Consumer Cooperative Union
NEP	New Economic Policy
NK	People's Commissariat
NK Trud	People's Commissariat of Labour
NK Tyazhprom	People's Commissariat of Heavy Industry
NK Legprom	People's Commissariat of Light Industry
NK Put'	People's Commissariat of Ways of communication (Transport)

Nomenklatura	Nomenclature (list of appointments)
Obkom	Regional party committee
Oblast'	Region
Oblispolkom	Regional executive committee
OGPU	Central State Political Administration (i.e. political police)
Opros	Decision-making by correspondence or oral agreement *in absentia*
ORS	Workers' Supplies Department
Partorggrup	Party organizers group
Podmaster'e	Senior worker
Politburo	Politburo Bureau of the Central Committee
Politotdel	Political department
Promakademiya	Industrial academy
Pyaterka	Five-person committee
Rabfak	Workers school (providing training for entry to higher education)
Raikom	District party committee
Raiispolkom	District executive committee
Raiony	Districts
RzhSKt	Workers' house-construction association
Seksiya	Section
Shefstvo	Patronage
Sovnarkom	Council of People's Commissars
Sovpartshkoly	Soviet Party schools
STO	Council of Labour and Defence
Treugol'nik	Triangle or three-member group of an enterprise (Party secretary, Manager and chair of Trade Union)
Uchastkovie Kommendanty	Area Supervisors
VKhBO	Cotton Association
VSNITO	All-Union Scientific-Technical Association
VNSKh	Supreme Council of the National Economy
Vydvizhentsy	Promoted workers
ZhATK	Rented housing cooperative association
ZRK	Restricted-membership workers' co-operative

1 Moscow: History, Geography, and Society

1.1 HISTORY

Moscow's history goes back to the twelfth century; in the fifteenth century it became the capital of the Russian state and retained that status until it relinquished it to St Petersburg in 1712. Thus its history is closely tied to the development of Russian culture, government and economy.

Together with St Petersburg, Moscow dominated Russian industrial development. The textile industry had its beginnings there in the late eighteenth century and has remained strong ever since. In the latter half of the nineteenth century, Moscow became a major centre of the expanding railway network. Trade and commerce occupied a commensurately important place. Culturally, Moscow was the centre of the orthodox and other churches. Urbanisation resulted in the city's population rising from 602 000 in 1871 to 1 617 700 in 1912.

The working class, with its burgeoning political life had become a major feature of the Moscow scene by the end of the nineteenth century. By 1890 there were 667 factories in Moscow, employing 77 000 workers, and at the beginning of the twentieth century there were more than 120 000 workers.[1]

In 1885 there was a big strike at the Morozov establishment in Orekhovo-Zuevo (Moscow Province); this is regarded by many historians as the beginning of the workers' movement in Russia. Although the first active workers' movement was organised by Populists, the latter were soon followed by Russian Marxist groups. The Marxists took root in Moscow in the last two decades of the nineteenth century.

In the 1905 Revolution the workers for the first time organised a soviet of workers' deputies, which they revived after the February 1917 Revolution. Meanwhile, the working population grew, and by 1917 Moscow factory workers numbered about 187 000, mostly young and to some degree introduced what Koenker called a 'new urban youth culture', although many of them retained strong ties with the rural areas.[2] In any event, radicalisation of young workers would be both a cause and consequence of the 1917 Revolution.

In Moscow, unlike Petrograd, it took several days of armed struggle for the revolutionary masses to win power. The Moscow Bolsheviks were led by moderates like Rykov and Nogin. Young radicals such as Bukharin and Osinskii were also active,[3] and were energetic members of the 'left communist' trend, which advocated a revolutionary war against German militarism in opposition to Lenin's effort to secure peace with Germany.

In March 1918 Moscow became the capital of Soviet Russia when the Party Central Committee and the Sovnarkom (Council of People's Commissars) moved in from Petrograd. In 1919 the Comintern (Communist International) was founded in Moscow. During the period of War Communism from mid-1918 to March 1921 the city was the nucleus of Soviet power and sent thousands of young workers to the front and into the countryside.

Despite the perilous civil war situation, the Moscow Party organisation was divided by dissident tendencies, and several major disputes occurred. The Ignatov group, the Democratic Centralists and the Workers Opposition all challenged the orthodox line. At the end of 1920, the role of the trade unions divided the Central Committee; several factions, including Lenin's 'Group of Ten', debated the place of the trade unions in the 'dictatorship of the proletariat'. The Moscow Party committee (MK henceforth) at one time favoured Trotsky-Bukharin's line.[4] Even after the introduction of New Economic Policy (NEP) and the sharp condemnation of deviationists at the Xth Party Congress in March 1921, the strong tradition of grassroots radicalism lived on in Moscow.

NEP brought a swift economic recovery; industrial output between 1921 and 1925 increased some five times, while the working population almost doubled.[5] Agriculture was the main concern of NEP, and the policy of 'revitalising the [rural] soviets' was important in this. This pro-agriculture attitude of the leadership was accompanied by the defeat of Zinoviev's 'New Opposition' of 1925, which criticised the pro-agricultural, or what was called 'pro-kulak', line of Stalin and Bukharin. Zinoviev's close ally Kamenev lost his chairmanship of the Moscow soviet after the XIVth Party Congress of December 1925. This signified the victory of Uglanov, first secretary from 1924, advocate of the Party's pro-agriculture tendency and eventually a supporter of Bukharin's line. Moscow became the stronghold of Rightist tendencies within the Party. This was in conformity with the predominating interests of the local textile and other light industries. More than half of all Russia's textile workers lived in the Moscow region, and Uglanov identified himself with their interests when he stated:

As secretary of the Party committee for Moscow, where the textile industry occupies an important position, I have to put forward the problem of the textile industry ... I must argue, exert pressure, and make a row to get money from the appropriate Soviet supreme organs or from the Central Committee.[6]

A decisive change came about when general secretary Stalin, who had supported the pro-agriculture and pro-light-industry policy against the 'super-industrialisation' proposals of Trotsky and the Left opposition, changed his stance and supported the industrialisation drive at the end of the 1920s. The technological level was low, and the USSR badly needed to industrialise. Some economic organisations, notably VSNKh (Supreme Council of the National Economy), responsible for industry, demanded a faster tempo of industrial investment. This was also necessitated by the worsening international situation which culminated in the fiasco of the Chinese revolution and the break in Anglo-Soviet relations in 1927.

In turn, this implied a change of agricultural policy. The grain procurement crisis of 1928 was the real turning point, and extraordinary measures to collect grain became the main weapon in place of NEP's market mechanism. There was strong discontent among the peasantry, while that part of the working class, including the Donbass miners, which had strong ties with the countryside, wavered. Industrial disputes became keener.

The Moscow leaders had special reason to criticise this policy change, for the local importance of agriculture and textile industries demanded moderation both in industrialisation and in relations with the peasantry. After the Stalinist-Bukharinist coalition collapsed, the Moscow Party organisation, together with the ideological apparatus and the trade unions, provided the targets for Stalinist party officials (*apparatchiki*) intent on undermining the Right's power-base. Between the summer and autumn of 1928 there was a struggle between Uglanov's supporters and Molotov, who had been despatched by the Central Committee. By November 1928 Uglanov and his adherents, including Ryutin, had lost their positions in the Moscow Party organisation, and Molotov and Bauman became the new leaders.[7]

In 1929 the MK leadership passed into the hand of Bauman, who had specialised in agriculture at the central level. By the administrative reorganisation of the Russian Republic (RFSFR), Moscow region (*oblast'*) was created from neighbouring regions. By the end of 1929, radicalist tendencies had won, and the collectivisation policy was suddenly adopted at both the central and local level. The 'liquidation of the kulaks as a class' commenced at the beginning of 1930.[8]

FIGURE 1.1 *Administrative subdivision of the Moscow region in 1931*

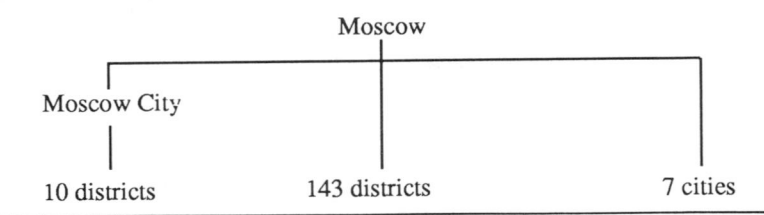

But the sharp and unprepared policy change deepened the crisis faced by the Soviet economy. Early in 1930, Bauman's policy in Moscow of collectivising more than the centrally-prescribed percentage led to 'Potemkin-village' collectivisation – on paper only. After Stalin's letter of March 1930, which ascribed responsibility for 'excesses' to local leaders, the Moscow kolkhozes collapsed and Bauman was sent to another post in Central Asia.

Stalin's close colleague Kaganovich was appointed Moscow leader in April 1930. A tough and orthodox Stalinist, Kaganovich condemned excesses by 'leftists'. His policy, essentially, was to continue existing activities, but with modifications here and there. Collectivisation was resumed, several years being taken to complete the task. A 'Cultural Revolution' was begun, involving the destruction of historical monuments, which included the Cathedral of Our Saviour (5 December, 1931) and the Chapel of the Iberian Virgin. Church bells had already been silenced in January 1930.[9] From 500 churches at the time of the Revolution, the number diminished to 143.[10] New factories were built and old ones reconstructed. Moscow was remoulded into a city of metal and engineering industries, with textiles and light industry taking second place. By 1931 the general outline of the future Moscow had been established. One journalist commented:

> The Soviet Union is a country of rapidly vanishing landmarks. Anyone who visits Moscow at the present time, after several years' absence, will be struck by the changes in the physical appearance of the city.[11]

1.2 GEOGRAPHY

The Moscow oblast', or region, was organised in 1929 from the previous Moscow, Ryazan', Tula and Tver' provinces and part of the Kaluga province. This new region would be eventually divided into the Moscow, Tula and Ryazan' regions in 1937; Tver' (after 1931 Kalinin) was already detached in 1935. Between 1929 and 1935 this region (excluding Moscow city, which had a somewhat independent status, and other cities) was divided into some 145 raiony, or districts. At 151 741 square km. the region's territory was vast, almost as large as England and Wales.[12]

The Moscow region at the beginning of 1931 accounted for about seven per cent of the territory and population of the USSR. The proportion of city dwellers was notably high, and the region was responsible for roughly one quarter of the USSR's industrial output.[13] At this time Moscow city was administratively separated from the region, becoming semi-independent of the latter. Party, soviet and other organisations were formally separated by the middle of 1931. However, this quasi-autonomous status was very limited, because the Moscow region leader, Kaganovich, was also the city leader, and both leaderships sometimes held joint meetings to solve common problems.

Ryazan', the area in the south-east of the Moscow region, was typically agrarian, with more than 90 per cent of its working population being engaged in agriculture. This was also an area of *kustar'* (handicraft) industry; even the workers were largely recruited from the peasantry. Industry was related to agriculture, with Ryazselmash, a typical factory, producing agricultural machinery. There was also some coal mining, centred on Skopin.

Tula was in the south of the region and was an agricultural area. Tula was a large town, and had an important metallurgical and weapons industry: its traditional samovar production was no longer dominant. Like Kaluga, Tula had also a coal industry.[14] The agricultural population was very dense in the southern part of the region; and there were 30 districts in the Moscow region, mainly in Ryazan' and Tula, where more than 90 per cent of the population was engaged in agriculture, which was orientated mainly towards grain and potatoes. From Kaluga (also included in the Moscow region) through Tula to Ryazhsk there was a mining belt known as the Sub-Moscow Coalfield.

Tver', north of Moscow, was renamed Kalinin after the Soviet president in November 1931. Integrated in the Moscow region, it was an area of textile industries that were partly dependent on the flax-growing of its extreme western parts. In 1935, however, the area was reorganised into a new Kalinin region, embracing parts of the Moscow, Leningrad and Western regions.

The city of Moscow had developed radially, from the Kremlin in the centre. There were three major rings (the boulevards, the Sadovoe

Chaussee, and Kamer-Kollezhskii Val) which had the effect of dividing it into four concentric zones, with the fourth zone, beyond the Kamer-Kollezhskii Val, expanding after the Revolution. The population of each zone roughly doubled between 1912 and 1933. There were ten districts at the beginning of the 1930s, and these are described in Chapter 4.[15]

Around the city there developed a suburban horticulture, providing fruit and vegetables. The development of this area was tightly controlled, and there were only a few industries, including some textile works and the Lyubertsy agricultural machinery factory. There were also some important

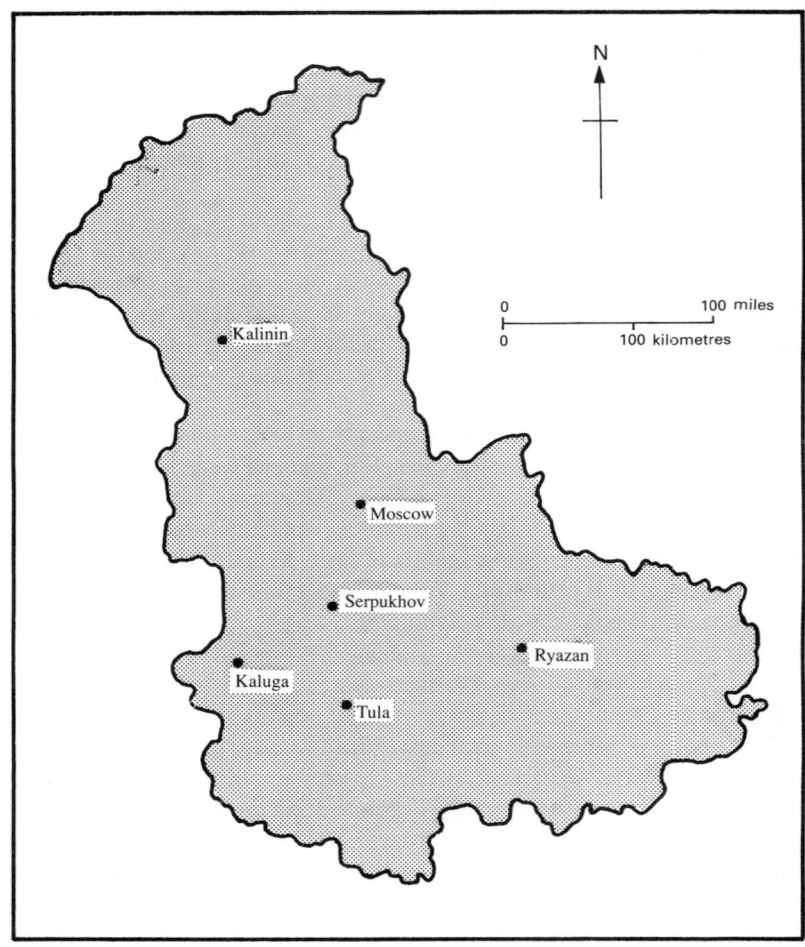

MAP 1.1 *Moscow Region*

towns in the outer suburban areas: two thirds of the region's towns and urban workers' settlements were here. Serpukhov, south of the city, and Orekhovo-Zuevo to the east were well-known as textile towns. Other towns were developing to the east and south, including Mytishchi (railway car-building), Shatura (peat), and Kashira (electric power).[16]

1.3 SOCIETY

The population of the Moscow region was 11 359 300 in 1931, of which Moscow city accounted for about 2 781 300; the city population rose to 3 416 500 in 1933. In 1933, almost a quarter of the population lived in Moscow city and three quarters in the rural areas of the region outside the city. In 1931 almost 61.6 per cent of the region's population was engaged in some kind of work, while 39.4 per cent were dependents. Among the working population, 39.9 per cent were classed as workers, while 25.9 per cent were employees (office workers), 5.6 per cent were in *kustar'* (industry) and another 5.6 per cent were students.[17]

The tempo of urbanisation was fast, and the rural population shrank from two thirds (66.9 per cent) in 1926 to just over half (53.2 per cent) in 1933. This high degree of urbanisation, however, lagged behind that of the Leningrad region (50.5 against 55.7 per cent in 1933). Urban population as a whole (including urban-type settlements) increased by 355 per cent between 1897 and 1933, and 72 per cent between 1926 and 1933. The urban population of the USSR as a whole grew by about 29 per cent between 1926 and 1931, while the 19 industrial cities, including Moscow, rose by 44 per cent in the same period. Cities like Tula and Tver'/Kalinin (61 per cent) grew especially fast, while Moscow (35 per cent) and Leningrad (38 per cent) were comparatively slow in their speed of urbanisation.[18] The rural population only slightly increased between 1897 and 1926, and actually decreased thereafter.[19]

TABLE 1.2 *Population of Moscow region, 1897–1933*

Year	Moscow city	Other cities and urban settlements	Rural	Total
1897	1 038 600	611 700	5 720 100	7 370 400
1926	2 025 900	1 383 300	6 883 100	10 292 400
1933	3 663 300	2 206 000	6 682 100	12 557 400

SOURCE: *Ekonomiko-statisticheskii spravochnik po raionam Moskovskoi oblasti*, vyp. 2 (1934) p. 49.

For Moscow city, the population was about 1 665 800 in 1913, and the rapid increase of the war years was followed by a decrease in the years of revolution and civil war, although the fall was not as drastic as in Petrograd. The low point was reached in 1920, and the population in 1921 about 1 148 000 was almost half of that of 1917. In the first half of NEP there was a rapid increase, and by 1927 a population of about 2 031 800 was recorded. The fast increase of the city's population continued thereafter, especially after 1930. In 1932 the figure rose to about 3 135 000. A peak of about 3 663 300 was reached in early 1933, just before the passport system was introduced to restrict urban populations.[20]

From the ethnic point of view, the predominant nationality in both city and region was Russian (95.2 per cent in the region and 87.5 per cent in the city). Jewish residents amounted to 6.5 per cent in the city. Karelians were concentrated in certain areas of the region, while Tartars and Ukrainians each amounted to 0.8 per cent in the city.[21] The Moscow Party apparatus had had a national minorities sector, and in 1933 the Moscow Soviet's presidium set up the inter-nationality commission for the minorities.[22]

Table 1.3 shows the substantial increase in the number of workers. The elimination of the unemployed is also impressive, (some of these, however,

TABLE 1.3 *Social composition, city of Moscow (thousands)*

Social groups	1926	1931	1933
Workers	293.2	673.0	823.4
Employees	263.3	437.6	649.9
Young service staff	91.4	160.7	214.6
Domestic servants	42.2	54.2	52.6
Co-op. *kustar'*	91.1*	78.7	70.2
Non-co-op *kustar'*	*	15.6	6.0
Grant-aided students	34.9	98.1	89.1
Pensioners	39.8	74.2	85.9
Unemployed	130.3	–	–
Transitory	–	32.2	25.2
Unhired	35.0	3.6	1.3
Other independent	65.4	64.8	59.0
Dependents	939.3	1088.6	1339.3
Total	2025.9	2781.3	3416.5

SOURCE: *Moskva v tsifrakh* (1934), p. 16.

* The 1926 figure includes both co-operative and non-cooperative handicraft workers.

may be recorded as transitory or unhired). Domestic servants were entirely female. Women constituted almost 40 per cent of all hired persons in 1933.[23]

Moscow in 1926 was a city of administrations, and this was reflected in the circumstance that employees (essentially office workers) accounted for 36.5 per cent of the working population whereas industrial manual workers accounted only for 27 per cent. In Leningrad the corresponding figures were 27.7 and 33.0 per cent. All the same, the proportion of manual workers was higher than in Odessa, Khar'kov and Tashkent and was close to the average level for cities in the USSR.[24]

In these years of great change, the social composition of Moscow city was also changing. Traditional citizens of the old regime (merchants, the so-called 'parasites' – those who were idle and supported by others – and the petty bourgeoisie) either finally disappeared or changed their characteristics. Nepmen (private entrepreneurs) and speculators were repressed by administrative or financial measures, even though Bauman's slogan 'Eliminate the Nepman!' was regarded as a leftist error.[25] In their place, new classes or strata emerged. Social mobility was high and people changed positions and places, both permanently and temporarily. This continual change of employment, particularly among communists, was characterised by one foreigner as 'the old Russian nomadic instinct'.[26]

Some major features of the changes in the Moscow social strata should be noted. Firstly, workers changed their characteristics as their ranks grew. During NEP the Moscow workers were predominantly in textiles and light industry, but in the 1930s new heavy industry created new groups of metal workers, and others. The expansion of heavy industry was accompanied by a 365 per cent increase of workers in engineering (540 per cent in electrical engineering).[27] This sharp increase in heavy industry contrasts with the stagnant light-industry workforce: textile workers hardly increased at all between 1929 and 1933.[28]

The proportion of industrial workers among the gainfully employed grew from 27.0 per cent in 1926 to 39.6 per cent in 1933 (it still remained lower, however, than in industrial towns like Leningrad, Ivanovo, or Chelyabinsk). Workers in general were mainly recruited from proletarian sources, but the social origins of workers in heavy industry were slightly biased towards the peasantry. In textiles, 60 per cent of workers had been born into the working class, as against 54.4 per cent of metal workers.[29] Building and seasonal workers were mostly of peasant origin.

Workers living outside the city were a majority. They had stronger ties with the countryside, but faced an accommodation shortage more serious than that of the city.[30] The workers' living conditions were very poor in these years, and deteriorated greatly until 1933; real wages fell to far below the NEP level.

Being a huge administrative centre, Moscow had a high proportion of office workers (employees); in 1926 they amounted to 36.5 per cent of the total working population. This was higher than any other city, apart from Sverdlovsk (41.3 per cent). By 1933, the employees amounted to 31.3 per cent of the city's gainfully employed; they tended to live in particular districts and on average their living conditions were superior to those of workers in general.[31]

So far as peasants were concerned, after the departure of the leftist Bauman, the collectivisation process was relaxed, with collective farms dropping to a mere 6 per cent of all peasant households. But by mid-1931 38 per cent had been collectivised, and 50 per cent was achieved by the end of that year.[32] But by mid-1932 the proportion had dropped again, although by the end of the year it did reach 55 per cent.[33] An unknown number of kulaks were deported. The average Moscow kolkhoz was small, and it should be remembered that the region's agriculture was primarily directed towards local consumption; its general economic importance in the region was relatively low.

The old capitalist strata fared worst of all. The bourgeois class had in the main been eliminated. Merchants had either disappeared or been transformed into co-operative or state trade workers. In the economic from October 1928 to September 1929 private traders in the region diminished by about two thirds, compared to the preceding year. Kalinin pointed out that private trade had almost disappeared by the end of 1929, and had completely disappeared by 1932.[34] People who had no productive role were not favoured, and had to obtain even the necessities of life from the so-called 'Mikoyan shops', where prices were very high.[35]

The large number of students, and of workers attending training schools, were a distinctive feature of the social face of Moscow. About 190 000 were studying in VUZY, VTUZY, and Tekhnikumy, while some enterprises, like the vehicle factory AMO, had large factory schools.

1.4 THE JUNE PLENUM RESOLUTION ON MOSCOW

Moscow was both the biggest city and the capital of the USSR, so its development was different from that of industrialising cities like Magnitogorsk and from that of rural areas. Moscow had to solve many problems unknown to other Soviet cities; urbanisation is not the same as industrialisation, although both share common features. On the other hand, being the capital, Moscow enjoyed favourable conditions in terms of resource-supply and political authority.

The Central Committee plenum of 11–15 June 1931 had the effect of elevating the Moscow municipality to the status of a major current problem. The resulting document was the first in which a Soviet socialist strategy of urban construction and reconstruction was formulated. Moscow city was separated from the regional system of administration in February 1931 and the new city leader, Kaganovich, described important sectors of the city's administration as 'laboratories' of the socialist city.[36] In his report to the plenum Kaganovich pointed out that progress in the municipal economy was lagging behind industry and agriculture, and had hitherto been regarded as only a 'second-rank' problem.[37] He insisted that collectivisation and especially industrialisation had made the problems of this city more important; housing, water supply, urban transport, public catering, heating and other municipal functions had become important parts of the struggle for the Five-Year Plan.

Kaganovich admitted that achievements in the municipal economy had not kept pace with the rapid expansion of the working class and its needs. He listed six concrete guidelines concerning Moscow. First, new dwellings for half a million people needed to be built, with appropriate provision for shoppers and children. Second, public catering and bakery facilities should be enlarged. Third, energy supply and district heating required attention, local coal and peat resources being important for this. Fourth, city transport must be radically improved, with the construction of the Metro and the development of bus lines. Fifth, road construction should be carried out. Sixth, water supply had to be improved; the construction of the Moscow-Volga Canal would result in a radical improvement.[38]

This ambitious strategy also proved facile and bureaucratic. 'Gigantomania', typical enthusiasm for large-scale projects at that time, harmed the construction schemes: the new canal and Metro suffered especially, and the central heating projects proved expensive. The housing strategy was ill-defined and unrealistic; the proposed five-storey blocks with two- and four-room units were too expensive to cope with what was emerging as a housing crisis. Care of the environment, and of historical architecture, took second place, to put it mildly. In fact, Kaganovich rather crudely destroyed parts of the Kitaigorod Wall, and also the Sukharev Tower and several churches.[39] The future, and its planning, was the main consideration, and in particular the concentration of people and services into small areas, was to be avoided.[40]

Municipal construction has another dimension, the central-local relationships. The period after 1929 was one of centralisation, and initiative came mainly 'from above'. *Komandovanie* and *administrirovanie* soon became common terms for economic management.

This did not prevent, for the moment, local heroism and initiatives from playing an important role. There was a certain flexibility in the municipal economy, with local initiative being strong in some areas. The June plenum resolution was itself initiated in the MK (the regional committee) and the Mossoviet (Moscow city soviet) and was elaborated before being submitted to the Politburo.[41]

Moreover, a local newspaper publicised the problems of the municipal economy prior to the plenum.[42] A public discussion about whether or not to build the Metro appeared in the newspaper.[43] A week after the plenum, it was the Moscow Party and soviet which gave the go-ahead for this project, and Kaganovich addressed a meeting of activists about it.[44]

In each policy area the extent of the involvement of the central organisations (Central Committee, people's commissariats, Gosplan) varied. The building of the Metro and the canal needed their direct participation, but the local Party and soviet were still expected to play a role (see Chapter 3).

2 Moscow Party Organisation and Membership

2.1 PARTY MEMBERSHIP

In the USSR as a whole 1931–34 witnessed a sharp increase in Communist Party membership, followed by a sudden reversal when the 1933 *chistka*, purged 'alien' elements from party ranks. The enthusiastic recruitment of 'proletarian youth' in the 'revolution from above' phase was followed by severe measures against those who were considered to be 'hostile' or 'passive'. USSR party membership, including candidates (probationary members), increased from 2 212 225 in 1931 to 3 555 338 in 1933, and then diminished to a level of 2 701 008 in 1934.[1]

An analysis of communist party membership makes clear the impact of the 'revolution from above' and its consequences on the party and society. Above all, among the *vydvizhentsy*, or promoted workers, who survived this period were many who would become part of the Stalin and post-Stalin leadership.[2]

The Moscow party organisation conformed to this general trend. By January 1932 there were 395 104 party members in the city and region, more than double the membership in 1928, and accounting for 13.7 per cent of the USSR total (see table 2.1). The rapid growth in membership in the region as distinct from the city is largely due to boundary changes. The new Moscow regional organisation established in 1929 included Moscow, Ryazan', Tula, Tver' and parts of the Kaluga region.

Candidate numbers in both city and region increased by more than 50 per cent between 1931 and 1932. The increase was more marked in the city; the 'revolution from above' evidently attracted many young people. Though the rural increase was less impressive, Party strength in the countryside also grew, from two communists per 1000 people in 1930 to 6 per 1000 two years later.[3] In total, the increase in the number of full members rose from some 20 000 in 1929 to 58 050 in 1932. The acceptance of further full members terminated at the end of 1932. At candidate level, the peak in new membership had already occurred in 1931.

The Moscow leadership made great efforts to recruit workers to the Party throughout the period up to 1933. The MGK adopted a policy of

TABLE 2.1 Membership trends in the Moscow Party Organisation, 1928–35

	1928	1931	1932	1933	1934	1935
CITY						
Full	84 225	126 740	162 665	190 280	138 532	134 839
Cand.	19 796	39 372	62 889	51 938	37 737	30 902
Total	104 021	166 112	225 554	242 218	176 269	165 749
REGION						
Full	24 507	70 636	92 884	112 577	78 537	66 476
Cand.	10 860	50 114	76 666	67 384	34 362	26 120
Total	35 367	120 750	169 550	179 961	112 899	92 596
TOTAL						
Full	108 732	197 376	255 599	302 857	217 069	201 315
Cand.	30 656	89 486	139 555	119 322	72 099	57 022
Total	139 388	286 862	395 104	422 179	289 168	258 337

SOURCE: *Moskovskaya gorodskaya i Moskovskaya oblastnaya organizatsiya KPSS v tsifrakh* (1972), p. 28.

recruiting up to 95 per cent of new members from people whose social origins were industrial working class; in the first half of 1933 94.4 was the recorded proportion. Despite these endeavours, the proportion of industrial workers fell from 53.8 to 46.7 per cent between 1930 and 1932, a fall which attracted some attention at the time. The MGK also actively promoted candidates to full membership, and in July 1932 a bureau decision reproved those districts where members even after two years were still only candidates.[4] This decision noted the diminishing number of new recruits in the first half of 1932 and called for greater recruitment among activists and shock workers. The economic difficulties of 1932 may explain the declining enthusiasm for Party membership among the workers. The slow recruitment continued until the Politburo decision of December 1932 terminated new recruitment altogether.[5]

The membership structure of the Moscow Party on 1 January 1932 can be analysed on the basis of the incomplete statistical data available. There were 395 104 members, of which 35.4 per cent were candidates and 18.7 per cent women. Compared with the all-union level, the candidate percentage was low, and the proportion of women high. By social origin, 74.5 per cent of the members were classified as workers, 13.2 as peasants, and 12.3 per cent as employees.[6] The percentage of peasants was at almost half the all-union level (26.1 per cent), whilst that of employees was higher.

The high proportion of industrial workers and the low proportion of

TABLE 2.2 *Occupational classification of Party members, 1 January, 1932 (per cent)*

	Moscow	All-union
Workers:	46.8	43.9
Industrial	35.1	25.5
Transport	5.9	8.3
Agricultural	1.2	3.9
Other workers	4.6	6.1
Kolkhozniks (collective farmers)	6.1	18.0
Individual peasants	0.1	0.5
Employees	29.6	26.9
Students	14.8	7.8
Others	2.6	2.9

SOURCE: *Partiinoe stroitel'stvo*, No. 9 (1932), 50–51.

kolkhozniks in the Moscow Party is evident, and obviously reflects the social structure of Moscow and its region. At the candidate level, this particular feature of the Moscow Party is even more obvious. Of 137 559 candidate members in the Moscow region who entered the Party between the first (1930) and second (1932) conference of the MK, 76.1 per cent were workers, whilst only 2.5 per cent were peasants. The low influx of peasants and high influx of workers attracted some attention.[7] The MK policy of recruiting 95 per cent of its candidates from those born into the working class contrasted with the 90 per cent level recommended at all-union level.[8] 74 per cent of the region's members were located in the industrial districts, and 26 per cent in the rural districts.

Table 2.3 clearly shows the effect of the 'Lenin enrolment' of 1924 and the 'revolution from above,' on the structure of Party membership.

TABLE 2.3 *Party members in Moscow, 1 January, 1932, according to year of entry (per cent of total)*

1917 and earlier	1.3
1917–20	14.2
1921–23	3.1
1924–26	23.3
1926–28	17.4
1929–30	24.0
1931	16.7
Total	100.0

SOURCE: *Moskovskaya gorodskaya* . . . (1972) p. 57.

2.2 THE PARTY PURGE (*CHISTKA*) OF 1933

The purge of 1933 is the main reason for the decline of Party membership in 1933. On 10 December 1932 the Politburo decided to prohibit further recruitment in 1933, as well as promotion of candidates to full membership.[9] In the event, until November 1936 there was virtually no new recruitment. Although the underlying reasons are not entirely clear, the deteriorating agricultural situation and resulting confusion among the party rank and file no doubt played a major part. 'Kulak sabotage' was said to be threatening the new kolkhozy; and the North Caucasus, especially Kuban, purge, carried out by the Shkiryatov commission in 1932–33, was probably the model for the 1933 general purge.[10] The Shkiryatov commission was appointed not by the Central Control Commission but by the Central Committee, and was stiffened by a delegation headed by Kaganovich at the end of 1932; it purged about 42.8 per cent of the entire Kuban membership.

The general *chistka* did not begin in practice until the spring sowing was complete. The decision of the Central Committee and the Central Control Commission on 28 April 1933 established the Central Purge Commission, headed by Rudzutak and consisting of Rudzutak, Yaroslavsky, Shkiryatov, Stasova, and four others. These commissioners relied heavily on the support of high party officials, especially Kaganovich, Kirov and Ezhov. The specially appointed membership of the commission, and its procedures, were very different from those of the 1929 purge, which had been executed in a more regular way by the normal control commissions.[11]

A striking feature of the 1933 purge was its irregularity. Local purges in the Kuban, Khar'kov, and Petropavlovsk were already under way in 1932, and the 1933 purge was conducted mainly in regions giving greatest concern to the central leadership.[12] The first area of concern was territory vulnerable to foreign attack (the Far East, East Siberia, Byelorussia, Karelia). The second area was that of the Ukrainian famine, around Odessa, Kiev and Vinnitsa. Other areas were Moscow, Leningrad, and the Urals. There was also a purge in the Red Army.[13] The 1933 purge was in effect a continuation of the 1932 local purges, and was itself repeated in 1934 in other regions.

The head of the Moscow purge commission was V. G. Knorin, a MK member in the 1920s and best-known as a hardline Comintern official. Other members included Peters, Filatov, Karavaev and Sol'ts (Sol'ts was from the Central Control Commission presidium). The Moscow commission set up three-member purge commissions at the district level. For example, the head of the Frunze district purge commission was Drizul of the MGK cadres department, and the head of the Bauman district was Gei, a secretary of the MK.[14] Each district committee bureau participated in the selection of commission members.

The purge proper began in June. After a city conference on 22 May in which Knorin, Peters and Sol'ts participated,[15] Kaganovich made a lengthy speech, and closed meetings were held at factories. The newspaper *Rabochaya Moskva* reported the progress of the purge, paying particular attention to the power station in the Lenin district, where the Metrovick affair had been based. The evening newspaper *Vechernyaya Moskva* also reported the purge, announcing that in the Agriculture Administration of the Moscow Soviet heads of sectors were reported to have been defending 'kulaks'.[16]

Purge methods were described by Knorin in a joint session of MK and MGK to which district secretaries and political department chairmen were invited. In September, the bureaus of the MK and MGK met with the regional purge commission, and the progress of the purge was reported. From these reports the real aims of the Moscow purge can be established.

First, the purge was related to the serious difficulties in the economy. For example, a meeting with the railway political department revealed that the purge of the Moscow railway centre had not been carried out in conformity with the Central Committee and Sovnarkom decision on the railway crisis. One station committee bureau was dissolved because of this failure. This emphasised the need to co-ordinate the purge with Party and government directives, so that the purge by the railway political departments (*politotdely*) would be in conformity with the work of the purge commission. Thus the work of the purge commission involved the political department as an extraordinary Party organisation, introduced at that time on the railways and also on the machine and tractor stations.[17]

Second, purges took place at locations where worker morale was low. The purge at the Frunze district's 'Tenth Anniversary' factory was typical here. The rapid expansion of this factory over two years had created trouble. More than half of its workforce were recent recruits from the countryside with less than a year's work experience, and more than two thirds of the Party members here were also new recruits, with less than two years' membership. The purge was said to have improved labour productivity, enabled the production/finance plan to be realised, and led to the discovery of those who had stolen property.[18]

A third type of purge occurred at the Voitovich railway repair works in the Proletarii district. This was an intermediate-level works that had grown from an old workshop. At this works the previous 'bad' custom of allowing excessive pay for non-working time benefited, among others, even the communists, who accounted for almost a quarter of the workforce. No instructors from the MGK or district committee had paid any visits there in the second half of 1932. Some members had been critical of purges that resulted in the silencing or suppression of self-criticism. As a result of the commission's endeavours, the Party secretary was ousted and the district committee was instructed to strengthen the Party leadership in medium or small-scale factories. The principle of one-man management was also emphasised. As for the excessive payments, the stress was put on proper application of the decree on protection of socialist property, the notoriously harsh law promulgated by Stalin on 7 August 1932.[19]

Finally, a purge in the consumer association in Tula city served to control this sector by repressive means at times of shortage. Some section heads were accused of being 'class enemies', enjoying the support of the chairman. Even after this situation was disclosed, a warning issued by the Tula city committee (*gorkom*) had little effect. Eventually, 14 communists out of 73 were purged, and seven demoted to candidates. The MK cadres department received a warning, and its organisation-instructors' department was required to make a report on the implementation of the decision to the MK bureau meeting a month later.[20]

Popular attitudes towards the purge on the shop or factory floor varied, but were typically apathetic and indifferent. At the Elektrokombinat works, where a fair number of workers had been dismissed in connection with the issue of passports (see Chapter 6. 2), the purge allegedly had a 'good' effect on output. But at other factories, like the Frezer (cutting tools) works, the Party organisations were said to have been only passively carrying out the purge. The Frezer manager was consequently reprimanded by the Stalin district committee bureau,[21] and the latter was criticised in its turn because 17.2 per cent of those purged were revealed to be 'alien elements'. In this district four factory secretaries and 17 shop secretaries, as well as 25 Party organisers were expelled, and the need to strengthen shop-floor Party organisation was emphasised. Party secretary Khrushchev pointed out shortcomings in the selection of Party secretaries in this district.[22]

Involvement of the ordinary workers in the conduct of purges was encouraged. At the Kauchuk (rubber) factory in the Frunze district more than a hundred non-Party workers were mobilised each day for one and a half months. But it seems doubtful whether this was a genuinely voluntary phenomenon. At the Krasnaya Roza factory, where mass participation was the best in the Frunze district, the district committee secretary intervened when the initial mass turnout was meagre.[23] In the Bryansk locomotive depot of the same district even the district committee bureau member did not take part, and the cell bureau allegedly sabotaged the purge.

Moscow Party Organisation and Membership

There was evidently also some active resistance to the purge. An 'abnormal' situation was reported in the Institute of Soviet Law during the purge, and several of its members never admitted their errors even after the decision of the district committee.[24] After a meeting of the secretariat and the purge commission of the Frunze district, several Party members were again purged.[25]

The relative significance of mass participation, passivity and resistance to the purge is unclear, but the high rate of expulsions must point to confusion, and even conflict, within Party ranks.

'Deviationist' groups were particularly strongly attacked, although the intensity of this is unclear. Some Party members were critical of Stalinist policy in Moscow, and Moscow Party leaders were probably keen to sniff out 'Right deviationists' because this had once been a stronghold of Uglanov, and anti-Stalinists like Ryutin held important positions. At the end of 1930, some action by the 'Right opposition' was reported, and at the beginning of 1932 several economists in the Institute of Red Professors were alleged to have committed 'Right deviationist' errors.[26] These tendencies seem to have culminated in the Ryutin affair, revealed in the Autumn of 1932; Ryutin distributed a pamphlet in which Stalin's policy of forced collectivisation and super-industrialisation was criticised. Even Stalin's right to remain Party leader was questioned. In consequence of the affair, Zinoviev, Kamenev and Uglanov were reprimanded. Before the end of 1932, some high officials like A. Smirnov, Eismont and Tolmachev were also pushing for policy changes; Rykov and Tomsky received warnings from the Party authorities at the beginning of 1933.[27]

All these developments had their repercussions in the Moscow organisation. According to one official report after the January 1933 plenum:

> In the discussion on the conclusions of the Central Committee and Central Control Commission, there occurred in many Moscow Party cells several attacks by the 'Right opportunists', who said 'What kind of victory is it when factories are working a three-shift system . . . there is no time for rest; the tempo is extremely fast; there is not enough meat and agriculture is deteriorating'.[28]

The director of another institute complained that 'Our agriculture is deteriorating and the kolkhoz is unprofitable'.[29] This critical mood may have been fairly widespread. Filatov, the chairman of the city control commission, mentioned that 'many such cases' were revealed, and even claimed that Trotskyist activity was discovered.

The result of the purge in Moscow was reported in general terms by

TABLE 2.4 Reasons stated for expulsion from the Party in Moscow
(per cent of the total)

Hostile elements and class aliens	13.4
Double-dealers	5.1
Violators of Party or government discipline	27.3
Passive members	23.7
Suppressors of self-criticism and inner-party democracy	2.2
Degenerates in personal life, and demoralised persons	27.6

SOURCE: *VI Moskovskaya oblastnaya* . . . , (1934) p. 300
(data imperfect and do not add up to 100).

Knorin to a joint plenum of the MK and MGK in December 1933. He criticised the weak leadership provided by the district committee for the small cells especially for the rural cells. The MK, MGK, and district committees were instructed to use the information collected during the campaign; members of local purge commissions were to contact each cell, and the culture and agitation-propaganda departments were asked to ensure intentions were carried out. Each district committee was to report to the MK within two weeks on how to carry out the task.[30]

The figures for the results of the purge are sometimes contradictory and confusing. According to Knorin, 11.7 per cent of the Party members (including candidates) were expelled in the Moscow region, while Moscow city lost 10.4 per cent.[31] However, Rudzutak, at the XVIIth Party Congress, stated that 13.6 per cent were purged in the Moscow region; this evidently includes those who were reduced to sympathiser status.[32] At a local Moscow conference, Khrushchev gave a different set of figures: 10 per cent of full members and 17 per cent of candidates expelled.[33] Khrushchev's figures would suggest that some 30 000 full members and 20 000 candidates were expelled; in addition, 9000 were demoted to candidates in the region as a whole.

The totals arrived at from the three sets of figures are not identical, pointing to some confusion in the purge. Probably Rudzutak was right when he pointed out the gap between registered and actual members.[34] This problem would be raised again in 1935 and 1936, when verifications of Party documents had to be carried out.

More detailed figures are available for certain districts of Moscow city. In the Stalin district, of 16 959 members (including 3707 candidates), 1521 or 8.9 per cent were purged, (8.1 per cent of full members and 11.9 per cent of candidates).[35] 7.4 per cent (989 members) were demoted from full to candidate status. In addition 3.6 of the full and 17.5 per cent of the candidate members were reduced to sympathisers. Of those purged, 72.2 per cent were classed as workers, and these were mainly from the 1929–32 recruits.

The apolitical character of the purge, as reflected in the figures in Table 2.4, seems perhaps surprising. Interpreting such figures is not at all simple. Western experts in this field have put forward two different interpretations. Thus T. H. Rigby regards the political side of this campaign as a first step towards the elimination of the 'Old Bolsheviks', which came to a head in the great purge of 1937–38.[36] But a more novel view has been propounded by J. A. Getty, who considers this purge to have been a continuation of that of the 1920s, and to be lacking in political implications.[37] My own view is that while the political aspect of the purge has been overemphasised, Getty has somewhat oversimplified the effects of the purge. In particular, he did not make the necessary connection with the social upheaval of 1932–33. He also failed to note the more political purge carried out concurrently by the control commissions, to which I now turn.

2.3 THE CONTROL COMMISSION AND PARTY SANCTIONS

There is a considerable difference between the number of Party members purged in 1933–34 (not more than 57 400 in the Moscow region), and the reduction of party membership in the same period (about 133 000). Records of the 4th regional and 3rd city Party conferences give the following explanation for the abrupt fall of party membership:

> The reduction may be explained by the termination of Party admissions following the declaration of the purge, the diminution of the flow of communists into Moscow combined with the significant outward flow connected with transfers to jobs in other parts of the Soviet Union (MTS, railways).[38]

This explanation, however, does not entirely clarify the reasons for and extent of the decline in membership. The political department workers who were sent away were not numerous (about 3000 were sent to the MTS).

This question was also discussed in a report of the chairman of the city control commission, Filatov, to the city Party conference. According to Filatov, the control commission, had purged some 4.4 per cent in 1932 and another 6.7 per cent in 1933.[39] These actions had nothing to do with the purge (*chistka*) of 1933, although their effects might have been similar. The function of the control commission, Filatov stressed, included:

... fighting for the Party line, for ideological purity against all kinds of deviationists from the Party line, against the distortion of the line in theory and practice, against trouble-dealers, against eye-wash, against the suppression of self-criticism, against bureaucratism in the soviet apparatus and the inadequate attention to the workers' needs on the part of Party bureaucrats, and against all other unhealthy tendencies inside the organisation.[40]

According to Filatov, in Moscow city alone about 9900 members were purged by the control commission in 1932, and 16 000 in 1933. The number of members investigated was far larger than this in those two years, with about 18 600 investigated and 7000 expelled in the city for deviationism or other anti-party manifestations alone.[41] Filatov's figures are fragmentary, and those purged for other reasons are not fully enumerated. Nevertheless, these figures go some way to explain the sharp decline of party membership.

More detailed figures for the effect on membership totals of the activities of the district control commissions are available for the Stalin district. The collegium of its control commission investigated 1226 individuals in 1932, and 1994 in 1933. Of these, 368 were expelled and 46 reprimanded in 1932, and 844 and 642 in 1933. The causes varied widely, from drunkenness to ideological deviation.[42] Violation of Party discipline was the most frequent reason of investigation, whereas passivity was by far the most common cause for expulsion. As this district had about 16 900 Party members in 1933, these figures indicate that five per cent were expelled in 1933 alone. Moreover, another 8.9 per cent were sifted out of the district by the above-mentioned purge campaign.

Thus, the purge in 1933 should not be confused with the control commission purge, which removed 4.4 per cent of the membership in 1932 and 6.7 per cent in 1933. Table 2.1 shows a reduction of about 51 700 full members, or 65 900 including candidates.[43] The 1933 purge removed at least 25 200 members in Moscow city, and the control commissions were responsible for a further 16 000 expulsions. In addition, about 3000 members were sent to rural areas outside the city. A gap still remains, part of which may be explained by ordinary lapses of membership.

A more detailed examination of trends in one district lends plausibility to these suggestions (see Table 2.5). The reduction in membership in Frunze is attributed to the purge and to mobilisation. About ten per cent of full members were expelled, 7.8 demoted to candidates, and about three per cent reduced to sympathisers. In this district, 329 activists were sent away to take charge of political sections in the MTS and state farms.[44]

Moscow Party Organisation and Membership

TABLE 2.5 *Party membership in the Frunze District, 1931–34*

	Full members	Candidates	Total
1931	13 124	4069	17 193
1932	15 898	7166	23 064
1933	16 605	4162	20 767
1934	14 056	3880	17 936

SOURCE: *Ot pobedy k pobede* (1934), 118, 120.

A further 598 were mobilised either by the Central Committee or the MK for permanent rural work. It should be added that this area had a high concentration of higher educational institutions.

To conclude, the critical situation of 1932–33 caused confusion and turmoil in Party ranks in Moscow just as it did in the USSR as a whole, and this was part of the reason why the purge was carried out in the latter half of 1933. However, other Party sanctions were also applied, in the form of control commission investigations that had the effect of causing a further drop in membership. A third reason for the diminution was the posting of communists to rural areas outside the Moscow region and to the railways. There were also some members who dropped out for various mundane reasons.

The decline of party membership continued after 1933–34; it reached a trough in 1938, when the number was little more than half the 1932 level.[45] The decline in Moscow city was not quite as drastic as in the region as a whole. With very few exceptions, there was no enrolment from end-1932 until 1936.

Finally, it is interesting to note that there was a slight relative increase of women members, from 18.9 per cent of the total in 1932 to 21.9 per cent in 1933. This could imply that women members were less affected by the purges and the expulsions.

2.4 PARTY EDUCATION IN MOSCOW

While the purge commission and control commission were concerned to maintain an obedient and efficient membership by cutting out unsatisfactory members, the system of party education was primarily concerned with the positive work of political training.

No modern political system can sustain itself without massive recruitment and training of an elite. In Moscow in the Stalinist regime, Party cadres and activists, and also citizens outside the Party, were exposed

TABLE 2.6 The trend of Moscow Party membership, 1933–38
(1932=100)

	1933	1934	1935	1936	1937	1938
Entire Moscow region	106.8	73.2	68.9	57.4	62.2	53.9
Moscow city	107.4	78.1	72.1	62.3	70.0	70.4

SOURCE: calculated from *Moskovskaya gorodskaya* ..., 128 ff.

to vastly expanded Party and general education. Moscow, the centre of the Soviet Communist Party and of the world communist movement, contained high-level Party institutions like Sverdlov University and the Communist University of Eastern Peoples, run by the Central Committee, where Comintern and Soviet communists were trained.

At the regional and city level, there were the regional Communist Higher Educational Institutes (KOMVUZ). There were three regional institutes in Moscow, Tula and Ryazan' in 1932; a fourth was due to open in Kalinin to offer a three-year course to 920 students, but this had to be modified (see Chapter 7.3).[46] In the Ryazan' KOMVUZ, opened in 1930, about 350 students attended the three sectors (Party organisation, propaganda, soviets), and the first graduates of the propaganda sector were at work by 1932.[47]

However, serious shortcomings were pointed out by the MK culture and propaganda departments; some students were said to have developed 'consumer instincts' in that year of acute shortages. In 1931 the 'Case of the 17' was reported, concerning some students of this institution who had refused to be mobilised into an important campaign (apparently in agriculture), and had come back. This was followed by a tightening of discipline.[48]

In 1932 there was a change in policy towards the regional-level educational institutions. In view of the mounting importance of agriculture at this time, the central authority abruptly transformed all the higher communist educational institutions into agricultural institutions; only the two Comintern institutes were untouched. According to a special commission headed by Postyshev, of the Central Committee, some 12 000 cadres were trained in the communist institutes for agricultural work.[49] In Moscow, the three regional communist higher education institutes were be transformed; this was handled by a commission headed by Party secretary Gei and including the heads of the culture and propaganda department and of the Moscow soviet's agriculture department.[50] The MK secretariat decided that well-disciplined communists should be selected for these institutes, and by December 1932 of that year about 450 students had been recruited on the recommendations of district committee bureaux. The Moscow KOMVUZ specialised in farm organisation, flax, and livestock, Tula in grain, and Ryazan' in livestock and potatoes. The first 144 students of Moscow's Kaganovich Higher Communist Agricultural Institute were posted to political departments and to state farms in July 1934.[51] The Kalinin institution originally intended as the fourth regional KOMVUZ, was transformed into a higher educational institute for textiles at the request of the MK, and was thereby deprived of its status as a communist institution.[52]

Apart from this full-time higher education system, part-time higher education courses for Party-cell secretaries were held in Moscow on the initiative of Kaganovich, and each city district had its branch.[53] In addition, at the regional level, seven branches were opened in industrial cities in order to improve the qualifications of Party-cell secretaries. About 675 secretaries of the region attended once-weekly over four months. This programme was largely supervised by secretary Gei, but with the co-operation of the district organisation. The number of branches more than doubled.[54]

Shorter-term re-education of cadres was carried out at a variety of establishments. The Zvenigorod House of Party Education was mainly concerned with district officials: secretaries, heads of district committee departments, chairmen of district executive committees and soviet department heads. For example, to cope with the difficult situation in the textile industry in mid-1932, a six-week course for cadres in that industry was held in August. Three-month courses for 500 district cadres were arranged by the MK secretariat in 1932, and 30 district committee secretaries as well as 110 heads of district departments were invited.[55] Before the difficult spring agricultural campaign in 1933, the joint bureau of the MK and MGK organised three-week courses for district committee secretaries, and 40 chairmen from district district executive committees and control commissions were also invited.[56] The main organiser was Malenkov, then head of the MK organisation-instructors department. In the winter, a ten-day course for rural cell secretaries was organised, where Mikhailov, the MK secretary for agriculture, and Malenkov were among the speakers.[57] The House of Party Education in Skopin was adapted to specialise in the re-education of shop-floor workers of the Sub-Moscow coalfield. The House of Party Education in Sakharov educated some 600 activists every year.[58]

Below this level a similar system existed in the form of district communist higher educational establishments. Their main task was the cultural enlightenment of factory-and cell-level officials and activists. In Moscow city there existed eight district communist higher educational institutions, where 3082 students were attending two-year evening courses in 1932.[59] In Frunze district, for example, two institutions taught 280 communists, mainly Party-cell secretaries.[60] In the region as a whole about 8000 attended, with ten evening courses in Moscow and 40 in other areas in 1934.[61]

So far, the discussion has dealt with the educational system for communist middle- or lower-level officials. However, there was also another system for general communist education. Sovpartshkoly, or Soviet Party schools, were one-year schools for soviet and trade-union activists and workers; by 1934 there were 12 schools with 2000 students.[62] Around them, for some months, various kinds of circles were organised, covering both theoretical and contemporary topics. In Frunze district, there were ten branches with 512 students registered; courses in agricultural technology and languages were provided.[63] 'Candidate schools' were designed for three-month courses for non-Party members and candidates, to teach the programme and rules of the Party. Those completing these schools progressed to elementary Party schools, where a six-month course imparted basic information for Party activists. In all, some 150 000 were embraced by the communist educational network in 1931–32.[64]

In carrying out the programme of the various circles and groups for communist and citizen education, the propaganda cadres were of enormous importance. However, the district committees were apt to divert them into other areas. Of 941 propagandist cadres whom the MK posted to the districts, only 350 were in the same job some time later.[65] The MK bureau in November 1933 recalled these propagandists, who were directed by the district committees to another area.[66] This move was given extra impetus by the despatch of 1000 graduates of the regional Sovpartshkoly, as well as worker-instructors.

The MGK bureau decision, two months later, also emphasised the need to consolidate the propagandist situation. For this purpose it instructed the district committees to set up commissions, headed by district committee secretaries and including heads of departments.[67] Propagandist leaders were to be personally checked by the district committee secretaries and to be approved by the district committee secretariats.

Printing pamphlets and documents was an important part of the duties of MK and MGK departments.[68] In the MGK editorial board for cultural affairs, young Stalinists like Mekhlis, N. Popov, Knorin, Soms, and Mitin assumed important roles, together with the head of the culture and propaganda department.[69] By the end of 1931, with the publication of Stalin's famous article in *Proletarskaya revolyutsiya*, these culture hardliners, with the Institute of Red Professors as their bastion, became dominant.

3 Decision-Making in the Party

3.1 PARTY LEADERSHIP

Moscow, political and economic hub of the USSR, is the home of the major administrative, economic and cultural institutions. The Moscow Party organisation was the largest of the local units and its membership included some of the most urbanised, proletarianised, and politically active people. In 1931–34, which included the 1932–33 crisis, the organisation was led by L. M. Kaganovich, the key figure in Stalin's Politburo and secretariat after July 1930. This appointment was made as a consequence of the preceding 'deviationist' trends; the 'Right opportunist' leadership of Uglanov (1924–November 1928) had been followed by the 'leftist excess' of Bauman (1929–30 April 1930), (see pp. 3–4 above).[1]

The victory of Stalin and his supporters was not complete. Firstly, the dissidents Uglanov and Ryutin, former Moscow Rightists, continued to resist the consolidation of the Stalinist system in 1930–32. In the spring 1930 retreat from collectivisation prior to the XVIth Party Congress the 'leftist' Bauman was removed from the position of first secretary of the Moscow Party organisation, and at this time Uglanov again criticised the forced collectivisation policy. Then at the end of 1930, Ryutin and others were reprimanded when Syrtsov and Lominadze were attacked as a 'Rightist-Leftist bloc'.

Second, there were further oppositionist moves in 1932. The excessive and forced character of collectivisation, together with other factors, caused a serious crisis in the spring of 1932, and a policy of appeasement towards the kolkhoz peasants was introduced, although it was soon replaced by more coercive methods. Former Right oppositionists such as Ryutin began to organise a group against Stalin. There was even a polarisation of opinion among former oppositionist leaders themselves. The willingness of Bukharin and Rykov to co-operate with Stalin was criticised by Ryutin in his well-known anti-Stalin pamphlet. After the September plenum in 1932, Ryutin and Uglanov were among those who were purged together with Zinoviev and Kamenev.

TABLE 3.1 *The MK Bureau in 1932–34*

L. M. Kaganovich*	First secretary of MK and MGK
Ryndin	Second secretary of MK
Kaminsky*	Chairman of Oblispolkom
Gei	Secretary of MK
Mikhailov*	Secretary of MK (agriculture)
Donenko	Secretary of MK (Transport)
Egorov	Secretary of MK
Agranov	OGPU
Drozhinin	Trade union chairman
Kalygina*	First secretary of Kalinin gorkom
Sedel'nikov*	First secretary of Tula gorkom
Veklichev*	Red Army (Political administration)
Ruben	Secretary of MGK
Khrushchev*	Secretary of MGK
Kogan*	Secretary of MGK
Davidson*	Secretary of MGK
Bulganin*	Chairman of Mossovet
Malenkov	Head, MGK org. – instructors department
Guberman	Chairman, planning commission #

* Position still retained in 1934
\# From February 1933
SOURCE, *Pravda*, 31 January, 1932; *Rabochaya Moskva*, 26 January, 1934.

Two months later another move against Stalinist policy was reported: A. P. Smirnov, candidate member of the Orgburo, and other high-ranking officials allegedly organised an oppositionist group with the backing of Tomsky and Rykov.

In this process the Moscow Party organisation as a whole followed the orthodox hard line of Kaganovich, who was struggling against allegedly 'kulak sabotage' in the rural areas.[2] The Party organisation at the Moscow level, and the Party full-time apparatus, were geared to this purpose.

(i) The MGK and MK

In February 1931, the MGK (Moscow city Party committee) was formed as a body semi-independent of the MK (Moscow region Party committee). However this quasi-autonomous status was limited because some officials were members of both committees. Kaganovich himself was the first secretary of both organisations. Moreover, members of the MGK bureau (the executive sub-committee) were often also members of the MK bureau.

Decision-Making in the Party

The two organisations sometimes held joint plenums and they always held a joint conference.[3]

The MGK and MK nevertheless differed in character, the MGK being mainly concerned with urban matters, and the MK with rural. Their agendas differed correspondingly. According to the work plan of July 1933, the MK dealt with such matters as agriculture, peat, construction and public catering while the MGK dealt with municipal economy, public catering, and collection of potatoes and other vegetables.[4] When their staffs were sent out to deal with urgent tasks, most of the MK staff were sent to assist with the harvest, while MGK staff were allocated to the municipal economy.

In parallel with the central party, a bureau and a secretariat of the Moscow Party organisation dealt with routine matters. According to the Party rules, the regional bureau had a minimum of five members for current work. In January 1932 the third regional conference appointed as many as eighteen bureau members: six MK secretaries, five MGK secretaries, the chairman of the *oblispolkom* (regional soviet executive committee) and of the Mossovet, two local *gorkom* (city committee) secretaries, and members from the military, OGPU, and trade unions (Table 3.1). In 1933 the chairman of the planning commission (*oblplan*) was also co-opted on to the bureau. Bureau candidate members were drawn from the Komsomol, district secretaries and other officials.[5]

But the large size of the bureau was unwelcome to Kaganovich, and at the XVIIth Party Congress in February 1934 he proposed a reduction.[6] The effect of this is shown in Table 3.2. The most important members were kept on. Other important changes in 1934 included the departure of the second secretary, Ryndin, who became first secretary of Chelyabinsk Regional committee. Redens, the Moscow OGPU official newly appointed in 1934, was a relative of Stalin's wife. The promotion of Khrushchev in 1934 is also worth noting. In 1934 the representatives of the trade unions and planning commission and also the heads of the political departments of the MTS (Machine-Tractor Stations) and railways, were demoted to candidate membership of the bureau.

The MGK bureau contained 14 members and six candidate members in 1932 (Table 3.2). They included six MGK secretaries and six secretaries of important districts, Bulganin (chairman of Mossoviet), and Badaev (chairman of consumer co-operatives). The nomination of Badaev reflects the crucial role of supply problems at that time. The most important departmental head of the MGK, the head of organisation-instructors department, was promoted to full membership of the bureau in 1933.[7]

TABLE 3.2 *The MGK Bureau in 1932–34*

Kaganovich	First secretary of MGK
Khrushchev*	Second secretary
Ruden#	Secretary
Kogan*	Secretary
Davidson	Secretary
Voropaev#	Secretary
Bulganin*	Chairman, Mossoviet
Badaev*	Chairman, Moscow Consumer Co-operative
Soifer*	Secretary, Lenin district
Margolin*	Secretary, Stalin district
Gaidul'	Secretary, Zamoskvorets district
Trofimov	Secretary, Bauman district
Starostin	Secretary, Sokol'niki district
Kulikov*	Secretary, Proletarii district
Il'in#+	Head of org. – inst. department
Karpov+	Secretary, Frunze district
Andreasyan+*	Secretary, Oktyabr' district
Korytnyi+	Secretary, Dzerzhinsky district
Bukharin+*	Secretary, Krasnaya Presnya district

* Position retained in 1934
# To August 1933
+ From May 1932
SOURCE: *Pravda*, 31 January, 1932; *Moskovskaya Pravda*, 26 January, 1934).

The importance of the Moscow gorkom as a model for other organisations is exemplified by Kaganovich's initiative in reducing the number of bureau members by 30–40 per cent. This was taken before the standard national pattern of eleven bureau members was recommended by the XVIIth Party Congress.

(ii) **The Main Leaders and their Roles**

The outstanding leader was, of course, L. M. Kaganovich, first secretary of the MK and MGK who was a member both of the Politburo and of the secretariat of the Central Committee after the XVIth Party Congress. His importance as a national leader is emphasised by his appointment as head of the new Central Committee agriculture department, created in early 1933 to deal with the deteriorating situation in kolkhoz agriculture, which in some areas had already led to famine. Evidently his leadership in Moscow was limited to broad guidelines, and did not include the day-to-day running of party and soviet affairs. But he certainly intervened intermittently in various specific Moscow matters. The vast range of issues with which he dealt included, for example, the co-ordination of the leather industry with related commissariats, attending commissions on textile workers' supplies, and consulting with the Transport Commissariat about retaining the reserve army on the Moscow-Donbass railway. He played a crucial role in the construction of the Metro, sometimes acting against the advice of the specialists.[8] He was eventually replaced in his Moscow role by Khrushchev at the MGK level in 1934 and at the MK level in 1935.

The second secretary of the MK, Ryndin, was mainly responsible for heavy industry. A former metal-worker, he worked in the Urals during NEP and moved to the Central Committee in 1928 and to the Moscow Control Commission, before being appointed Moscow second secretary under Kaganovich.[9] His activities in Moscow and its region as described in Soviet documents included such varied matters as the development of Tula metallurgy, chairing a commission on the engineering industry, supervising the construction of the Moscow-Donbass railway, Party work in the Sub-Moscow coalfield, and reorganising the engineering industry trade unions.[10] For some reason, he was demoted to a mere district secretary in the Urals; soon after, however, he was appointed first secretary of Chelyabinsk regional committee.

Agricultural and related matters fell to another secretary: Mikhailov. But the functions of party secretaries were not precisely definited. Mikhailov was also concerned with chemical and railway construction and took an active part in procuring firewood during the fuel crisis.[11] Gei, another secretary, was primarily concerned with culture and propaganda work, and controlled the relevant departments.[12] Secretary Donenko's speciality was railways and transport, and by the autumn of 1933 he was transferred to work for the railway political departments (*politotdely*). Another secretary, Egorov, had previously worked in economic administration (in VSNKh): in Moscow he was concerned with supplies.[13]

In the MGK the rise of Khrushchev was perhaps the remarkable event. Born and bred in the Donbass mining area before the Revolution, he moved to Moscow in the late 1920s as a *vydvizhenets*, to study in the Industrial Academy (Promakademiya). In 1931 he was already a district secretary; he became MGK second secretary in 1932, and MGK first secretary and a Central Committee member in February 1934. His function before 1935 was relatively modest; he was a kind of adjutant to Kaganovich, particularly dealing with city transport, including work on the Moscow Metro, and on constructing and planning the new trolley-bus lines. He was mainly to be found in the corridors of power, on financial, budgetary and control-figure (planning) commissions and committees.[14]

In the MGK as in the MK there was a broad division of labour between the secretaries. Davidson specialised in worker's supplies, commodity supplies and the public catering system.[15] Kogan worked mainly in mobilisation and construction.[16] Ruben was also involved in construction (he was transferred to the Central Control Commission in autumn 1933).[17]

Bulganin, representing the Mossoviet in the MK and MGK bureau, was a conspicuous figure; he played an important part in such matters as compiling the control figures for Moscow.[18] The bureau made decisions after hearing from Bulganin in his capacity as a representative of Mossoviet. In practice the MGK bureau was the highest decision-making body in Moscow city, although the soviet was nominally the 'highest organ of power'. This does not mean, however, that the soviet played no part in the bureau, or that 'the bureau merely represented the secretariat in a somewhat enlarged guise', as Fainsod found in Smolensk.[19] The viewpoint of the soviet or of its planning commission sometimes played an important or even vital role, especially when a decision backed by technical or specialised knowledge was required.

The diminishing role of the trade unions was reflected in the decline in their status on the bureau: in 1932 the trade union leadership was represented in the regional bureau, but this was no longer the case by 1934. In Moscow the trade union leadership was now concerned mainly with such matters as administration in the fields of supply and mobilisation.[20]

Representatives of the soviets and other organisations on the bureau were not necessarily confined to the narrow brief of representing their organisations. Kaminsky, chairman of the regional soviet executive committee, is a good example. He consulted with the secretariat on the details of soviet work, but also had his own job as a bureau member.[21] Bulganin dealt with the central government in seeking building materials for the canal, and with the Central Committee on the import of pipes.[22] The military and OGPU representatives also had important work on behalf of the bureau assigned to them.[23]

Similarly, the role of local secretaries in the regional bureau was not limited to the defence of their local interests. For example, Kalygina, secretary of Kalinin gorkom, joined the commission on municipal construction when it was compiling the economic plans, and also joined a commission on the status of textile workers. The same was true in the MGK bureau: Kul'kov, secretary of a city district committee, was a member of the fisheries commission even though his district was not particularly concerned with fishing. However, on the whole, the role of local representatives was mainly concerned with their particular interests.[24]

This narrow approach to the role of the MK bureau members was later criticised on the grounds that the 'former' MK leadership had been somewhat decentralised and that the leadership style was that of 'a feudal prince' (*knyaz'*) running his fiefdom independently and that the MK was a 'federal meeting of boyars'.[25] After this criticism in 1934, control was tightened from top to bottom.

However, governing a huge and complicated society like Moscow is beyond the capacity of amateur politicians and is always accompanied by role differentiation among the leadership. In another words, it cannot be totally subjugated to the political will of the single leader or 'quasi-independent satrap' as is suggested in the case of Smolensk first secretary I. P. Rumyantsev in Merle Fainsod's classic analysis.[26] This contradiction of the Stalinist system was to become salient in 1950s.

(iii) Procedures of the Bureaux

This section will investigate the routines of the bureaux: who participated, when meetings took place, and what was discussed. Both full members and candidates were entitled to discuss all the issues on the bureau agenda, but only full members could vote. Representatives of other institutions and organisations, as well as specialists, were invited to report or advise. Some were given instructions, often with deadlines, and in some cases they were penalised for failing to carry them out. For example, the MK bureau in its agenda of 20 November 1933 heard a report by the chairman of the Control Commission on house repairs, naming 23 tardy district secretaries. Each was given instructions to take the necessary steps within five days.[27] Personal responsibilities were fixed in this case and plenipotentiaries were sent from the regional level. Two district secretaries were severely reprimanded for allegedly neglecting the notices, and a factory director was taken to court. The case illustrates three aspects of the bureaux' role: firstly, secretaries were held responsible for trivial matters like house repairs; secondly, concrete measures were demanded within certain time limits; and thirdly, the bureau could decide to send someone to court.[28]

Although the bureau discussed the matters listed in its agenda, summoning the persons concerned, it did not stick to the agenda. For example, at the meeting Kaganovich unexpectedly raised the question of the Moscow-Donbass railway which had already been decided upon more than a year previously, on 26 October 1933. The railway had in fact not been completed and the heads of the MK departments were warned of Party sanctions that might be applied. Similarly, Kaminsky was asked as a matter of emergency to mobilise 4000–5000 kolkhozniks. The implementation of the decision had to be reported to the next bureau meeting, and bureau members were assigned to check the work of each department. The Party *fraction* of the soviet (the group of members of the soviet who were Party members) was also directed to pay attention to it, and until the project was completed, the progress of the construction had to be reported 'on every two bureau meetings'.[29] Similarly, the question of mass mobilisation was placed on the agenda 'as an extraordinary item'. Thus, although the agenda was presented in advance, this did not prevent urgent matters being raised. Assigned persons were specified, as well as their supervisors. Internal sanctions could be applied even to bureau members.

Bureau meetings probably took place every ten days or so. Between January and April 1933, twelve bureau decisions were taken and published on different dates, which suggests a ten-day interval between bureau meetings. From April 1933, the MK and MGK regularly conveyed the main decisions to the press, although not all were published.[30] Joint meetings of the MK and MGK were sometimes held, especially in the latter half of 1933.

(iv) Activities of the Bureaux

One characteristic of the Moscow decision-making process was that bureaux frequently organised various commissions for the investigation and resolution of complex problems. A typical example may be found in the preparation of the economic plan and budget for 1933. By a decision of 4 January the MK bureau set up seven commissions: three were concerned with the construction or re-siting of factories, three were related to specific planning matters, and the other to the fulfilment of Moscow planning. Kaminsky attended four of these commissions, Guberman (of the planning commission, a bureau member from February 1933) attended three, and Ryndin and Mikhailov two each. These commissions invited district secretaries, representatives of trusts or even OGPU officials.[31]

The same practice was followed by the MGK bureau. By a decision of 4 January 1933, six commissions were organised, and they included the bureau members and the representative of the Mossoviet.[32] More commissions were established on 23 January to plan development of factories for clocks and watches and for ships' engines, and in the latter case district secretaries were also invited.³³ After consulting the chairman of the district executive committees, the plan for each district was to be evaluated by Mossoviet presidium before being presented for approval to the MGK bureau.

This system of decision-making was not confined to planning or budget formation, but was also used for *ad hoc* issues. For example, to cope with the deteriorating condition of the textile industries, the MK formed two commissions. One of these, on the status of *podmaster'e* (senior workers), was chaired by Gei, a secretary, and attended by one gorkom secretary and representative of trusts and trade unions. The other, more powerful and including Kaganovich and Ryndin, was on the supply problems of the textile workers. While these commissions were working, every bureau meeting discussed these matters.³⁴

In short, the bureaux set up various commissions to investigate and formulate policy with the participation of bureau members and representatives of institutions concerned. In this connection it is worth noting that the secretariat itself seldom initiated such commissions, apart from selecting workers to be despatched to the countryside.³⁵

Those commissions in which specialists participated are particularly worth of attention. A significant example is the commission for architecture and planning, or Arplan, which was a permanently active commission formed by decision of the MGK bureau and the presidium of Mossoviet in September 1933. This commission included both political figures such as Kaganovich, Khrushchev, Kaminsky and Bulganin, and also the heads of Mossoviet departments. The architect Zholtovskii and several other specialists were heads of the planning work group.³⁶ This commission, which could exercise control over the Metro construction, embraced both policy and the plan in general; the result of this labour was presented to the Politburo in July 1934. This may have been the background which inspired one bold district secretary (Margolin) to advocate in 1934 the inclusion of specialists and technologists in the leadership.³⁷

This style of decision-making by commission, with specialist advice, had lost favour by the end of 1933.³⁸ It is possible that this was due to the impact in the Party apparatus of the politotdel way of working, for which Kaganovich was mainly responsible. Certainly Kaganovich was sceptical about involving specialists in decision-making. In 1934, he said:

> Some people are posing the questions of involving engineers in the Party apparatus. However, the slogan we shall put forward is 'engineers to production'.³⁹

This negative attitude towards the commission system and the involvement of engineers in the commissions was reinforced by the decision of the XVIIth Party Congress that no more special commissions should be established. This case again suggests that functional differentiation is more visible in urban and industrial policy-making, though it was not consistently pursued in Moscow and there were set-backs.[40]

3.2. THE PARTY APPARATUS

The Party apparatus at each level mainly consisted of full-time, paid officials (*apparatchiki*), whose importance had been enhanced since 1928–29. In Moscow the apparatus of the Party Secretariat was in fact the core of the party organisations, and tightly controlled other organisations, especially the soviets.

The secretariat was assigned routine organisational and executive work with a narrower jurisdiction than the bureau. It lacked institutional representatives from the soviets, OGPU and military. Running day-to-day Party administrative work, it met, like the bureaux, about every ten days.[41] Minor items filled its agenda, and these were sometimes dealt with by correspondence (the *oprosnyi* method).[42]

The secretariat's decisions were mostly concerned with personnel. It did not deal with economic planning, and rarely dealt with industry. But it made many decisions about agriculture. Thus, in general, bureau decisions mainly related to planning and industry, where specialised knowledge and institutional involvement were needed, and secretariat decisions were concerned with subjects that required mobilisation, especially mobilisation of Party members.[43]

But too great a stress on the different areas of competence of bureaux and secretariat would be misleading. Through their agents, the secretariat could issue instructions and orders to economic and governmental organisations, and sometimes did so. For example, the MGK secretariat issued decisions on trolley buses to Bulganin, representing the Mossoviet, who was not even formally a member of the secretariat.[44] The roles of bureau and secretariat could be interchangeable. Thus the bureau decision of 23 April 1933 on the Moscow-Donbass railway required the bureau itself to check implementation two months later; but in the event, the report was made not at the bureau meeting, but at a secretariat meeting. Similarly, a decision about sugar supply was made by the bureau, but a decision about wheat and oats supply by the secretariat; this was surely only a matter of convenience.

In practice, the secretariat was an auxiliary of the bureau. The city Party employed about 150 full-time officials. This number was reduced by Kaganovich to 99 by 1934.[45] The size of the regional secretariat is not known; but the total number of full-time officials would have been some 300–350 in the city and region taken together. This figure includes numerous chauffeurs and typists as well as political appointees. In addition, city district committees each employed a staff of about 35–40 people, while the staff of rural district committees rarely exceeded 20.[46] According to Kaganovich the regional committee should supervise 10–15 leading workers of the apparatus of each district, and the district secretary at that time.[47]

(a) Inner structure of Moscow Party organisation

The Party apparatus at each level was divided into a number of departments. During NEP, the influence of the Party organisation in the economic sphere was limited and the Party apparatus was not so directly involved in the day-to-day control of the state apparatus. But political changes between 1928 and 1930 resulted in a change in Party organisation. By a Central Committee decision of January 1930, the Party apparatus was organised according to the 'functional' principle. Instead of the several branch departments which had existed in an undeveloped state in 1920s, there were established, at all levels of the Party structure, functional departments dealing with such matters as cadres and culture and propaganda.

In the Moscow Party organisation there were four departments (organisation-instructors, culture and propaganda, mass-agitation, cadres). Other secret departments were also established at the MK, but little is known about their work.[48] This system existed between 1930 and 1934. It was abolished at the XVIIth Party Congress on the strong recommendation of Kaganovich, leaning on his Moscow experience. A *de facto* departure from the functional principle can be discerned in Moscow as early as 1932. But Kaganovich's involvement in agriculture in 1932–33 was surely the turning point away from functionalism. These developments will now be considered in more detail.

(i) The Organisation-instructors Department
In Moscow, as elsewhere, the core of the Party bureaucracy was the *orginstr* department, which dealt mainly with the Party organisation itself. The increasing political importance of this department is reflected in the co-option of Malenkov, the regional head of the department, and Il'in, its

city head, as bureau members at this time. They controlled both information and appointments to lower Party organisations.

There were at least four sections in this department at the MK: they dealt with routine contacts; leadership and statistics; Party activity and Party construction; and Party cadres. Of twelve responsible instructors of the MK, seven were under this department.[49] To strengthen economic activities, a territorial-production sector was established under *orginstr* in 1932. This sector supervised the economy in each district. This was a new development in Party organisation, a departure in practice if not yet in principle from the functional principle replacing it by the production principle.

To facilitate information-gathering, an information sector was organised in summer 1933 at regional level; this was in contact with each district and with the Party organisations of 100 enterprises.[50]

The political influence of the *orginstr* department derived from its control of Party personnel, including promotion and key information about Party members. The Party-cadres sector of the department eagerly sought to promote heads of district *orginstr* departments to secretaries: according to one account Party activists from proletarian areas were promoted to the post of secretary even when their experience was inadequate in terms of official Party requirements.[51]

An important decision about the department and its work at district level was adopted by the MGK bureau on 27 July 1932. Relations between Party and managers had deteriorated, and the decision emphasised the lack of contact with enterprise Party cells, and urged district committee department heads to check, instruct and train the cell secretaries, and keep them informed, rather than merely providing general economic leadership.[52] This decision was also noteworthy because it classified industrial cells according to their branch of industry (metals, textiles and transport, etc); each branch had its own instructors. Thus, a *de facto* production-branch principle began to appear in the Party apparatus, even though the latter had been reorganised on a 'functional' basis at the beginning of 1930. The same tendency had been evident earlier in agricultural matters, but was quite new for industry. It was in Moscow that the tendency for specialised instructors to deal with particular industries first appeared; this principle later flourished throughout the Party apparatus.

This decision also made it clear that the MGK department should exercise control over the org.-instructors departments at the district level. The former was instructed to obtain better information from districts and enterprises; for this purpose an information sector was set up with three reporters and 65 informers.[53] The stenographic reports of meetings of the district committee and of important enterprises were directly checked by the head of the department, or by responsible instructors. These changes produced rather poor results. An auditing commissioner of the MGK noted that the department was merely investigating middle- and lower-level activities.[54]

(ii) The Cadres Department

While the *orginstr* department dealt with full-time workers in the Party apparatus, the cadres department dealt with the personnel of the government and non-party organisations: for example soviets, trade unions and economic institutions. The cadres department was also divided into sectors; in 1930 there were five sectors in the MK. Its supervisors investigated individuals and were supposed to appoint them to jobs suited to their competence. For example, industrial sector of the MK cadres department investigated 142 candidates and the city construction sector investigated about 100 persons. As only about a third or quarter of those investigated were actually promoted, the numbers covered were rather small.[55]

The activity of Statsevich, the head of the MK cadres department, covered a huge variety of major and minor appointments. Thus he allocated personnel to warehouses, to the chairmanship of hog-raising sovkhozes, and to politotdely.[56] It was under his chairmanship that a commission was organised to select Party activists for despatch to kolkhozes. The department also sent 90 engineers to the Moscow coal-mining areas, and responsible workers to vehicle factories. Sometimes personal responsibility for urgent appointments was imposed upon individual members of the staffs of the department: one was given the task of finding personnel for the supply department of a key factory, another was given orders to supply 20–25 engineers, 30–40 technicians and 50–70 foremen for construction work with the help of the labour department of the soviet.[57] At this time of shortages, special attention was paid to supply and co-operative personnel.[58]

In the MK, the role of the cadres department was very similar. The tasks assigned to Drizul, its head, included the training of brick-making specialists, the mobilisation of some 20 000 workers for Metro construction, the selection cadres for the Moscow-Volga canal; the selection of deputy managers specialised in supply for enterprises. He was also required to assist the fisheries, and strengthen the procuracy.[59] A certain Dmitriev was a member of a troika that checked canteen staffs, while somebody else checked the leading cadres of a bicycle factory that was supervised by the Mossoviet.[60]

(iii) The Culture-propaganda Department

At the end of 1931, cultural affairs were reorganised and control over them greatly strengthened after the criticism of Yaroslavskii's Party history and Stalin's intervention over the journal *Proletarskaya revolutsiya*. The new militant tendency in history and philosophy was strong in Moscow. The new head of the culture-propaganda department in the MK, Dubyna, was a historian strongly critical of the Pokrovsky school.[61]

The education of lower and middle Party workers was carried out under her direction. She organised the education of Party secretaries jointly with Malenkov; she also educated rural district secretaries and selected district cadres to be taught in the course for Party junior-leaders in the House of Zvengorod where Party cadres were trained.[62] She took charge of the reorganisation of the Communist Higher Education Institute into the Communist Agricultural Institute, under the general guidance of secretary Gei (responsible for culture-propaganda work in the Secretariat).

Angarov, the head of the equivalent MGK department, had similar functions. His remit included the training of people's judges and procurators in the Stuchka Soviet Law Institute and the Institute of Red Professors. The responsibilities of the department also included the theoretical training of Party propagandists and the organisation of workers' clubs. Party papers and journals like *Rabochaya Moskva* and *Vechernyaya Moskva* were under the supervision of the press sector of the department.[63]

The function of this department was thus not restricted to narrow Party education. It was also entrusted with the broader political-civic education of the masses, particularly in periods of crisis. Thus in connection with the 1933 decisions about the Donbass, the department organised education among peat workers, railway workers and other mass audiences.[64] It also supervised the education department of the soviets, which at the time was reorganising the school system. An important but difficult task was looking after homeless children. This department was also concerned with education in the countryside and among the national minorities.

(iv) The Mass-agitation Department

This was responsible for a variety of major campaigns, including mass industrial campaigns, rural campaigns, and work among woman and kolkhozniks. Mass campaigns often took place to cope with the agricultural crisis. The department was also concerned with the situation in factories. The head of the MGK department, Ratner, embarked on urgent enquiries about large enterprise in the spring of 1932, following reports of labour unrest.[65] The department was also supported to train

Decision-Making in the Party

agitators at the shop-floor level, and to organise patronage or *shefstvo* in rural areas.

(b) The Nomenklatura

We have seen that the allocation of personnel was handled in this period by both the *orginstr* and the cadres departments of the MK and MGK. At the heart of the selection, training and distribution of cadres was the nomenklatura.[66] There was a nomenklatura, a list of appointments and of suitable candidates, at each level of the Party organisation.

So far as Moscow was concerned, there were two or three kinds of nomenklatura within the MK and the MGK, with separate lists controlled by the bureau, the secretariat and the department. This division was flexible; the decision as to which *nomenklatura* should list a particular post was made by various MK and MGK institutions. The MGK plenum decision on the factory departments of workers' supply (ORS), dated 25 January 1933, may be taken as an example. This required the checking of 13 warehouse managers of various co-operatives: the cadres department carried out the work, and the secretariat approved it.[67]

On the other hand, a bureau decision of 9 December 1932 noted that the post of the deputy director in charge of supply was on the secretariat's nomenklatura.[68]

In a third case, the MGK secretariat decided to put the deputy procurator, the senior assistant and assistant procurators into the MGK nomenklatura, forbidding their removal without the approval of the secretariat.[69]

Thus a variety of institutions were concerned with what should be included in the secretariat nomenklatura. But it was the bureau and the secretariat that had the ultimate power to decide in which nomenklatura a particular post should appear.[70]

More important posts were on the nomenklatura of the secretariat, less important on the nomenklatura of the departments. For example, the MGK bureau decision on housing administration of September 1933 distinguished between posts approved by the secretariat and posts approved by the cadres department. The head of the Moscow Housing Trust (Moszhiltrest) administration, the chairman of the Moscow housing union and their deputies were approved by the secretariat. Their assistants, the director of the enterprise, the managers of Moszhiltrest houses and the inspectors were approved by the cadres department.[71] But even in the latter case, candidates were often confirmed at secretariat or bureau level. An example is the MGK bureau decision on the local brick industry: all directors were listed in the cadres department nomenklatura, but candidates were to be approved at a secretariat meeting.[72] Every meeting of the bureau and secretariat in 1933 confirmed between 10 and 20 names of appointments to posts in middle-level administration and economic management.[73]

3.3 THE 1934 REORGANISATION

The organisational structure of the Party was thoroughly revised at the XVIIth Party Congress in 1934, less than four years after the reorganisation of 1930. Both the reorganisation on functional principles in 1930 and the reorganisation, based on the branch principle in 1934, were launched by Kaganovich.

The 1934 reform had three major principles, all tried out in a preliminary way in Moscow in the previous two years.

First, the secretariat system was abolished except at the central level. All questions were to be presented directly to the bureau, whose membership was reduced to eleven (this change had already taken place in Moscow).[74] This reform turned out to be short-lived. The MK secretariat was never abolished; the MGK secretariat disappeared until March 1935, and than re-emerged.

Second, the 'commission system' was abolished; this had played a significant role in Moscow as a place for communication and decision by Party elites, specialists, and other institutions. No explanation of this move was given by Kaganovich, and there was no discussion of it at the Party Congress.

Third, it was recommended that the 'functional principle' of the Party apparatus be replaced in favour of a line and staff or 'production-branch' system. Kaganovich pointed out that the functional principle had weakened the party activities, and proposed to establish branch-industry departments:

> We need an integral department [for each branch], in charge of the primary Party organisations, Party work, mass agitation, selection of cadres, distribution of personnel, investigation of people, professional work, and so on.[75]

Following these decisions, several new departments were organised in the MK: agriculture (Statsevich), industry/transport (Makar), Soviet/trade (Leikand, former head of the MGK orginstr department), culture and propaganda of Leninism (Dubyna), leading Party organisations (Malenkov), and a so-called special sector. A financial-management sector was also set up.[76]

At first glance this change looks like a return to the system which existed before 1930, when each organisation had the production-branch system. However, this was not a mere revival of the old system. After the 'revolution from above', Party organisations were much more involved in the industrial sphere than they had been in the 1920s. Role differentiation in the Party apparatus was much more sharply-defined after the 1934 reorganisation than in any previous period. Possibly Kaganovich derived the idea for this reform from his experience in the agricultural department, and in the associated politotdel, in coping with the famine and the crisis of kolkhoz agriculture at the beginning of 1933. In any case, after 1933 the command structure, coupled with the subdivision of the organisation into narrow branches, became a firm characteristic of Party leadership in the social and economic fields.[77]

This reorganisation in Moscow resulted in the direction of the Party being concentrated in the hands of regional elites, and the semi-autonomous status of the MGK was subordinated to this. Kaganovich's organisational scheme required the abolition of departments at district level and their replacement by various systems of responsible instructors. Cities and districts of large cities were supposed to be excluded from this arrangement. But the Moscow leadership followed an even more centralising policy and abolished the departmental system at district level in Moscow itself, despite the resistance of 'some comrades'.[78]

On 7 March 1934 the Central Committee approved the 'initiative of the Moscow and Leningrad regional committees' which had reorganised the city and district-level apparatus, abolished the departmental system, and recommended that other cities should follow suit.[79] Except for the department for the culture and propaganda of Leninism, all the departments disappeared. In the MGK, two groups emerged in their place: a registry/information and a daily assignment/mobilisation group. The instructors system was used more intensively in compensation. For example, in industry two instructors were assigned to every 15 sub-divisions. It will be recalled that the instructor system was developed in Moscow city apparatus. The instructors were selected at the gorkom level but appointed at the MK level (another indication of centralisation). In total there had been about 550 instructors in Moscow; about forty per cent lost their jobs in the reorganisation.[80]

Whether these arrangements were rational is another matter. Within a year the Party cadres department was restored and this was followed by the revival of the secretariat.[81]

Compared with many other regional committees, which were overwhelmingly agrarian and simple, the Moscow organisation was differentiated and complex.

The tasks of the MGK differed substantially from those of the rural regional committees. But Kaganovich himself was also responsible for the rural areas in general in 1932–33, when Moscow had to provide politotdel workers to cope with agricultural difficulties. In this sense, Moscow could be regarded as a kind of avant-garde organisation for the Party as a whole.

4 The Party at the District Level

4.1 CHARACTERISTICS OF DIFFERENT DISTRICTS

Between 1931 and 1936, Moscow city was divided into ten districts (*raiony*), each of which had a larger population than a large regional city like Kalinin.[1] These city districts varied considerably in their social and economic characteristics. Frunze and Bauman districts, for instance, were similar in their social structure, with a fairly small proportion of workers and fairly high proportion of white-collar employees. The Bauman district had some textile and instrument-making factories, but its general character was that of an administrative and educational centre.

The Stalin and Proletarii districts in the Eastern part of Moscow were typical heavy-industrial areas in process of further industrialisation. A third of the metal industry was in Proletarii district, including ball-bearing, bicycle and electrical engineering (Dynamo) factories. Most of the electrical engineering industry, however, was concentrated in the Stalin district. The leaders of these districts were primarily concerned with the construction of factories, houses and roads.

Sokol'niki district included three railway terminals. Transport and related industries were located in this district, together with some light industries. The Dzerzhinsky and Oktyabr' districts, to the north of Moscow, were not primarily industrial areas; however, the Kalibr factory was situated in the Dzerzhinsky district and the Oktyabr' district had some chemical works.

Krasnaya-Presnya in the West, once famous for its revolutionary spirit, was the centre for textiles, food and other light industries. Khrushchev was first secretary there for a time in 1931. The Lenin and Zamoskvorets districts were newly expanding areas. Food and metal industries were located in the Lenin district, and footwear, textile and leather industries in Zamoskvorets. Both districts had a dense working-class population.[2]

4.2 CONTROL OF THE DISTRICT BY MK AND MGK

The abolition of the *okrug* (the intermediate administrative unit between district and region, established in 1929) in mid-1930 extended the authority of the district Party organisation and gave greater opportunity for the regional Party to control the district Party organisations.[3] The MK bureau became more directly involved in district affairs. According to one report, the MK bureau and secretariat discussed district matters 661 times in 1932–33, as compared with only ten times in 17 months between 1929–30.[4]

There were several channels through which the MK and MGK could control district affairs. First, local officials, and especially the raikom (district committee) secretaries were promoted or demoted under the auspices of the MK or MGK. Thus, following unsatisfactory grain and potato procurements, Utkin, secretary of Efremov district, was dismissed by the MK bureau and the MKK (Moscow Control Commission) presidium, with the endorsement of the MK plenum.[5]

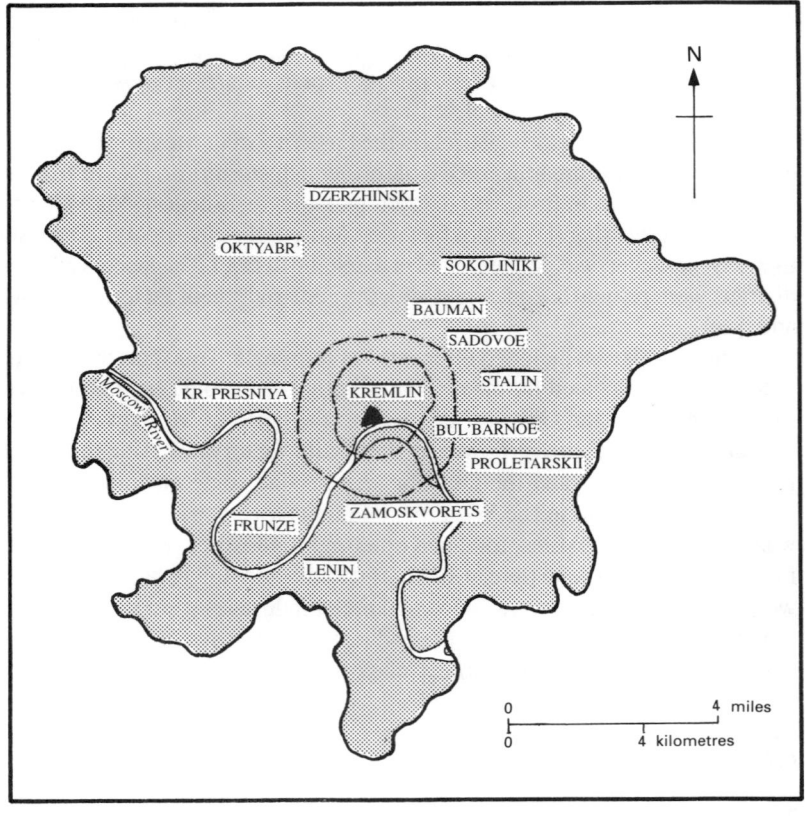

FIGURE 4.1 *Moscow City*

This shows that the secretary of a district committee in the region was listed on the nomenklatura of the MK bureau.[6] Moscow raikom secretaries in the city as distinct from the region were sometimes dealt with at a higher level. In the case of Ryutin and Pen'kov, the tough 'Right deviationist' secretaries dismissed in October 1928, the Central Committee directly intervened.[7]

The first secretaries frequently changed in this period. Of ten district committee secretaries in 1932, only one held the same position in 1934. Several changes in personnel are particularly noteworthy. At least five among the 10 secretaries in 1931 were moved to the city or regional level in 1932 (Filatov as head of MGKK, Moscow City Control Commission; Khrushchev, Egorov and Ruben as secretaries; Dubyna as a department head). Karpov worked as both Frunze raikom secretary and Mossoviet presidium secretary for some time in 1933–34. Trofimov was closely related to Postyshev, Central Committee secretary.[8] Korotchenkov later became Moscow secretary and eventually Ukrainian head of state in the 1950s, apparently under the patronage of Khrushchev. Apart from him, no district committee secretary of 1934 survived, at least politically.

The second channel of control by the MK and MGK was the common practice of direct dispatch of regional officials to local areas. In 1932–33, 220 long-term missions by regional bureau or secretariat members were recorded; this implies that every district was visited by top MK officials more than once.[9] As many as 8156 short visits were recorded; this was the equivalent of visiting each district once every two weeks.

TABLE 4.1 *District Committee Secretaries in Moscow City, 1931–34*

District	1931	1932	1934
Lenin	Filatov	Soifer	Soifer
Oktyabr'	Egorov	Andreasyan	Andreasyan
Sokol'niki	Bessonov	Starostin	Starostin
Dzerzhinsky	Soifer	Korytnyi	Korytnyi
Bauman	Khrushchev*[1]	Trofimov	Korotchenkov
Krasnaya-Pr.	Dubyna	Khrushchev*[2]	Bukharin
Zamoskvorets	Kul'kov	Kul'kov?	Volkov
Stalin	Trofimov	Margolin	Margolin
Frunze	Ruben	Karpov	Karpov
Proletarii	Gaidul'	Gaidul'*[3]	Kul'kov

* 1 Khrushchev was replaced by Margolin.
* 2 Khrushchev was replaced by Bukharin, K. I. (*Pravda*, 26 March 1932)
* 3 Gaidul' was replaced by Kul'kov (Rabochaya Moskva, 6 March, 1933)

For example, Orekhovo-Zuevo district, celebrated for its textile industry, was visited by secretaries Mikhailov, Ryndin, and Gei.[10] The MKK chairman Peters, instructed by the MK bureau, is said to have visited the barracks reconstruction in this district 'almost every day'. The MK criticised the inadequate control over shop cell secretaries by the district committee, and ordered Shurov, the district committee secretary, to see shop secretaries individually for two or three weeks in the spring of 1933. This decision also listed the secretaries of the shop cells in the nomenklatura of the district committee. The MK even summoned shop cell secretaries in large enterprises to headquarters, and MK officials in turn visited shop-cell secretaries.[11] The MK bureau, primed by Kaganovich, even noted and issued a warning about the Mosnarpit canteen in this district.[12]

In general, however, it was agricultural matters which involved the strict regional control of district affairs. In the Udomlya district, lack of 'class vigilance' and the poor control of the kolkhozes were condemned by the joint September 1932 decision of the MK and MKK.[13] The district committee secretary was warned, and four officials from the MK cadres department were sent to strengthen the soviet apparatus. In the rift between the politotdely and the district committees (see Chapter 9), the district committee secretaries were threatened with dismissal.[14] In addition, the MK and MGK selected 1000 large kolkhozes for observation and direct communication.[15]

A third way in which control was maintained was the grouping of districts into zones by the Central Committee and the MK. Each zone had specific economic characteristics. By 1931, for example, linen, textile, and grain zones were distinguished in connection with the bureau cell election campaign.[16] To handle this differentiation in guidance leadership, a territorial-production sector was established in the MK orginstr department. MGK bureau decision in July 1932 on the district orginstr departments insisted on stronger connections between the districts and important cells.[17]

A fourth channel of control of the region and city over the districts was known as the 'passport' system; it was in the Moscow region that the term 'passports' was originally introduced (not to be confused with the internal passports issued to individuals). The characteristics of each district were summarised in its so-called 'passport'. While the system was supposed to facilitate the study of personnel, it also investigated districts, enterprises and kolkhozes as a whole.[18] In the 'passport' for each unit, Party and economic information was set up so as to enable the MK and MGK to obtain a 'wider, comprehensive knowledge of each unit'. The passports were stored in the new information sector of the orginstr department.[19] The passport on each district committee contained reports, documents, newspaper cuttings, regional decisions applicable to that district, personal details of '20–30 cadres'and economic and geographical characteristics.[20] Passports were compiled in the passport section (*chast'*) of the orginstr department. In the region, 146 districts and 100 enterprises were covered by this work; in the city there were some 30 enterprises and, subsequently 300 passports were compiled.[21] The Central Committee recommended the passport system for wide application.

Fifthly, the extent to which the nomenklatura system controlled district or lower units was significant but should not be overestimated. At that time personnel files and records were classified and held not at the centre but at the district or cell of the member concerned. The MK or MGK merely collected quarterly statistical data on the composition and trends of membership.[22] Direct control from the MK centre over individual members was uncommon, except in the case of certain officials and members.

Finally, the leadership of those districts which contained major enterprises was of vital concern to the MK or MGK. The performance of the district was measured by the plan-fulfilment of these enterprises, so district committee secretaries willingly co-operated with them. According to the regional leadership, this co-operation sometimes resulted in nepotism (*semeistvennost'*). In the Kaganovich ball-bearing works, the major enterprise of the Proletarii district in the city, the party secretary of the factory committee interfered in operational management, and in autumn 1931 the MGK proposed his dismissal. But the Proletarii district secretary protected him. Eventually in May 1932, the MGK succeeded in dismissing this factory secretary and prohibited him from taking another important job for two years.[23] The district committee leadership was strictly warned. Khrushchev commented that: 'We dismissed the secretary of this committee and brought the Moscow organisation into line.'[24]

The responsibility of the district committee for factory performance was frequently emphasised. At the Yakhroma textile factory in Dmitrov district the summer 1932 plan was not fulfilled, although the MK had issued several warnings. The MK complained that mass Party activity, and concern with the daily material interests of the workers, was insufficient, and in an open letter even hinted at labour unrest in this factory: 'Communists, instead of assuming the ideological and political offensive against the hostile and backward mood, followed it.'[25] The MK secretariat warned the Dmitrov district secretary that he was personally responsible, and sent the warning to all Moscow district committees.[26]

4.3 THE FRUNZE AND STALIN DISTRICTS: TWO CASE STUDIES

This section examines in more detail the socio-political settings at district level. Frunze district, formerly Khamovniki, was located south-west of the city centre in a bend of the Moscow river, and was a traditional dense-populated area with about half a million inhabitants. Textile and artisan industry predominated up to the end of the 1920s. A quarter of Moscow textile workers were employed here; its original name indicates that it was a cotton-weaving quarter. In 1933 51 000 were employed here in 41 enterprises; half of them were female.[27] Three quarters of them had been recruited in the previous three years, mainly from the countryside. Workers of 15 or more years experience amounted to only 2.5 per cent of the total. Labour turnover was high. Nevertheless, one eighth of the workforce were communists.

In this district, in spite of this substantial industrial presence, the proportion of white-collar employees was higher than in any other district, and the proportion of blue-collar worker was lower. There were 4000–5000 technicians, of whom 31 per cent were communists; this was a very high concentration. Many educational establishments, at all levels from primary to higher, were located here. There were about 25 000 students in the higher educational establishments.[28]

By contrast, the Stalin district was a newly-built area, far distant from the city centre and located in the East. Its population was initially quite small, but grew rapidly, from 110 000 in 1928 to 260 000 in 1933.[29] The proportion of the white-collar employees, 55–65 per cent, was lower than in any other district. This was a district of newly-developing metalworking and clothing industries, and two-thirds of Moscow's electrical engineering was located here.[30]

The district took first place among the ten districts for new building floor-space in 1933.[31] There was a planning scheme for this district even before the plan for Moscow as a whole. But living conditions in the district were particularly poor.

(a) The Party in the Frunze and Stalin districts

About 23 000 communists (including candidates) were working or studying in the Frunze district, but the purge reduced numbers by 26.6 per cent.[32] The Stalin district, with its smaller population, had a maximum of 17 000 members; about 2000 were purged in 1933.[33] The proportion of students in the Party membership of the Frunze district was particularly high; in 1931 41.7 per cent were classified as students.[34] After the purge the proportion fell to 32.7 per cent; the proportion of workers was then higher at 36.8 per cent. This decline in the number of communists students was ascribed not to the purge but to mobilisations for various agricultural campaigns: the Central Committee and MK recruited about some 600 members from this district to work in rural areas as politotdel heads or managers of MTS and sovkhozes.[35]

As elsewhere, the Frunze and Stalin districts held Party conference every two years to 'select' district committee members (i.e. to approve their nomination).[36] The bureau consisted of 5–7 members, including the district committee secretaries, the chairman of the district soviet and the heads of major enterprises and institutions. The first secretaries of Moscow city district committees were in fact appointed by the MK or the Central Committee. The Frunze district secretary Ruben was appointed as MGK secretary in 1932 and replaced by Karpov, former chairman of the district soviet executive committee. Karpov, in his turn, was appointed secretary of the Mossoviet from March 1933, retaining his job as party district secretary for some time.[37] The secretary of Stalin raion, Margolin, had been the secretary of the Bauman district committee. Probably because of the importance of this industrial base, Margolin was elected and remained an MGK bureau member. In 1934 some new members of the MGK came from these districts: Babushkin (Frunze district) became a candidate of the MGK, and the second secretary of Stalin district became a full member.[38]

The district committee bureaucracy had the same structure as the city or regional organisation, although it was small, the staff never exceeded about 35.[39] The Stalin district committee bureau in 1932 had 13 members, of whom five were secretariat members. The secretariat was notorious for its reluctance to convene meetings, decisions being made by correspondence (*opros*).[40]

Until the abolition of functional departments in 1934, four departments existed in the district committee. The orginstr department of Stalin district committee, for example, checked and recruited party members of economic organisations. The cadre department of the same raikom also sent some 52 members to be heads of politotdely, and as many as 50 000 were mobilised for short-term campaigns. 134 were sent for Metro construction work.[41] After the abolition of the department system in 1934, the instructors system was introduced; each district committee had some 12–15 instructors in various production areas such as chemical and transport.[42]

Apart from the full-time apparatchiki, the district Party consisted of leading Party members from a variety of enterprises and institutions. From a political point of view, an important group were secretaries of enterprises, soviets, and higher educational institutions. In the Frunze raikom, the information sector directed its attention to the 78 enterprise secretaries, 36 secretaries of higher educational institutions, and the 48 party officials in the soviets.[43] Enterprise secretaries were required to have eight years Party membership. The secretaries in the higher educational institutions had even longer Party experience; most had entered the Party in 1916–20. The high turnover of secretaries was notorious in these years of transformation and crisis.

The lower level of district Party cadres was the group *partorg*, located in the factories and on the shop floors in 39 enterprises. There were about 550 group partorgs in Frunze district, most of them having been recruited during the 'revolution from above'.[44]

For the Stalin district, data on the middle and lower party cadres is rather vague. The 134 secretaries of enterprises and factory cells must have been an important, or even dominant group.[45] These were mainly of worker origin (77.3 per cent, according to unreliable statistics), and about sixty per cent had been Party members for five or more years. Some 40 per cent were said to have higher education.

Secretaries of factory shops or departments were also important in this working-class district. As many as 138 secretaries out of 293 were full-time Party officials. About 40 per cent had been Party members for more than 5 years. 1415 members were classified as 'grouporg' and 'partorg', and usually worked on the factory floor.[46]

The Stalin district had great trouble selecting enterprise and factory secretaries. Four secretaries were ousted after the 1933 purge. In the Komega factory, the shop secretaries turned out to have been purged from another district. Khrushchev criticised the lack of vigilance in the work of the raikom orginstr department at the beginning of 1934.[47]

No less important than the allocation of Party workers was the selection of managers, ostensibly conducted by the raikom cadres department; this was somewhat formal procedure and in reality appointments were made at the commissariat (ministerial) level or by the Central Committee. In the case of Frunze district 53 managers in 56 major enterprises were Old Bolsheviks, recruited by the Party in the Revolution or Civil War, aged 40–45, and educated in the primary school.[48]

They had occupied their positions for more than five or more years. Even at the level of shop-manager or foreman, almost half were communists. On the other hand, at the technical director level, 15 out of 21 were non-communists.

In the Stalin district, on the other hand, the Party affiliation of economic officials is less certain. Of 653 communist-managers and foremen, 624 were of worker origin; 218 were classified as higher education graduates, and a further 110 were attending the Promakademiya.[49] The purge commission recommended a strengthening of the communist presence in the Stalin district; and in Narpittrust, for example, communist strength quadrupled after the purge.[50]

(b) The Soviet in Frunze and Stalin districts

The structure and function of the district soviet system (*raisovety* and *raiispolkom*) replicated the regional and city soviet in miniature. The raisoviet congress selected the ispolkom (executive committee), which included up to 45 members and candidates. The raiispolkom in its turn selected a presidium; according to the 1931 statute the presidium should include not more than nine full and four candidate members.[51]

The raiispolkom was required to organise a minimum of six sections (soviet construction, education, industry/labour/supply, agriculture, finance/budget and health). But this was a minimum figure: the Stalin district had as many as 16 sections.[52]

A centralising tendency was obvious from 1929 onwards. The Mossoviet or Mosgorispolkom (Moscow city executive committee) proposed that new district departments should be established.[53] These were subordinated to the corresponding Mossoviet department as well as the district soviet presidium. Even city planning felt this tendency, although it showed some resistance. An outspoken chairman of the Frunze district soviet, Kirillov, criticised 'the tendency among Mossoviet department to concentrate and centralise the various separate service branches': the Mossoviet department allocated land without consulting the district which was involved. This was rejected by Perchik, head of the city planning department, who frankly defended centralisation, arguing that 'the problem of replacing and rebuilding Moscow can and must be resolved not on the scale of the individual district but on the level of the city as a whole'.[54]

However, this centralising tendency should not be overestimated. Among 500 projects initiated by one district soviet, only two or three were submitted for the approval of the Mossoviet, according to the raiispolkom chairman.[55] Even though the Mossoviet's activities at the district level increased, the district soviet could still by-pass Mossoviet and run its own district affairs. But in general the range of freedom of the raiispolkom was too narrow to allow any development of initiative. Bulganin acknowledged that the district soviet should be strengthened in order to cope with current economic problems, but no effective change took place.[56]

5 The Governmental Process in Moscow

5.1 THE SOVIET AS UNIT OF GOVERNMENT

As already mentioned, Moscow city was detached from the regional system at the beginning of 1931, and henceforth enjoyed a semi-autonomous status.[1] Even before this, the city was a powerful component of the regional administration. According to an RSFSR (Russian Republic) decree on the relationship between the regional executive committee (oblispolkom) and the city executive committee (gorispolkom), the city had considerable autonomy vis-à-vis the region. The chairman of the oblispolkom could not simultaneously be chairman of the gorispolkom. This trend was strengthened when the city was detached from the region.[2]

This division between region and city was finally confirmed by the Central Committee plenum resolution of June 1931 on Moscow city. The trade unions, the Party and the co-operatives were also separated out from the region, although sometimes this separation was only nominal.

However, separation of regional and city organisations gave rise to some difficulties in the suburban and satellite areas of the capital. To protect the interests of the city in the 14 neighbouring districts, permanently working commissions, embracing both the city and its suburban districts were established in 1933. The presidium of the meeting consisted of Kaminsky (chairman), Bulganin, and the Mossoviet secretary. In these areas the development of forestry and factories needed the special permission of this presidium.[3]

5.2 THE OBLISPOLKOM PRESIDIUM AND MOSSOVIET PRESIDIUM

According to the formal procedure, each soviet plenum elected by the full soviet congress appointed the ispolkom (the executive committee that could act in the name of the soviet), and the presidium of the ispolkom. For example, the February 1931 plenum of the Moscow city soviet (Mossoviet) selected 63 gorispolkom members as well as a presidium of 14 full members and three candidate members.[4] At that time the presidium met three times a month, the ispolkom twice a month, and the plenum once a month.⁵

The presidium included the main Party leaders and secretaries, and the heads of important soviet departments. Among the most important members were the oblispolkom and Mossoviet chairmen. Kaminsky was appointed oblispolkom chairman in 1932; Bulganin was Mossoviet chairman at that time.⁶ These two were not only leading members of the MK, but were also elected as candidate members of the Party Central Committee in 1934. They acted in effect as oblispolkom and Mossoviet factions within the Party; their role was just as important as that of the second secretaries Ryndin and Khrushchev.⁷

According to the MK decision on the oblispolkom, dated September 1933, the duties of the chairman were regularised as follows:

> Leadership in all matters, checking implementation, summoning heads of departments and institutions, collecting information before presidium meetings about the items on the agenda, checking execution and chairmanship, defence problems and representation in higher governmental organisations, signing presidium decisions and issuing visas.⁸

Kaminsky also had control over the agriculture, industry and construction departments, as well as banks and procurement institutions. It is not clear whether Bulganin had the same jurisdiction. As he was in charge of obtaining materials and resources for the various construction projects, he was probably responsible for industry and construction, but there are few references to his work in agriculture.⁹ One of Bulganin's major functions was to handle appeals for resources and materials with higher institutions like the Central Committee or the Commissariat of Heavy Industry. He was also involved in planning and obtaining the resources needed for construction.¹⁰ It would be simplistic, however, to regard the role of soviet chairman, especially at the city level, as that of a mere servant for the Party apparatchiki. Bulganin was no mere subordinate to Khrushchev. Kaganovich's role was considerable, however. In spite of his obligations at the central level, he frequently intervened in Moscow affairs.¹¹

The daily routine of each presidium was handled by its five-man sub-committee (*pyaterka*).¹² In the case of the oblispolkom, the *pyaterka* was confirmed by the MK bureau decision on the function and internal structure of the oblispolkom in September 1933.¹³ This committee comprised Kaminsky, Ter (deputy chairman), Guberman (head of the regional planning committee or oblplan), Peters (head of the regional control commission, or MKK) and the oblispolkom secretary (this was probably Kuchimin). There was a division of labour between the *pyaterka* members. The deputy chairman controlled finance, supply, health, light industry, education, forestry, communal services, handicraft industry and co-operatives; Guberman was in charge of fuel and transport; Peters was in charge of the procuracy, courts, foreign trade and exports.[14]

The membership of the Mossoviet *pyaterka*, which was formed in August 1932, is less certain. Bulganin, Khvesin (deputy chairman) and Filatov (MGKK, or city control commission) were no doubt members. Khvesin often acted in the name of the party *faction* of Mossoviet, while Filatov compiled the control figures for Moscow trusts and institutions.[15] Mel'bard (of the city planning commission) was probably also a member of the presidium. He was co-opted as MGK bureau member in February 1933 and was deputy chairman between 1934 and 1936. The Mossoviet secretary, Shurov, was succeeded by Shternberg and Brezanovsky in 1932, and eventually by Karpov in 1933. The secretary had to co-ordinate the work of the presidium as well as the pyaterka, and was also the head of the Mossoviet organisation department.[16]

The pyaterki met every two or three days to discuss routine affairs.[17] Every five days they met department heads, and in any case they maintained daily contact with the departments. One of the five was available every day for meetings with the chairmen of the district soviets and other officials.

The presidium included about 11–15 members: the pyaterka, the Party secretaries, and the heads of departments and administrations.[18] Under the system of 'dual subordination', each department was subordinated both to the presidium and to the next highest branch organisation level. Heads of important departments had often been deputy chairmen until the reduction of officials in 1933.[19]

With the approval of the Party bureau, the presidium could establish new departments. At the end of 1931 departments were organised for social security; supply; fuel and energy; and the construction of the Metro.[20] Additional departments followed in 1933: construction; culture and civic education; work among adults; veterinary services.[21] The department for city land and land allocation was reorganised in 1933 (see Chapter 10).[22] There were also eight administrations, mainly concerned with the management of specific enterprises.

The oblispolkom organisation department was crucial. It dealt with co-ordination with other institutions, the checking of the allocation, recording, informing and preparing of cadres. In view of its significance, the department was chaired by the presidium secretary.[23] In Moscow, this department and its instructors had already been reorganised on the production-branch principle by 1932.[24] By 1934 it included 43 paid officials, including 24 instructors. Sub-groups within the department were responsible for such matters as record-information and cadre rationalisation. Special attention was paid to information collection.[25]

The presidium also set up *ad hoc* commissions for particular tasks, or appointed plenipotentiaries. In 1933 the main administration of the militia set up the passport department and at the presidium the head of this department proposed to establish a special commission.[26] To regulate the markets during the period of extreme scarcity in January 1933, the presidium established a special commission which had the right to close, or take measures to 'normalise' the marketplaces.[27] The struggle with 'speculators' was dealt with by sending officials from the supply department to the markets.[28] To check the potato warehouses, about 400 people were mobilised under the guidance of the supply department and the Workers' and Peasants' Inspection. A commission headed by the city procurator was responsible for checking the repair of houses for the winter; another commission was established to prepare a plan for the development of public transport.[29]

A special official, Khoroshilkin, was appointed as plenipotentiary of the Mossoviet for vegetable storage, and could call upon the help of other

TABLE 5.1 *Mossoviet Presidium, March 1933*

Kaganovich	MGK first secretary
Khrushchev	MGK second secretary
Bulganin	Mossoviet chairman
Khvesin	Deputy chairman
Mel'bard	Deputy chairman, city planning commission
Filatov	Deputy chairman, chairman of MGKK
Karpov	Secretary
Kogan	MGK secretary
Shternberg	Water supply
Samoshikin	Tramways trust
Usov	Public services organisation
Badaev	Consumer co-operative, or MSPO
Perchik	Department of city planning
Romanov	Department of finance
Konstantinopol'skii	Construction administration
Komarov	Department of agriculture
Shulyakovskii	Housing administration

Of the members of Mossoviet presidium listed above, Mel'bard and Usov became deputy chairmen under Bulganin, while Filatov was elevated to replace Kaminsky, chairman of the oblispolkom (*Rabochaya Moskva*, 17 March 1933).

departments.[30] The MGK bureau also appointed plenipotentiaries with responsibility for the workers' dormitories, both at the Moscow level and in the districts.

In the Stalin district committee the bureau appointed twenty-one plenipotentiaries to deal with the dormitories problem; the appointments were made by the Party bureau itself.[31] The head of the fuel and energy department was appointed special plenipotentiary of Mossoviet to deal with the urgent question of mobilising energy sources. He could demand all the required measures from the 'special apparatus' as well as from members of Mossoviet and other organisations.[32] Plenipotentiaries were appointed for agricultural matters such as rabbit farming or the transport of horse fodder. Thus the permanent departmental structure was supplemented by *ad hoc* arrangements to deal with crises and temporary problems.

5.3 THE SECTIONS

A characteristic of soviet administrative activity, with no equivalent in western society, were the sections (*sektsii*). These were intended to involve the population at large and institutions in the various fields of soviet activity. The sections were a point of contact between the government, social institutions, and the population. According to the 1931 statute on the city soviet, there were to be sections for communal construction, finance, education, social culture, co-operation and trade and other matters.[33] Other sections established in Moscow dealt with housing, the Red Army, the Metro, automobile and horse transport, railways, and tramways. Thus there tended to be a section for each soviet department.[34]

Participants in a section included soviet members, candidate members and delegates, and also activists from the general public, and from the institutions such as trade unions.

Soviet delegates were required to be members of sections (*sektsionery*). Section meetings usually took place once or twice a month, and discussed the activities of the departments, their planning, and their supervision and checking. Sometimes their responsibilities included the promotion of personnel (*vydvizhenie*), and the rationalisation of the apparatus. In October 1932 the Mossoviet included 3000 delegates and 7000 section members.[35] The same structure existed at district level: the Stalin district, for example, had 16 sections with 1564 section members in 1933.[36]

Sections had the important function of mobilising the public. Thus various Mossoviet sections – including those for tramways, municipal economy, health, transport, public catering and supply – made a joint appeal to the trusts to prepare for May Day.[37] Active support for campaigns was also encouraged.[38] As one illustration, about 300 section members were mobilised to supervise the stables.

Sections worked intermittently, and sometimes were quite inactive. Kiselev warned the All-Union Executive Committee in January 1933 about the need for an 'urgent and decisive turn'.[39] In the following months the MGK and Mossoviet joint plenum discussed the work of the sections, and subsequently the newspapers, reflecting the result of the plenum, criticised some sections and delegate groups for not working on a daily basis.[40]

But in general the activity of the sections in Moscow city had some real substance.

5.4 PLANNING: SYSTEM AND PRACTICE

The Moscow planning agencies, oblplan and gorplan, were the local planning and co-ordination institutions. The planning agencies were faced with serious problems. Their organisation was weak and their burdens enormous. Communication with other organisations, including Gosplan, the people's commissariats and the enterprises was poor. Checking of the implementation of plans was neglected. Control agencies like Rabkrin severely criticised the planning agencies for failing to secure mass participation in the form of counter-plans. The oblispolkom tended to regard the planning agencies as mere secretariats of the presidium. A serious purge was undertaken in 1931.[41]

The drafting of the 1933 control figures and financial plans for Moscow, however, was delayed, and was carried out against a background of deepening crisis. Poor grain procurement results after the 1932 harvest in the USSR as a whole threatened the plan for 1933, even though Moscow's results were exceptionally good.

I will illustrate decision-making in local planning by examining the drafting of the 1933 Moscow city economic plans as a case study. In this age of centralisation, basic planning took place at the central level. Economic decisions were made in the commissariats for heavy and light industry. Thus little room was left for the regional or city planners to develop their own initiatives. Nevertheless, some significant decisions were made at the local level.

Planning for each year started in the middle of the preceding year. The Sovnarkom of the USSR set the timetable. Planning was usually completed before the end of the previous year. Thus the 1934 economic plans were approved by the MK and the MGK joint bureau on 19 December 1933.[42]

So far as the oblplan is concerned, each trust and institution under its control was scheduled to present its plan by 20 September, to be incorporated in the oblplan by 1 October. However, the 1932–33 crisis delayed drafting, and the economic plan for Moscow was not finally complete until in January–February 1933.[43] The initial budget for Moscow was prepared by the Mossoviet financial department, and then presented to the presidium, with the gorplan participating in the process.[44]

On 4 January 1933 the MGK bureau approved the 'Moscow 1933 control figures'.[45] The decision was divided into 15 items. First came the item on population, in relation to the introduction of the internal passport system. Other items included heavy industry, light industry, housing construction, dormitory reconstruction, housing repair, municipal economy, culture, health, the Moscow-Volga Canal and the Metro. Each item was subdivided into detailed instructions. For example, the item on municipal economy was followed by specific points for (1) tramways, (2) buses, (3) highways, (4) embankments, (5) drainage, (6) city cleaning, (7) outside lighting, (8) trees and plants, (9) public bath and wash houses, and (10) the Mosmekhpromgruz trust.

The bureau meeting on 4 January made significant changes in the initial proposals. First, in accordance with the policy of reducing the city population, the Moscow maximum was cut from 3.6 to 3.3 million by the end of 1933.[46] For that purpose, a transfer of the higher education system was planned, and a commission was requested to submit a proposal at the next bureau meeting. Internal passports, although a powerful control mechanism, were not decided at the city level.

Second, in industrial policy, increased investment in the two watch factories and the bicycle factories was recommended; these all came under the city jurisdiction.[47] In light industry, increased production by the Mosbel'e and Mosgorkozh trusts, both producing consumer goods, was emphasised. A commission was also established to expand the footwear industry. But the effect of city-level decisions by MGK or Mossoviet on Moscow industrial production as a whole was very limited. Most investment decisions were made at a level beyond the reach of city organisations.

When formulating economic policy and control figures, various institutions played an influential role. First, as the pivotal organisation in city politics, the MGK secretariat was instructed to convene the meeting for an increase of consumer goods production.[48] The secretariat was also instructed to propose at the next bureau meeting the formation of an association for consumer goods, including handicraft industry, taking the MGK bureau's opinions into consideration.[49]

The Mossoviet fraction (in the person of Bulganin), was asked to prepare the house-construction financial plan for the January – March quarter, and present it to the next bureau meeting.[50] Two Mossoviet deputy chairmen, in consultation with the planning commission, were ordered to prepare a plan for the location and priorities of building, including hotels. In its turn, gorplan was evidently an active participant in bureau meetings. It proposed the electrification of snow-clearance operations, and increased electric lighting. It was also asked to prepare project lists for the health service.

However, no one institution could totally control city-level decision-making. A system of commissions, comprising the MGK, Mossoviet, gorplan and other institutions formed the centre of decision-making. The roles of Bulganin, Khrushchev, and Mel'bard (of gorplan) were crucial; Mel'bard was appointed to become a member of the bureau in February 1933. There are several examples illustrating the role of the *ad hoc* commissions. Light industry resource allocation was entrusted to Khrushchev, Bulganin and gorplan.[51] The question of transferring higher education facilities to suburban areas was put to a commission headed by Kogan, Mel'bard and the head of the MGK culture propaganda department.[52] With the tramways, a city transport bottleneck, the secretary Voropaev was commissioned to investigate transport volume with the assistance of a deputy chairman of Mossoviet and a representative of the railways.[53] One troublesome trust (Mosmekhpromgruz) was entrusted to the care of Bulganin, Davidson (supplies secretary) and Filatov.[54]

This process of achieving a consensus about decisions through the commission system was again illustrated at an MGK bureau meeting some time later which it discussed the 1933 control figures for the Moscow economy and the Moscow budget. For the watch factories, a commission was set up consisting of Khrushchev, Mel'bard, and the district secretary; this had the power to convene special on-site meetings to take appropriate measures.[55] For the building of ships' motors, Bulganin, Voropaev, Filatov and others were asked to compile a plan for 1933, inviting relevant people.[56] A commission for the compilation of project lists consisting of two Mossoviet deputy chairmen was set up on 4 January, and enlarged by the addition of Khrushchev, Bulganin, Filatov and others on 23 January; the enlargement presumably reflected the importance of this question.[57] This new commission was, when necessary, to involve chairman of district executive committees and district secretaries for formulating district-level plans. On that same day several commissions were constituted or reorganised, including Mel'bard's wages commission and Filatov's labour-productivity commission. Khrushchev took part in the agricultural commission.[58]

The process by which plans were implemented, once they were on the agendas of the commission and bureau meetings, is also worth describing. Thus, the bureau decision of 4 January required the Mossoviet fraction to present revised draft control figures to the next bureau meeting, after an exchange of opinions.[59] Each enterprise and administration of Mossoviet was asked to present its quality index of the plan to gorplan, and this was to be examined by the Mossoviet presidium fraction, and eventually by the MGK bureau. Investment plans for each area or sector in the first quarter of 1933 were also handed for elaboration to the Mossoviet presidium, for approval by the MGK bureau by 15 January. In its turn, gorplan was regarded to play an important role in practical questions like the distribution of materials, subject to the approval of the Mossoviet presidium and the MGK bureau.

This procedure shows clearly that the MGK Party bureau was the final decision-making body in Moscow city and regional politics; even the Mossoviet presidium needed its approval to carry out its plans. Use of the Mossoviet reserve budget needed the sanction of the MGK secretariat as well as that of the Mossoviet.[60] But this does not necessarily imply that the local soviets were powerless, mere puppets of the Party bureaucracy. It only concerned the lower stages of the decision-making procedure. Actual policy formation was initiated by the Mossoviet fraction or departments, together with gorplan, so far as the plans and the budget were concerned. Without their help even the powerful apparatchiki could not have governed the city or localities.

More concretely, for the project list of the construction plan the bureau decided on 23 January that the procedure to be followed by the commissions would be as follows: discussion at the Mossoviet presidium, followed by final approval by the MGK bureau meeting.[61] Initially, this commission had been formed by two deputy chairmen of Mossoviet on 4 January, and later Khrushchev, Bulganin, Filatov and a secretary were co-opted. Thus the plan evidently originated in the apparatus of the soviet and was then revised by the more authoritative members such as Khrushchev and Bulganin before being finally agreed by the MGK bureau.

A year later, the project list was divided into three parts. The first part was to be approved by the MK and MGK, the second by the Mossoviet, and the third (minor construction) to be directly planned by the economic organisations.[62] In the first group, the construction plan was to be submitted to the Mossoviet, before approval by the MK and MGK. Thus, in this important and typical instance, the relationship between political party and executive was directly opposite to that in western society.

6 The Party and Social Problems

The patterns of links between central government and Moscow local government were very varied. As we will see in Chapter 7, industrial decision-making was largely undertaken at the centre; only implementation and its control was left for the regional or local authorities.

At the other extreme, 'decentralised' decision-making was permitted in such areas as social and welfare functions, and in the municipal economy, which will be described in Chapter 10.

In some major matters of central policy, the central government referred specific aspects of policy to the Moscow government. In 1932, the Central Committee and Sovnarkom planned to build housing for specialist workers, and some months later the MGK bureau submitted proposals for building ten blocks of flats to the Central Committee.[1] This was also the case with the construction of the Moscow Metro (see Chapter 10). But in such cases this is a matter of convenience; the housing for specialists and the Metro were both almost entirely financed by the national budget and controlled from the centre.

We shall discuss some examples of the varying role of the local authorities in this chapter: law and order; education; the internal passport system; the treatment of homeless waifs. In all these cases, the hand of the central government was rather strong, allowing limited room for regional or city-level government to bring influence to bear.

6.1 LAW AND ORDER

Judicial and militia organisations, as an essential part of the 'dictatorship of the proletariat', were all the more important after the XVIIth Party conference of 1932, which emphasised the need to strengthen the state apparatus.[2] In the years of stress, 1932–34, judicial and militia organisations were assigned a greater role, especially in the countryside. The notorious decree on socialist property of 7 August 1932, which took an extremely harsh stand against those who stole public or socialist property, or even their own harvest, was strongly recommended by the MGK secretariat as a subject for careful study.[3] This decree was followed by the law on 'speculation', empowering local authorities as well as the procuracy and OGPU to deprive a person of freedom for 5–10 years.[4] The confusion in the countryside at that time gave plentiful opportunity for these institutions to exercise their powers, and to abuse them.

The militia also tended to be centralised. There were about 50 offices and 1000 police stations (*uchastki*) in Moscow city in 1933.[5] In August 1932 the MGK secretariat issued a decision by which district committees and district soviets were forbidden to mobilise the militia without the approval of the head of the regional militia administration.[6] This was an especially strict rule in the case of the political militia. In Moscow city the administration also took measures to improve public order on the streets, by increasing the presence of mounted militia and establishing area supervisors (*uchastkovie kommendanty*); the latter were introduced for the main streets from May 1932.[7]

District leaders in the Moscow countryside did not always follow central directives. In some districts the militia were in fact mobilised at district committee request without the prior approval of the region. The MGK secretariat therefore again warned the militia to observe the existing decision.[8]

During the crisis months of the winter of 1932–33, the Moscow authorities directed the judicial organisations to pay greater attention to the situation of shortages and growing crime. The city procurator, Filippov, and the city judge, Smirnov, were asked to uncover and punish thieves and speculators as a means of dealing with the food shortage among Moscow workers. The MGK bureau decision of February 1933 insisted on the application of the harsh August 1932 decree for the protection of socialist property.[9] One people's judge who neglected to use this strong decree was dismissed and the district committee had to select another.[10]

Economic functions of the court and procuracy were no less important. To combat defective production, a strong decree was introduced, with scores of managers and economists being sentenced to five years or more. Control over wage-funds was also a concern of the procuracy, and 73 overpayment cases were sent to court.[11]

The MGK bureau urged the procuracy and Filippov in particular to involve themselves in important cases. The latter was urged to act against abuses of the housing fund and in cases of delayed repairs to communal living quarters.[12]

A lively article in *Vechernyaya Moskva* of 5 February 1933 clearly suggests that crime had not diminished, and that swindlers still survived even after the closure of the Sukharevka market; Lenin's words were cited about workers not being ' . . . isolated from the old bourgeois society by a Chinese wall'.[13] According to the article, crimes against property were especially increasing at this time: in large industrial cities, swindlers, ex-officers, and bandits flourished because 'dekulakised' elements flooded into the city. This article justified the introduction of the internal passport.

The tension in both the countryside and the city raised the problem in 1933 of controlling more closely the judicial and court system. In a characteristic example of Stalinist centralisation, the excessive pressure exercised on the peasants by the local authorities at the behest of the central authorities provided a pretext for further strengthening central control. The Central Committee and Sovnarkom secret instruction of 8 May 1933 urgently requested local authorities to reduce the pressure on the kolkhozniks.[14] This move was followed by the establishment of the All-Union Procuracy in June, which was supposed to supervise militia and OGPU organisation. The OGPU allegedly deviated from the official line at this time.[15] These developments implied the necessity to impose tighter control over the militia, and in fact the MGK secretariat in September decreed that district procurators specialising in militia affairs should be established. The same decision also appointed two city procurators to supervise houses of detention.[16]

Simultaneously, the MGK secretariat investigated the city procuracy personnel. About a hundred procurators, including district procurators and deputy procurators, were checked with the help of the city procuracy.[17] 'People's interrogators' were also checked. It transpired that district procurators were sometimes sub-standard, and some were dismissed. The MGK cadres department, in the person of Drizul, selected new personnel. Special attention was devoted to the low qualifications of district procuracy secretaries.

An interesting point in this decision is that it clarified the nomenklatura level to which procurators should belong. The city deputy, higher deputy, and district procurators were listed in the MGK nomenklatura.[18] The city procurator, Filippov, was evidently listed in the Central Committee nomenklatura.

The MGK secretariat also expressed concern about Moscow court personnel. Of 145 judges under study, 99 per cent were Party members, but their technical and political qualifications were poor.[19] Following various scandals involving district-level judges, a third of the judges were dismissed. The MGK cadres department and Smirnov, the city judge, were instructed to substitute more reliable and better-informed people. Higher district judges and area (uchastok) judges were listed in the MGK nomenklatura. The strengthening of the court system at city and regional level was further encouraged by a decision of the MK bureau in November 1933. People's assessors were to be newly selected by the 'Ryndin Commission', with the help of Mikhailov and Peters.[20] This was to be followed by an all-region meeting of people's assessors, and a course was organised by the MGK secretariat. All these measures tended to shift powers from the district to the regional and city authorities, who were in turn closely linked to the central Party machinery.

6.2 THE INTERNAL PASSPORT SYSTEM

On 27 December 1932 the Soviet government issued its notorious decree introducing the internal passport. This decree claimed that the new system aimed at restricting the populations of cities, workers' settlements, and newly-built areas, and also at removing those who were not engaged in 'socially useful labour' by being attached to production, institutions, or schools; it would reveal 'kulaks,' criminals, and anti-social elements.[21] In other words, this system prohibited the rural population from moving into the city.

The new system was immediately enforced in Moscow, Leningrad, Khar'kov and other cities. According to the instruction, residents of Moscow and its 100-kilometre zone were to be issued with the passport between 20 January and April 1932;[22] 367 issue-points were set up in Moscow.[23] The instruction sought to encourage militia enthusiasm for an unpleasant task by the provision that 10 per cent of the evacuated living quarters would be allocated to members of the militia.[24] Lepses, head of the Moscow militia administration's passport department, explained to the Mossoviet presidium that the passports would be initially introduced in enterprises and later in other population areas.[25] A special commission was organised in the soviet presidium, and called upon some 1800 workers from the Mossoviet labour department to stimulate these arrangements.[26] The measure was closely connected with labour discipline in the factory as well as events on the streets. It was aimed at eliminating speculators and parasites as well as combatting idlers and hooligans.

The main effect of this decree was the drastic restriction on the city population, which had previously been growing rapidly. A report from the British embassy stated that a 'well-known communist' had acknowledged that 700 000 were to be moved out from Moscow (apparently an overstatement). Litvinov admitted that 300 000 bread-ration tickets might be taken out of circulation. The 1933 Moscow control figures projected that the city population would be some 3.3 million, which was 300–400 000 less than the preceding year.[27]

The decree also tightened the screw on labour discipline. A report claimed that the passport system had resulted in the fulfilment of the industrial plan (Promfinplan). In the Elektrokombinat 4 per cent of the 20 000 workers were sifted out; of the 800 removed, 140 were allegedly Whiteguardists, 250 kulaks and 200 criminals.[28] They were obliged to move away from Moscow city and its accommodation. Internal passports were also a strong measure for controlling residents; housing administration documents were a prerequisite for obtaining a passport.

By May 1933 2 485 000 adults over 16 had been issued with passports in Moscow.[29] The number refused passports is not known. Some 100–200 000 may have left Moscow for a doubtful future elsewhere. But the net result was disappointing, insofar as the 1934 population was still 3.61 million. Population growth was halted but the total number living in Moscow was not reduced for more than a few months.

In spite or because of the importance of this measure, neither the MK nor MGK appear to have been directly involved in the campaign. This was a central matter in which local Party organisations had no authority.

6.3 EDUCATION

Education was also an area where central control was strong. The Mossoviet education department (Gorono) was subordinated to the People's Commissariat of Education.[30] The education system, and especially general education, expanded rapidly in this period. In 1929 there were 208 000 pupils in Moscow city; this grew to 367 000 in 1933 and 417 000 in 1934. They were attending some 380 schools in 1934, of which ten were for national minorities and 54 were special schools for the deaf and for orphans.[31]

There were few matters controlled by the local Party or the public at large. The only decision in this area by the MGK was taken at the May 1932 plenum, and was a joint decision with Mossoviet presented by Dubrovina, head of Gorono, rather than by an MGK official. It aimed to introduce a 10–year general-education (middle school), replacing the 7-year system. This had already been decided in principle by the Central Committee in 1931 and was a return to general education in preference to education concentrating on industrial skills.[32]

The method of provision of textbooks reflected the tendency towards centralisation in education. A Central Committee decision of February

1933 proposed that standard textbooks should be recommended, a policy rejected after October 1917. The education commissariat appointed a commission under its commissar Bubnov to adopt new textbooks in the RFSFR (and by implication the USSR as well).[33] Regions and national republics lost their right to develop their own textbooks. In this connection, a Moscow textbook publisher was criticised by *Vechernyaya Moskva*, and the MGK bureau dissolved the publisher. Some authors were purged.[34]

Some direct involvement of the regional Party organisation was discernible in the social sciences. Komvuz graduates were mobilised as teachers.[35] Each district had to re-educate teachers in seminars, and district education departments as well as the district committee culture and propaganda departments organised evening courses for this purpose. The appointment of social-science teachers in primary and secondary schools had to be reported to the district committee departments.[36] In Frunze district, about 85 per cent of the social-science teachers were communists or in the Komsomol, but this was regarded as 'insufficient'.[37] District committees were also involved clearly in preparing schools for the winter, with repairs and fuel supplies having priority. The MK also dealt with supplies for teachers; although precise figures are not known, about 10 000 'scientific workers' could use closed co-operatives at this time.[38]

6.4 THE PROBLEM OF WAIFS AND STRAYS

One of the most serious problems facing the Moscow authorities, and especially the militia and the teachers, was the large number of waifs and hooligans. This was a result of collectivisation and of the 1932–33 famine, and a renewal of a social problem which was already found during War Communism and NEP. As famine developed in the south of the USSR, the influx of homeless waifs into cities like Moscow increased and gave rise to serious difficulties. One disillusioned American communist who had worked in the USSR wrote:

> On almost every street corner in Moscow it is a common sight to find a scrawny woman seated on the sidewalk, in the mud or snow, with a baby in her arms and three or four children beside her, begging for bread. Begging is one of the chief occupations of the great mass of the poorer children.[39]

Although the Moscow authorities were reluctant to discuss this question openly, the second plenum of the MGK in May 1932 already resolved to eliminate 'finally' the waif problem when it decided to strengthen mass-cultural activity outside the schools.[40] By the end of 1932, however, the problem had become more serious with the onset of famine in the south.

In February 1933 *Vechernyaya Moskva* specially referred to this question, stating that the trade unions and the Party had to pay attention to it and complaining that insufficient out-of-school education was provided by the People's Commissariat of Education.[41] In February 1933 an RSFSR decree was issued about the waif problem.[42] The RSFSR education commissariat was instructed to take measures to reduce the number of waifs. Special inspectors of children were to watch over theatres, cinemas, railway stations and markets, and could detain children engaged in gambling.[43] Children found begging were severely reprimanded. To prevent an influx of waifs from rural areas like the Lower Volga, strict control over the selling of railway tickets to children was introduced.

In February 1933 the education and justice commissariats came to an agreement on how to deal with waifs, but 'hooliganism' continued, and the procuracy and militia were requested to deal with it.[44] The control of children through the housing administration was also strengthened. The nursery system was to be involved. In some districts, detention centres for child criminals were established under the city department of education; in these, the district secretary, educationists, teachers, and doctors were to investigate the family situation of waifs and hooligans. A special machinery for criminal investigation was organised by the militia, together with child reception and distribution points. Scientific research sub-departments were set up to study and register criminal and 'de-classed' elements'.[45] The militia and the Mossoviet education department established 16 permanent points for dealing with waifs.

In consequence of these measures, about 200 children were detained in five days in the Krasnaya Presnya district.[46] In one locality a 12 year-old boy was trading in tobacco, others were begging for money in front of the cinema, and another was stealing at the tram station.[47] In the Dzerzhinsky district a meeting of parents, teachers, and representatives of social organisations was held to discuss the struggle with waifs and hooligans.[48] At the suggestion of Mossoviet, 1500 childrens' areas were to be set up in housing complexes, to provide catering for 50 000. The joint presidium of the oblispolkom and Mossoviet decided to spend 30 000 roubles to prevent a food and products shortage in the children's homes.[49]

But scepticism and inactivity prevailed. The city housing trust and the Union of ZhAKTy were said to be passive, and some ZhAKTy were said to have claimed that 'we need no children's activities'.[50] Sovnarkom and

Mossoviet were instructed to build a 'children's house' in Moscow, but this was not done. The Komispor (the soviet's implementation control agency) of the RSFSR discussed the waif problem in the lower Volga and Moscow at the beginning of July, pointing out the delay in measures to deal with waifs.[51] On the suggestion of Sulimov, the chairman of the RSFSR Sovnarkom, it was decided to set up children's labour camps to hold 2000–3000 waifs.

Eventually, some 150 children's homes were set up in the Moscow region by 1934 for those children who were difficult to bring up. But life within this system was miserable. The MKK often investigated scandals in children's homes, sometimes involving children being 'beaten to death'. Twelve Party members were expelled, while one accused of murder was sent to court.[52]

Even after the end of the famine the problem remained, necessitating a decree of the Sovnarkom and Central Committee in May 1935.[53] Every Moscow district executive committee had a section for this problem by 1936. Ten children's homes were operating under the Mossoviet education department, and each district had a similar system.[54]

We have mentioned several examples of the activity of the MGK and Mossoviet in trying to deal with this problem. But in general, this question seems to have been dealt with by the People's Commissariat of Education, somewhat by passing the MGK and Mossoviet. Vertical control was stronger than horizontal.

7 Industry in Moscow

7.1 PARTY LEADERSHIP STRUCTURE AND INDUSTRY

The defeat of Uglanov in 1928 was followed in Moscow by a turn towards a policy dominated by heavy industry. New industrial centres were built in Moscow. The high rate of investment in heavy industry was slow to produce results and in 1932–33 output was poor and there were severe delays in construction. A complicating factor was the deterioration of the international situation following the 1931 Manchurian crisis. This enhanced the importance of heavy industry and the military sectors expanded at the expense of civilian consumption.

The proportion of heavy industry in total industrial output rose sharply. In Moscow, 'group A' production (means of production) rose from 20 per cent in 1927–28 to 37.1 per cent in 1931. About 81 per cent of industrial investment was directed towards heavy industry in the Five-Year Plan period 1928–32.[1] Some factories were constructed within Moscow itself, and others in the Moscow region; the Tula metal works and the Voskresensk chemical combine were two examples.

These were the years in which the Stalinist command economy emerged, in the form in which it has essentially survived up to the present time. Moscow factories and enterprises were largely controlled by the USSR economic ministries (VSNKh, and from 1932 NK Tyazhprom and NK Legprom, respectively the People's Commissariats of Heavy Industry and Light Industry). Decisions on important issues of economic construction and management were made at the central level in the name of the Central Committee, NK Tyazhprom or NK Legprom.

There was also a category of 'local industry', whose management was the responsibility of Mossoviet or of district soviet organisations. These were by no means trivial responsibilities. The bicycle and watch factories, for example, were under Mossoviet control, and construction materials like bricks also came into this category. In light industry, Mossoviet controlled sewing, stationary, haberdashery and other industries, a total of 51 enterprises with 50 000 workers. The light industry of Mossoviet produced about 40 per cent of the entire Moscow output of NK Legprom. These Mossoviet factories were directly supervised by the MGK.[2]

At the district level, in 1933 the Mossovet organised the Univerprom trust, which united semi-handicraft industries. Raipromkombinat united the district level patronage (*shefskie*) associations and others.[3]

The emerging pattern of centrally-controlled economic mechanisms reduced the role of local Party and economic organisations. In September 1931 VSNKh listed 25 important enterprises of Moscow (city and region) and 10 new construction projects for which the appointments of director required an order (*prikaz*) from VSNKh approved by the Party Central Committee.[4] Thus most of the key industrial bases were directly supervised from the central level. Although the former Moscow Party secretary Bauman complained in 1929 that VSNKh deprived the Moscow Party organisation of the power to control Moscow factories, his criticism had no influence on the overwhelming tendency to centralise economic management.[5]

At the central level, the Politburo and NK Tyazhprom were undoubtedly the most important decision-making bodies concerned with Moscow economic affairs. The Politburo often discussed Moscow factories; the discussion of the ball-bearing factory in the Politburo in March 1932 is a typical example.[6] In 1931, the Politburo approved the establishment of a government commission, headed by A. Andreev on behalf of Sovnarkom, to deal with the financial problems of Moscow industries.[7] This commission made suggestions to the Politburo about the management of the AMO automobile works. Ordzhonikidze, head of NK Tyazhprom, supervised those Moscow factories which were under central control. He was a member of the MGK, while the Moscow plenipotentiary of NK Tyazhprom was merely a candidate member of the MK. Moscow leaders like Kaganovich and Bulganin often appealed to the central authorities for help in the resolution of a specific problem.[8]

In spite of these sweeping central powers, day-to-day control was left in the hands of regional, city and district Party organisations, although they were not allowed to take over the economic role of managers.

In his capacity as MK and MGK first secretary, Kaganovich was constantly concerned with heavy and light industry, and often visited the plants and construction sites. The main responsibility for industrial decisions, however, rested with second Party secretary Ryndin, as chairman of an industry commission in the MK bureau and secretariat. This commission gave detailed instructions to city and factory committees when there were delays.[9] After Ryndin's departure for the Urals in the Autumn of 1933 this sphere of activity was probably taken over by Mikhailov.[10]

There was a rough division of competence between different Party institutions. The bureaux of the MK and MGK were concerned with major production problems, while the secretariat seems to have made rather minor decisions. Thus the secretariat decision of 8 September 1932 insisted that the Moscow metal combine should not waste metal shavings. Mossoviet was responsible for the provision of buildings and transport to put this decision into effect.[11] Another secretariat decision was to extract non-ferrous metals and building materials from slag; help was sought from NK Tyazhprom.[12] Its lack of economic competence prevented closer involvement of the secretariat in industrial decision-making, especially in heavy industry.

The MK and MGK cadres department were particularly concerned with the manning of important departments like planning, finance, supply and wages, with the help of the factory directors.[13] In view of the importance of good technical leadership, the MK and MGK cadres department also monitored the choice as well as the activities of engineers, as happened in the Mytishchi factory.[14] Political reliability was a major preoccupation of the authorities, most starkly visible in the 'Metro-Vickers' case in 1933, when a number of engineers were put on trial for espionage and sabotage.

In industrial districts, party district secretaries were judged by the progress of the factories in their jurisdiction, and especially by the fulfilment of the plan. The MK and MGK insisted on 'unremitting control' over the factories by the district committees.[15] Kaganovich convened special meetings of the MK bureau, at which district secretaries were summoned to discuss and decide on district-level matters.[16] In the years of shortages, special attention was devoted by the district committee to food supplies.[17]

Although key factory managers were appointed by the centre, they were also controlled by local Party organisations. The MK and MGK issued warnings to managers if their work was unsatisfactory. Thus the manager of Stankostroi was reprimanded for his delay in carrying out a decision to instal new machines. The manager of the bicycle factory was reproved for the 'demobilised atmosphere' in his factory. The manager of Mytishchi factory was very severely criticised for regarding himself as a 'temporary resident' of the factory.[18] In August 1932 the MGK bureau threatened the manager of Wiring factory with dismissal, fearing that more work delay would spread over to associated factories. A few key industrial managers were members of the MK and MGK, including Bodrov, manager of the ball-bearing factory, and Likhachev, manager of AMO automobile plant.

Party organisations also issued 'advice' which amounted to an order to trusts and soviet departments in the interests of industry. The matters covered were heterogeneous and sometimes very detailed. The communist fraction of Mossoviet was asked to assist a trust to supply good cooks to a Podol'sk factory. The MK bureau instructed the labour department of the regional soviet that excessive work should not be allowed in electrical factories.[19]

A particularly important function for the Party was to facilitate the movement of goods and semi-finished between factories. For example, the MK bureau helped Stankostroi to arrange with NK Tyazhprom that special steel should be supplied from another factory.[20]

In some cases the Party decision-makers in effect prepared the factory plan, by passing the manager. In the case of the production of Metro trains and cars at the Mytishchi factory, MK secretary Donenko was entrusted with the examination of the plan in consultation with the Oblispolkom communist fraction, and a representative of the trust.[21] The Party bureau would also act on behalf of the manager in negotiating with the trust or the People's Commissars. Thus the MK bureau asked M. Kaganovich (brother of L. M. Kaganovich), who was head of the NK Tyazhprom engineering glavk, to agree to despatch engineers to Moscow electrical factories.[22] With the hierarchical structure of soviet industry management and the limited authority of managers, it is hardly surprising that the city and regional Party institutions performed the role of an 'invisible hand' which co-ordinated economic activity and linked different levels of economic management.

At factory level, the primary Party organisation was vitally important. Communists were allocated to factory shops, or sent to lagging sections of shops. The Podol'sk factory organisation sent 40 or 50 communists to join shock brigades and about the same number of Komsomol members to an inactive foundry.[23] To get mass-party work in the Frezer and Kalibr factories, the MGK orginstr department appointed full-time Party secretaries. In the case of Stankostroi, the MGK bureau decided to organise cells in every shop.[24] In the bicycle factory, the Party organisation was criticised and *partorggrup* was sent from the district for one month in March 1933; this measures did not overcome the lag and both the manager and the Party secretary were dismissed.[25]

7.2 HEAVY INDUSTRY: PROBLEMS OF GROWTH

In 1931, the extensive development of heavy industry was downgraded in favour of the more intensive utilisation of newly built projects. Inside Moscow city the construction of new factories was prohibited after the June 1931 plenum of the Central Committee, and new factories were built mainly in the region outside the city itself.[26] But it was not easy to bring new factories into production, especially in the period of over-ambitious industrialisation, with its extreme shortages and bottlenecks. The problem of bringing factories into production (*osvoenie*) was a central issue of the later years of this period throughout the USSR.

(a) The Politics of *Osvoenie*

In these years the new factories and plants were not completed on time due to the shortage of labour, materials and technical assistance, and lack of co-ordination generally. The Moscow Party played a crucial role in overcoming these difficulties.

A characteristic example is provided by the Tula works. Although production started in 1931, output remained miserably low after a visit by Kaganovich in April 1933. Following this visit, the MK bureau discussed the Tula situation and its decisions provide an insight into the politics of osvoenie.[27] The bureau organised a conference headed by Ryndin, including Donenko, Kuchimin (deputy chairman of the oblispolkom), Manfred (plenipotentiary of NK Tyazhprom in Moscow), and a representative of metal *glavk*.[28] On the basis of the conclusions of this conference, the bureau assigned key Moscow political figures to particular responsibilities. Thus, Manfred was allocated responsibility for construction materials, turbines, manpower and worker's dormitories, and Donenko for railway transport, including the completion of a spur line. In Tula the gorkom sent one of its district bureau members to the construction site with 100 workers; the Tula gorkom secretary, Sedel'nikov, was responsible for supplies for the construction workers.

Kaganovich sought to complete the initial work by the end of the year, and called a special meeting at the end of April. Progress of construction was reported to the MK every ten days. To raise additional funds for investment, the MK asked NK Tyazhprom to agree that other factories in the region should have a cut of 15 million roubles imposed on their funds.

The Elektrostal' case was similar. Its excruciatingly slow construction was discussed in the MK bureau at a meeting of 10 April 1933. The trouble was an exodus of some 600 workers due to the deterioration of food supply and to the financial situation.[29] The manager and three members (*treugol'nik*) of the construction trust were assigned to labour recruitment, and progress was to be reported to the oblispolkom labour department every five days. The district secretary and MK cadres department were instructed to ensure food supplies for the construction workers. A plenipotentiary of NK Tyazhprom was assigned to brick supply, and an oblispolkom deputy chairman was made responsible for transport organisation.

(b) The Politics of Production

Production problems were by no means confined to the new factories. In the years of over-ambitious industrialisation, every factory, however long established, suffered from every kind of shortage, with serious consequences for the quality of production. Thus Serp i Molot, an old factory with a high reputation, was strongly criticised by its district Party bureau in March 1932, because as much as 60 per cent of its output was defective.[30]

These difficulties were made much more acute by the need to reconstruct established factories at a higher technological level so that they could produce new products. In May 1932, the MGK bureau, having noted the slow growth in the production of high-quality steel (known in Russia as 'quality steel'), recommended that the Serp i Molot factory should specialise in its production.[31] The head of Spetsstal' trust, Tevosyan, and the manager of the factory were urged to propose this change to NK Tyazhprom. It may be that NK Tyazhprom itself initiated this move behind the scenes. Several major steps were taken to improve the technological level of the factory: mobilisation of students from the Iron and Steel Institute, strengthening of the technical control department of the factory, and improving the wages and living standards of the workers.

The Elektrostal' factory followed a similar path. VSNKh decided in November 1931 to reconstruct the factory to supply special steels. Following the VSNKh decision, the MK bureau set up a commission for the reconstruction of the factory, and the bureau approved its proposals in December. Kaminsky was allocated to this work from the bureau. The first stage was completed in mid-1932 but, according to a Soviet historian, steel quality was 'very low, the only high percentage being the spoilage rate'.[32]

In March 1933, Ryndin again criticised the low quality of production.[33] The MK bureau pointed out that the plan had not been fulfilled, and that workers' morale was poor and labour turnover high.[34] The MK culture and propaganda department sent two officials to stir up the Party, and one hundred Party members were hastily trained as *partorggrup* members or shop secretaries.[35] On the production line, one-man management was strengthened, the post of deputy manager for production being abolished. A production department was set up, technicians were allotted to it, and technical control was tightened.

Such MK and MGK decisions on production and new technology in heavy industry clearly show that regional and city Party organisations were directly concerned with the construction and running of factories.

Even though the NK Tyazhprom had the final say, the local Party was actively involved. Party channels were used to obtain materials and other resources, and above all skilled workers and technical personnel, from both Party institutions (including the Central Committee), and from the Soviet and economic bureaucracies.

7.3 THE MOSCOW PARTY AND LIGHT INDUSTRY

Moscow was the centre of the pre-revolutionary textile industry, and the basic industrial policy favouring light industry remained unchanged in the Moscow area until the end of the NEP period. The MK leader Uglanov (1924–28) was strongly committed to the interests of the textile industry and a supporter of the moderate industrialisation policies advocated by Bukharin. After the defeat of the Rightists, both the new Moscow boss, Bauman, and Kaganovich pursued a super-industrialisation policy, criticising Uglanov's neglect of heavy industry.[36] After that, the main new developments in the textile industry occurred in Central Asia and West Siberia, with only a few Moscow textile factories expanding. Lack of interest in the textile industry is reflected in the limited increase of investment compared with the substantial increase in metal and other heavy industries (4.5 per cent in 1932–33, for instance, as against 25.5 per cent).[37]

However, light industry was still important. As much as 30 per cent of all light industry was located in the Moscow region.[38] In the case of the cotton textile industry, Moscow still accounted for 43 per cent of the total Soviet output.[39] The extent of decentralisation was also large; the plenipotentiary of NK Legprom in Moscow had more influence than the NK Tyazhprom plenipotentiary.

The low priority of light industry raised many problems in the critical years of 1932–33, particularly in the textile industry. Production often ceased altogether because of materials or fuel shortages. Facilities were old. Workers were largely recruited from the countryside and were therefore difficult to integrate into the factory system; there were particular difficulties with new women workers. More than a third of output was defective. The plan was never fulfilled.[40]

(a) Party Control over the Textile Industry: the Example of the Ivanovo-Voznesensk Strike

An alarming strike movement in the Ivanovo region in spring 1932 persuaded the Moscow leaders to modify their policy. Although this worker unrest was not officially reported in Soviet sources, a report from the British embassy in Moscow was as follows:[41]

> There are reports that quite recently the workers in the textile industry at Ivanovo-Voznesensk ceased work, had meetings at which they demanded more and better food, and sent representatives to Moscow to present their demands. Troops were sent to the spot and work was resumed. A Moscow factory which struck in sympathy with the workers at Ivanovo-Voznesensk was immediately brought to heel by GPU troops and fleets of lorries are said to be held in readiness at various points in Moscow in case similar troubles should arise in the future.[42]

After this strike, the Moscow leaders were naturally seriously alarmed about the textile industry. In the Party bureaucracy there was evidently nobody with a specialised interest in textiles parallel to Ryndin's role in relation to heavy industry. Kaganovich, Ryndin and others dealt with particular issues such as supplies.[43] Mikhailov reported on the situation in the industry at a meeting of the MK culture-propaganda department.[44] A kind of collective leadership was at work here. An MK bureau decision in June 1932, apparently based on consultation with various officials after the strike, vividly describes the Party's role in running the textile industry:[45]

(1) To ensure improved repair of textile machinery, iron must be obtained from NK Tyazhprom, and a commission including secretary Gei, Kaminsky (oblispolkom), Ivanov (plenipotentiary of NK Legprom), and Korotkov (cotton trust) was appointed. Manfred (oblplan) was allocated responsibility for transforming the metal into components.[46]

(2) Special technical inspectors were instituted within the MKK-RKI, and over ten technical inspectors worked to supervise the industry. These special inspectors were responsible for checking the implementation of the technical decisions made by the Central Committee and the MK. The MKK-RKI was itself responsible for workers' supply.

(3) The leadership took steps to 're-educate' middle and lower Party officials in the textile industry from the middle of 1932, after the participation of communists in the strike movement. At the second plenum of the MGK, conflict at the Sverdlov cotton textile factory was mentioned: some communists were criticised because they failed to counterattack 'class enemies' and followed the 'bad atmosphere'.[47] The June bureau decision required some

1000 textile Party workers and activists, including 100 Party secretaries and 550 shop secretaries, to be re-educated. A textile Party school was established at Orekhovo-Zuevo, for 200 students to follow a two-year course. The Serpukhov Soviet-Party school was reorganised to prepare Party cadres for the textile industry.[48] The newly-created Komvuz in Kalinin was given the special task of training Party cadres for textile work; there were 125 students, of whom 40–50 per cent were female.[49] The sudden decision in Autumn to transform all Komvuzy into agricultural institutions put this decision in jeopardy.[50] However, in view of the weight of the Moscow textile industry, the MK secretariat appealed to the Central Committee, and the Kalinin school was transferred to the jurisdiction of Narkompros in October 1932.[51]

The plans for training textile Party cadres were confirmed at the second plenum of the MK July 1932. In addition to the measures adapted by the bureau in June, the Zvenigorod House for Party education introduced six-weeks courses.[52] It was also decided to educate as many as 63 000 workers in study groups ('circles'), mainly for women.

The Moscow Party organisation also directed reliable Party workers to the rebellious factories. The MK bureau decision in June instructed the organisation instructors department to send, with the help of the MGK, at least 50 Party workers to enterprises for one month.[53] The intention was to implant Party influence in the shop Party cells with the help of the district committees. Factories with a workforce of over 3000, or with at least 350 communists, were to organise Party committees with shop branches.[54] Party officials were instructed to remain at the shop level, and factory committees were requested to enhance their work at that level. The MK mass-agitation department was to send 80 agitators, with the help of the district committees.[55] To cope with the problems of women workers, appropriate district committees were to establish womens' sections. The July plenum decided to send 10 organisation-propaganda groups and 100 qualified propagandists for attachment to enterprises, and 100 communists were sent off for agitation work.[56]

(b) Problems of the Textile Industry

While the Ivanovo-Voznesensk strike movement caused the Moscow Party to put into operation all its levers of control, chronic problems haunted the industry both before and after the spring of 1932. Four major problems received most attention from the Moscow Party: the management system;

the shortage of experienced personnel; defective output; and the poor quality of the workers' daily life.

(i) Management system
The administration of the textile industry was divided between the all-Union trust, which in 1933 controlled 51 factories in Moscow, and the regional trust, which controlled about 30 factories.[57] The factories were mainly managed on the 'functional' principle, which had been adopted in 1931 both for management and production. But this system seldom worked smoothly. After Kaganovich's visit to several textile districts, the 'functional principle of management' was severely criticised for giving rise to irresponsibility.[58] A decision of the MK bureau as early as September 1931, long before the nation-wide abandonment of the functional principle, proposed to change the functional system in the textile industry.[59]

However, there was considerable resistance on the part of the textile enterprises, and the functional principle was not in fact abolished until the beginning of 1933.[60] On 4 September 1933 the MK decided to set up a special commission to prepare a simple form of management to replace the functional principle.[61]

(ii) The shortage of experienced personnel
The low priority of the industry inevitably meant that other industries proved more attractive, even to those who were textile specialists. Perhaps the most serious personnel difficulty was the shortage of *podmaster'e* (roughly translatable as senior, experienced, worker). To supply them, a MK bureau decision of 4 June 1932 instructed the trusts to organise three-month courses for 1000–1200 persons.[62] But this was not easily achieved. These were traditionally workers who often had 20 years experience in the factory, and they were key figures in carrying out the work-plan. The shortage remained chronic. The conference on quality in the textile industry in September 1933 appointed a commission, headed by secretary Gei and including representatives of trusts and others, to look into the question of the *podmaster'e*.

The shortage of engineers and technicians was also serious. An MK decision of September 1931 ordered 800 engineers and 1800 technicians to be found, but it was not carried out. The June 1932 decision personally instructed Ivanov, plenipotentiary of NK Legprom, to carry out the decision within two months. The Central Committee also took action. It decided to set up an industrial-educational institute to prepare lecturers for the textile industry. The NK Legprom was entrusted with the reorganisation of the textile technical school into a departmental technical school, and instructed to set up an additional school in Moscow region.[63] To reduce the high turnover of textile engineers, the oblispolkom labour department prohibited the transfer of textile engineers to other spheres, and also ordered the recall of textile engineers who had moved away from the industry.[64]

(iii) Defective output

A third issue facing the textile industry was that of low quality and defective output. The defect rate rose in the Moscow textile industry; slight defects amounted to 10–30 per cent, and in some factories rose as high as 37.6 per cent at that time.[65] The MK leadership claimed that the cause of the trouble was that managers were oriented to produce more without consideration of quality. The problem was rooted deeply in the structural problem of industrialisation. In one Egor'ev factory, the proportion of defects rose to 44 per cent after the introduction of automation, due apparently to the workers' inability to handle the new machines.[66] In 1933 the situation became even more serious. In one factory in Nogin district 70 per cent of output had been lost in the first five months; in this factory absenteeism was reported as 6 per cent despite the harsh sanctions introduced at the end of 1932.[67] The MK secretariat instructed the cadre department that checks of the leading personnel should be carried out, and as many as two-thirds of communist party members failed to reach the required standard. In consequence the trade union branch at the factory was dissolved and the Party organisations were severely criticised.

In September 1933 a conference on textile quality was held on the initiative of Kaganovich in Orekhovo-Zuevo, where the unsatisfactory performance was attributed to 'extremely weak leadership' in both managerial-technical and Party-trade union activity.[68] At that time the textile industry was discussed at every MK bureau meeting. The bureau found that the shortage of materials was the main reason for delays and urged that the industry should receive priority in supplies. Lyubimov, the light industry commissar, was asked to raise the issue at the Central Committee's commission on this matter. The plenipotentiary of NK Legprom and the head of the cotton trust were to take responsibility for cotton supply, the shortage of which was particularly severe in the summer of 1933. But improvement was very slow.

(iv) The daily life of workers

The strike movement and other evidence of unrest among textile workers revealed the low standard of living of the workers, affecting food, pay and housing. The June 1932 decision of the MK bureau gave detailed prescriptions for these problems. It ordered supply departments to ensure that those with responsibility in the textile districts should be carefully selected. It also requested NK Snab (the People's Commissariat for Supply/Trade) to deliver the allocated resources punctually. In the crucial matter of food supply it decided to raise pigs in allotments attached to 28 textile factories, as well as 23 000 rabbits and 2275 cows.[69] Additionally, 6100 hectares were to be cultivated for vegetables. The plenipotentiary of NK Legprom was asked to find 20 million roubles for this, and the responsibility for the programme was divided between the trade-union, the textile trust, and the NK Legprom plenipotentiary. These were to present a improved supply programme within ten days to the MK bureau.

Checking the internal trade system was also important, and the June bureau decision suggested checks on co-operative warehouses and trade personnel; this suggests how much trades officials were suspect in this year of shortages. The district committees were prohibited from transferring approved trade and co-operative personnel. MK secretary Egorov was charged with checking the Moscow co-operative system and the NK Snab system. The MK cadres department was requested to institute and provide assistant supply managers in the textile factories. Related to the supply problem was the need for an improved public catering system, which the MK emphasised should be reinstated in the summer, parallel with the improvement of workers' canteens. It recommended the experimental organisation of a co-operative public catering trust in two or three districts.[70]

Wages were another important problem for textile workers. Their average wage was low, about 69.5 roubles per month in 1931 as compared to 95.5 roubles for workers in general and 116 roubles for metal workers.[71] The difficulties of the spring of 1932 were partly caused by low wages combined with high output norms associated with the introduction of piecework, coupled with deductions for defects. The MK bureau therefore proposed that proper wage relationships be introduced.[72] But collective assistance or individualised help for the poorer-paid workers was recommended, rather than a general wage increase. Under the strict conditions of constraint, wage increases brought about by worker pressure could have become a political issue, especially as the textile industry had a low priority in the minds of the political leadership. Nevertheless, the September 1932 plenum of the Central Committee apparently agreed to raise the average wage of textile workers by 15.9 per cent, although this was not clearly promised in the resolutions of the plenum as published.[73]

Poor housing and the unrewarding material and cultural life of the workers also caused the local authorities considerable concern. According to the June 1932 decision, 'In the past the large housing fund was not used to shift workers from basement garrets and cubicles or to reduce the number of worker dormitories', and this resulted in a situation where cadre workers were continuing to live 'in extremely difficult dormitory conditions' in many textile centres.[74] In 1932 140 000 square metres of living quarters were planned to be constructed in the textile districts. Because of the shortage of building materials, the standard was rather shoddy. Four-storey houses were prohibited, staircases were made of wood, and waterpipes were manufactured on the spot from wood or earthenware. Trade unions and the communal sections of local soviets were expected to exercise control through allocation of the housing fund, but sole responsibility lay in the hands of the managers. In the textile districts 70 per cent of municipal housing was allotted to textile workers.

However, in view of the high priority to investment in heavy industry, housing priorities were extremely low. In the first quarter of 1932 the cotton association (VKhBO) achieved only one eighth of the intended construction. The regional textile trust completely neglected housing. The bureau decision of June 1932 put responsibility on the institutions concerned, particularly on the deputy heads of trusts. The district secretaries and chairmen of district executive committees were also charged with a personal duty to see that construction and construction materials for this purpose were provided smoothly. The need to repair dormitories was also emphasised.

To take a typical district, Serpukhov, as an example.[75] The construction of 34 houses totalling 20 000 square metres was planned. Construction cost was to be financed by the textile trust (50 per cent), the local budget (20 per cent), and various banks. Two nurseries and the repair of local hospitals were planned, though the cost of using nurseries was astonishingly high, amounting to a third of a worker's wage. In the July plenum, a report from one factory of this district confirmed the line adopted by the MK bureau June decision. The politically backward atmosphere and prejudice which permeated the textile workers were to be eliminated by attending to their interests. Party cadres and Party influence were to be strengthened. To this end, Party cells were reinforced by despatching communists from the districts and factories.[76]

But these measures were not enough to fulfil the expectations of the textile workers in the situation of deprivation and shortage. Absenteeism and even sabotage resulted from this. A general decree on absenteeism at the end of 1932 took a most severe attitude towards unjustifiable absence: one day's absence was sufficient for dismissal, with consequent loss of rations and housing. Even this had little effect. In January 1933 the MK secretariat, after hearing a report from the regional official of the cotton industry, as well as from the mass agitation department, criticised the leadership of the cotton industry for underestimating absenteeism.[77] Some trade union officials who were 'soft' in this matter were dismissed. All trade unions had to report on the progress of the struggle against absenteeism to the secretariat.

Despite everything, the situation remained fundamentally unchanged. At the 1934 Moscow Party conference, Ryndin had to acknowledge:

> Among textile workers the remnant of the old capitalistic, dormitory and church influences have not been removed. They are all still strongly felt among many groups of textile workers.[78]

In industry, Moscow was thus an old centre for light industry, and continued to play this role. But heavy industrial bases were also developed, though not yet fully operational. The successful operation of the heavy industry factories was the crucial issue for the Party, especially as the international situation imposed an increased production of armaments and the agricultural crisis demanded a large input of machinery. In these fields, it was the economic ministries that controlled the factories and related facilities. The mechanism of the central command economy was being crystallised, and the role of the local Party was somewhat circumscribed. The MK and MGK, with their subordinate Party apparatus, acted as co-odinators or brokers in the attainment of goals. In light industry the local Party had a somewhat louder voice, and the need to improve the standard of living of the workers generally, and the disaffection in the textile industry due to the poor conditions of life and work, forced the national and local Party to pay more attention to light industry from the spring of 1932 onwards.

8 Transport and Energy

8.1 RAILWAY TRANSPORT

This section will deal with rail transport (urban transport and the Metro are dealt with in Chapter 10). Moscow, served by eleven main lines, was an important transport centre for the USSR and one of Europe's largest railway centres. The railways carried fuel, construction materials, grain and metals for the capital's industries and were beginning to carry metal and engineering products out of Moscow. Some of the suburban lines were being electrified.

But railway transport was in serious difficulties at this time. Like light industry, it was neglected in favour of heavy industry. In 1931–33 it had become a bottleneck for the whole economy. In this chapter the attempt of the Party to cope with the railway transport problem in Moscow will be illustrated from the experience of constructing the Moscow-Donbass line and of the use of the extraordinary measures, including the politotdely, to improve railway management.

(a) Moscow-Donbass Railway Construction

To provide a new route from Moscow to the Donbass coal and metallurgical industries, the government decided in April 1932 to build a new main line, which was not completed until 1938.[1] The authorities instructed NK Put' (the People's Commissariat of Communications) to give top priority to this project in the supply of resources, including labour. The oblispolkoms (regional executive committees) of Moscow, the North Caucasus and Black Earth regions were expected to co-operate fully. The STO (the Council of Labour and Defence) formed a committee headed by Rudzutak for the co-ordination of construction.

Following the decree of April 1932, the MK bureau decided to prepare a more detailed plan of work in relation to the Moscow-Donbass line within a month.[2] In the Party campaign, first priority was given to the mobilisation of manpower, technicians and, above all, Party members. The labour department of Mossoviet was given permission to recruit workers within fifteen kilometre zones of the line, and sent out plenipotentiaries on a recruitment campaign. NK Trud (the People's Commissariat of Labour) was requested to recruit 5500 workers from the Middle Volga and 6900 from Moscow region. The MK cadres department helped this work by sending three officials as plenipotentiaries to the Middle Volga and Central Black-Earth regions and to the Tatar Republic. In four districts of Moscow itself about 1700 workers were recruited within a week through Party and soviet channels.[3]

The MK apparatus played a major role in this campaign. The cadres department allocated 25–30 engineers and officials to the construction sections, and the further appointment of trade union and co-operative cadres to the construction was subjected to the approval of the MK secretariat. Malenkov, from the orginstr department, was placed in charge of the Party officials concerned with the construction. The district committees were also requested to play a full part. Each of the district committees directly involved in the work was requested to allocate one bureau member as a full-time official to work on the project, and the other districts were requested to send instructors. Districts, and some large enterprises, were entrusted with *sheftsvo* (patronage, or supervision) over construction sections. The secretariat later admitted that this work was badly organised; districts such as Kashira failed to provide 'real daily and concrete help'.[4]

Perhaps the most crucial issue in 1932–33 was the supply of food to the construction workers. The plenipotentiary of the Tsentrosoyuz transport section prepared a supply plan which included the use of 200 hectares for vegetables.[5] Accommodation was also a serious problem. The decision to provide accommodation for 7000 workers proved inadequate and the MK secretariat called for the building of dormitory-barracks for 12 000. The oblispolkom was charged with building material supplies. Each district soviet was asked to provide accommodation for technical personnel.

Over a year after these initial decisions, at a meeting of the MK bureau in October 1933, Kaganovich called for information about its implementation. It turned out that to a considerable extent they had not been carried out.[6] Malenkov and three other heads of departments were strongly warned that they might be subject to Party sanctions.[7] The chairman of the oblispolkom, Kaminsky, was assigned to the mobilisation of kolkhozniks for work on the construction with the help of T. R. Voroshilov (not to be confused with K. E. Voroshilov, the Commissar for War), and of the *politsektor*, or *politotdel*, of the agriculture department. The results were to be presented at the next bureau meeting. People involved who attended that meeting without preparation were warned that they might be ousted from it.

To strengthen labour discipline, the head of the MK mass agitation department, Shamberg, visited the scene of construction together with GPU officials; and Kaganovich was made personally responsible for negotiating with NK Put' to use low-category reservists on the construction.[8]

The senior officials of the Moscow Party were very closely involved in checking the implementation of these directives.[9] Ryndin was made responsible for economic personnel, Malenkov for Party personnel; Malenkov's work was in turn to be supervised by secretary Mikhailov. The work of the culture-propaganda department on the construction was controlled by secretary Gei. Until the completion of the construction, every alternate bureau meeting was supposed to receive a report about the progress of the work and questions about it were given priority in the agendas of the meetings.[10] But in spite of the direct involvement of the Moscow Party on this top priority project, completion was in fact delayed until the end of the Second Five-Year Plan.

(b) **Railway Transport Management**

The crucial problem in railway transport was to secure the effective operation of existing railway lines in spite of the huge pressure of increased freights and inadequate resources allocated to their maintenance. Eleven major lines radiated from Moscow, including the Kazan', Kursk, and Northern railways, as well as heavy-traffic suburban lines. The situation on the Moscow-Kursk line, particularly crucial for the national economy, was the most serious. The Party secretary in charge of transport, Donenko, was charged with the improvement of this line by a Central Committee decision of August 1932.[11] The poor repair work at the Tula depot was cited as a striking example of poor organisation, in which a low level of mass Party activity was combined with the imposition of labour discipline by 'administrative' methods. The MK secretariat approved the decision of the Tula gorkom to purge the Party officials at the depot. The MK orginstr department allocated at a new Party secretary to the depot, and the cadres department allocated a new director of the depot.

The situation on this line further deteriorated by the end of 1932, affecting the crucial freight items, grain and coal. In the name of the Central Committee Kaganovich and Kuibyshev sent a warning telegram.[12] The MK called on Donenko to bring about a 'fundamental change'. The Party district committee involved with this line each appointed one of the bureau members for a twenty-day period to seek to improve the operation of the line. The soviet official in charge of transport in Moscow, and the chairmen of the district soviet executive committees were appointed as plenipotentiaries to deal with the accumulation of freight. The MK secretariat instructed that the newspaper to devote more space to railway problems.[13] But the most startling development was an instruction to the transport procuracy to organise a 'show trial' (*pokazatel'nyi sud*) of those who hindered the normal flow of transport. This was not only used for the national campaign against the 'class enemies' but also as a weapon to strengthen labour discipline at the local level.

These harsh measures had some effects on the Kursk line. Despite the 1932–33 crisis, it was cited as a good example of mass activity at the 3rd All-union railwaymens' conference.[14] The MK secretariat claimed that working masses participated in the campaign, and the Order of the Red Flag was conferred. Other lines, where the Party campaign was less intense, fared worse. The Kazan' line, for example, had chronic labour-discipline problems.

It was against the background of constant crisis on the railways that the central authorities decided to institute politotdely (political departments) on the railways on 7 July 1933, similar to the politotdely for agriculture in the Machine-Tractor Stations. Polonsky, head of the orginstr department of the Central Committee, was put in charge of the railway politotdely for the USSR. Donenko was appointed as head of the politotdel in the Moscow, Baltic and Belorussian areas and Kuchimin, oblispolkom deputy chairman, was appointed head of the Moscow-Kazan' line politotdel.[15]

In the autumn of 1933 the Kursk line was again in serious difficulties. A joint meeting of the MK and MGK bureaux with the Party purge commission at the beginning of September to discuss the progress of the purge pointed out the confusion on the Moscow railways and on the Kursk line in particular. Several railway chiefs were put on trial by the transport collegium of the Supreme Court.[16] The Central Committee issued a decision on the Kursk line, which took the symbolic step of withdrawing the Order of the Red Flag.[17] The MK despatched 100 workers to the line. But despite all these measures few improvements resulted.[18] All the measures taken by the Party to improve management by threats and exhortations failed to eliminate a chronic crisis, which was seriously ameliorated only when substantial resources were allocated to the railways a year or two later.

8.2 THE FUEL AND ENERGY PROBLEM

Together with the crisis in food supplies and railway transport, the fuel problem was also what Ryndin called 'one of the most embattled tasks' of the Moscow Party committee.[19] With its expanding population and industry, Moscow needed enormous resources of energy. It was calculated that between 1930 and 1934 the amount of electric and thermal energy needed to be more than doubled.[20] The huge rise in demand was very difficult to meet in view of the poor performance of the Donbass coal industry and the difficulties with transport which had already been discussed. Fuel transport within Moscow was also a serious problem; only 50 horses were available for this purpose in Moscow in 1931, and there were very few lorries. Mossoviet set up a new department of fuel and energy in November 1931, and its head was simultaneously appointed special plenipotentiary for fuel.[21] But the acute energy shortage of 1930–31 was repeated in the following years.

To cope with the problem, the Moscow leaders sought to diversify their energy sources by introducing peat, and also to develop the Moscow coal-mining fields.[22] The MK bureau sought to administer the programme by the methods with which we have already became familiar in other sectors. Key Party officials were assigned to various responsibilities. Peters, chairman of the MKK, and a long-standing member of the Cheka and the OGPU, was responsible for securing supplies of Donbass coal. Bulganin, (who became Soviet Prime Minister twenty years later) was placed in charge of electricity supplies. Ryndin was made responsible for peat and Mikhailov for firewood. The very important problem of the development of Sub-Moscow coal-mining was allocated to Kaganovich himself.[23] The seniority of the Party officials involved in this work indicates the seriousness with which the fuel and energy crisis was regarded.

(a) **Peat**

Peat was used both for power stations and for home heating and accounted for about one-fifth of the total fuel resources in Moscow. As much as 45 per cent of power station fuel input was peat.[24] Peat extraction was a typical labour-intensive industry and relied mainly on seasonal labour. Mechanisation was necessary, but the labour force was half illiterate and technically ignorant and technical education was badly needed.

In March 1933 the MK bureau decision on the peat plan for 1933 planned to extract as much as 5.2 million tons.[25] For this work, 58 500 workers were required. Responsible officials of each trust were assigned the task of recruiting workers from the kolkhozes; those who failed to get results were to be dismissed. To compensate the kolkhozes for the loss of labour, each of the three peat extraction trusts was ordered to supply agriculture with 15–20 tractors, and about 20 workers were sent from each trust to help with the organisation and planning of the kolkhozes from which the peat workers were to be drawn. The peat trusts were required to repair the machines, and the plenipotentiary of NK Tyazhprom and one of the deputy chairmen of the oblispolkom were instructed to prepare caterpillar tracks and other components for this operation.[26]

As usual, housing was another important problem. For example, the Shatura trust was instructed to prepare 28 dormitory-barracks and other facilities by the beginning of the season in May. For this purpose a deputy head of oblispolkom and the manager of the Peat Administration were assigned to transport building materials from Ivanovo region, while the chairman of this district executive committee was to collect wood for the peat area.[27]

Also important was cadre allocation. Related district committees were instructed to check the Party organisations of the trust, while the regional trade union organisation was to check lower trade union organisations. In this regard, attention was to be paid to activities among female workers. The MK secretariat issued a decision 'On activities among mining workers', which recommended that sectors for women in the Party organisations were also to be instituted.[28] This decision also requested Malenkov to prepare a resolution for the following secretariat meeting on Party work and cadres in the peat-mining industry.[29] Dubyna, head of the MK culture-propaganda department, criticised those workers who regarded peat-extraction as 'supplementary work'.

A commission was also formed for labour productivity in the peat industry, its membership including Kuchimin (oblispolkom deputy chairman), the trade union, the head of the peat industry trust and the head of the soviet labour department. This commission was not only asked to make proposals for the labour force, but also to discuss the financial situation of each trust with the representative of Gosbank. Secretary Ryndin's role in this area is less clear, but he probably acted as a co-ordinator.

(b) **Electric power**

Another important energy source in Moscow was electric power, with the Mosenergo trust supplying 625 000 kilowatts in 1934 to industry (76 per cent, of the total supply, including 14 per cent for the trams) and to the general population.[30]

The shortage of electric power and other energy sources placed the Moscow leadership in a difficult position. By mid-1931 the MK was seriously concerned with delays to the construction of the Kashira power station. Lack of leadership on the part of the MOGES trust and the Kashira district committee was criticised.[31] Delays were caused by construction material shortages and the MK bureau requested Ordzhonikidze and

Rudzutak (deputy chairman of Sovnarkom) to include this project in the shock work category. It was finished in 1932 but by 1933 difficulties with electricity supply were acute, causing many stoppages.

The power crisis led to accusations of 'sabotage,' which in turn became linked to the international Metro-Vickers sensation. In April 1933 the procuracy announced the discovery of 'wrecking activities' by the British Metro-Vickers company.[32] Vyshinsky claimed that acts of 'sabotage' had been organised by foreign capitalists against socialist construction, and particularly against power stations. According to Vyshinsky, two engineers of Metro-Vickers, in collaboration with 'counter-revolutionary officials' in NK Tyazhprom, allegedly damaged the development of power stations in Moscow, the Urals and elsewhere. Just prior to this affair, dozens of high officials of NK Zem had been shot or sentenced to imprisonment because of grain-collection failures. A certain Konar was charged with having foreign links.[33] In March 1933 a decree was issued on the 'sabotage' activities of officials, and OGPU action against 'counter-revolutionaries' was publicised.

However, just as there were genuine reasons for agricultural difficulties which could not be attributed to so-called 'counter-revolutionary' activities, the power stations had their own problems, caused by difficulties with fuel supply, transport and manpower. Kaminsky, for example, complained that fuel supply ceased in some power stations despite the endeavours of the MK commissions. It was reported that a 'counter-revolutionary' power-station group in Kashira had been revealed in January 1933 in connection with the coal supply, although local people tended to believe that the particular incident was caused by 'objective reasons.'[34] Similarly the investigation of Bryansk power station by a government commission revealed ineffective fuel collection and shortcomings in the installation of new machinery.[35]

The Metro-Vickers case gave rise to international complications. The NK Indel (People's Commissariat of Foreign Affairs) was evidently unhappy with the accusation against British citizens. The sentences on the British subjects were relatively minor: one of the accused was given three years, while the other was merely expelled. Even the Soviet officials involved got off lightly, with the maximum sentence being ten years. These sentences reflected worries about international repercussions; the judgement referred to the 'local character' of the offence and the negligible damage to Soviet industry.[36] Some time later, Ryndin indirectly acknowledged that the power stations had their own problems when he said 'our bad work was *made worse* [my italics – N. S.] by the wrecking activities of our enemies'.[37]

An outspoken article in *Vechernyaya Moskva* asserted that 'our court is not guided by the formal requirements of law', and added that 'many circumstances' would have their effect.[38] The article continued by claiming that the fact that the wreckers were not shot was a sign of strength rather than weakness.[39]

Evidently the Metro-Vickers case was a kind of scapegoat for the electricity difficulties. After the affair, the MK bureau issued a resolution 'On the condition of power stations' on 14 July, which criticised the bad work of the MOGES trust which had led to delay and confusion.[40] Its head, Matlin, was instructed to strengthen workers' discipline and to send experts to the spot. He was also warned about the failure to reform wages. Amas, *partorg* of the MK, was entrusted with the Party leadership of the trust. To struggle against 'liberal' attitude towards shortcomings on the part of the Kashira power station, the MK sent out a group headed by Peters (MKK chairman) and including Voropaev, Matlin, Amas, and Malenkov. Reports of this group which spent two weeks at the power station, were heard at the bureau meetings. Amas and Malenkov organised a shock brigade conference in this power station.[41]

A few words should be added about the district heating system. This was quite novel and, operating in conjunction with power stations, developed rapidly after 1930. In 1934 the system was 15 times bigger than in 1930, and covered central areas in Moscow. It was quite modern in world terms, with hotels, theatres, and public offices heated with hot water from the Moscow power stations.[42]

(c) **Firewood**

Firewood was a by no means negligible fuel at that time. The June 1931 plenum of the Central Committee, which considered fuel supply as 'a special fighting task', was followed by a more detailed report and resolution by the July joint plenum of the MK and MGK; Ryndin characterised the firewood problem as 'not simply an economic but also a political question'.[43] The establishment of the Mossoviet fuel and energy department was apparently a result of the shortage of firewood in the autumn of 1931. The MK expressed interest in founding a 'special city trust for procuring firewood and distributing it among the population'.[44]

Moscow city alone consumed 400 freightcars of wood daily at that time.[45] It was also used in power stations. The leader who was mainly concerned with this area was secretary Mikhailov, whose sphere of work was agriculture.[46] But other leaders like Kaminsky, Ryndin, Peters and secretary Gei were also involved in obtaining firewood. Kaganovich gave approval to each procurement plan, and was in favour of threatening responsible individuals, including district secretaries and chairmen.[47] Individual responsibility for meeting the plan was also laid on officials like Mikhailov, Ryndin and Peters, as well as on Guberman of the planning commission.

This question was especially critical in the Autumn of 1932, when preparations for winter were coupled with general agricultural difficulties. The MK bureau several times discussed how to obtain and distribute firewood, and a detailed plan was formulated. In the seven key districts, one member from the district committee bureau and one from the raiispolkom presidium were appointed to act as plenipotentiaries of the MK and oblispolkom for collection and transport. Top district officials were responsible for rationing firewood in the populated areas. Kaminsky and others took care of special winter food and clothing. The distribution of firewood was supervised by the deputy chairman of oblispolkom, Kuchimin, and a plenipotentiary of the forestry commissariat.

The problem of firewood collection once again came to the fore in autumn 1933, in connection with the deepening energy crisis. In November 1933 the joint bureau of the MK and MGK approved the supply plan for firewood.[48] The relevant trusts and enterprises were held responsible for operating delays. Leaders of the district Party and enterprises were asked for assistance. In early November 1933 five meetings of forestry head managers were held, with the participation of Ryndin, Mikhailov, and Kaminsky.[49] After these meetings the chairman of each district soviet had to invite representatives of those kolkhozes and village soviets concerned with firewood. The chairmen were charged with 'special responsibility'. Manfred, plenipotentiary of NK Tyazhprom, was charged with planning the mechanisation of firewood procurement; for the time being he was to ensure the repair of tractors. Mikhailov was responsible for planning a progressive wage system with representatives of the trust and trade union.

These measures doubtless contributed to the comparatively well-organised progress procurement and distribution. The reserve of firewood on the railways tripled between October 1931 and 1933.[50] *Vechernyaya Moskva* in December 1933 reported that the preparation of firewood for winter use was satisfactory.[51] A Mossoviet report stated that the problem had been solved, which seemed optimistic but not entirely unjustified.

Shortage of energy resources was caused by the fact that Moscow industry and its population expanded more rapidly than other regions, while transport from other regions such as the Donbass was not well organised. District heating was possibly motivated by the ideological commitment to demonstrate the superiority of socialism, but was something of a luxury and not in accord with the real state of the economy. Moscow had to solve its fuel and energy problems somewhat independently; and this meant that the Moscow leadership had to get involved with fuel problems more than other local leaders, and to a greater extent than in some other sectors of the economy.

9 Agricultural Policy

9.1 KOLKHOZ AGRICULTURE

Agriculture in the Moscow area was oriented towards local consumption, and its relative weight in total production was quite small. During the first collectivisation drive of 1930, Moscow was in the third category, and collectivisation was supposed to be completed at some unspecified date in the future.[1] However, local activists were carried away by their enthusiasm: Bauman, after replacing Uglanov, who was sceptical about forced collectivisation, launched a grandiose forced-tempo plan in spring 1930. On paper this achieved the collectivisation of about 73 per cent of households by March 1930.[2]

Following Stalin's article 'Dizzy with Success', the percentage fell to 7.3 per cent a month later, and Bauman had to resign for 'leftist excess'.[3] However, collectivisation resumed under Kaganovich in 1931 and some 52 per cent of households were collectivised by the end of that year.[4]

In 1932 the main emphasis was placed on better organisation and improved economic management of the kolkhoz system. The MK secretariat admitted in February 1932 that 'some' kolkhozes had pursued a high percentage of collectivisation but had neglected organisation.[5] In the spring of 1932, some peasants left the kolkhoz system even though the authorities made some concessions, which included the legalisation of kolkhoz trade, more emphasis on 'democracy', and termination of forced socialisation. The kolkhozes included 61 per cent of households by July 1932, but this figure was again reduced to 55 per cent at the beginning of 1933.[6]

In February 1932, a MK secretariat decision on two district committees claimed that as a result of poor leadership by the party, two kinds of tendencies had appeared in the kolkhozes: simultaneously with an exodus from the kolkhozes so-called 'kulaks' were permeating the system.[7] Ten instructors from the region were despatched to Babyno district. But this decision produced little result, and no serious efforts were made to cure the defects. The MK Secretariat again paid attention to this district when the latter's bureau even failed to discuss the February decision.[8] Secretary Koshelev was dismissed and prohibited from taking up other responsible jobs for a year. The district kolkhoz union was also accused of making no effort to strengthen the kolkhoz system; the chairman of the union was also dismissed, and ten new officials allocated to work there.[9] This time, the MK

Agricultural Policy

cadres department was responsible for strengthening the district kolkhoz union, and the implementation of this instruction was to be reported to the secretariat.[10]

As seen by the central party authorities, the kolkhoz leadership faced deviations in two directions at that time. On the one hand the Party line was influenced by the pressure of 'kulaks', or well-to-do peasants who permeated the system. On the other hand, peasants were treated unnecessarily harshly as a result of the administrative approach of the 'leftists'. A typical example of the former was found by Rybnovsk district, where a 'kulak' group was occupying leading positions in the 'New-Life' kolkhoz, causing waste and insulting the kolkhozniks.[11] This situation was ignored by the district kolkhoz union chairman and even by the procuracy, and was 'discovered' by a worker who visited that kolkhoz. This was a rather strange accusation: 'kulaks' had already been deported massively and their numerical and economic power within the kolkhozes was certainly negligible. In fact the kolkhoz system failed to work not because of the presence of 'kulaks' but because of the absence of well-to-do peasants. All members of bureau of this district were reprimanded, and the procuracy purged. The MK secretariat decision in this case obliged all regional cells to discuss it, under the auspices of the MK orginstr department.

'Leftist' excess was allegedly found in the Lotoshinsk district. Here workers from the centre found that the 'middle peasants' were mistakenly purged in two kolkhozes.[12] Leaders of district institutions were allegedly corrupt in daily life, and their group was undisciplined. The district secretary, the raiispolkom chairman, and the control commission were all purged. In their place the MK recommended a certain Solob'ev as district secretary and seven other officials were also sent there. In these two cases two things are noteworthy; first, the facts were revealed by the workers who had been mobilised and sent from the MK. Second, new leadership groups were formed on the 'recommendation' of the MK.

During 1932, great tension developed between the authorities, who did not flinch from using coercive methods to get what they wanted, and the kolkhozes, which were most reluctant to hand over their harvests at the expense of their own consumption. This situation became more complicated because free trade in the kolkhoz market after completion of procurement was permitted in the spring of 1932.

Consciousness of a crisis was already apparent in the July 1932 plenum of the MK, where a resolution warned about the 'underestimation of all difficulties'.[13] The MK and MGK secretariat decided in August to send 500 Party members to the rural areas, including 300 from Moscow city, and 20 from Kalinin.[14] Their wages came from the enterprises in which they had worked. Each district committee set up a commission, under the head of its orginstr department, to deal with these problems, and the MK itself also set up a commission within its cadres department. In all this the regional leadership, following central orders, was on the offensive.

In September the MK and MGK presidium joint meeting expressed alarm about the 'kulaks' and 'alien' elements that had infiltrated into the Udomlya district kolkhozes through lack of vigilance, causing the collapse of kolkhozes and an exodus of their members.[15] Seven out of 20 kolkhoz secretaries were allegedly connected with 'kulaks'. The head of the raiispolkom financial department and the the chairman of kolkhoz union were dismissed, and the MK cadres and culture-propaganda department were instructed to involve themselves in righting the situation.

In the devastating crisis that unfolded over the Soviet countryside, in the winter of 1932–33, Moscow performed especially well in terms of the implementation of the imposed grain plan. By 2 December 1932, it had completed the grain collection plan and was allowed to sell grain on the kolkhoz market.[16] Kaganovich himself was away enforcing the grain collections in the Kuban and elsewhere; in January 1933, he was appointed head of the Central Committee agricultural department, a new organisation intended to master agricultural difficulties.[17]

Very strong pressure was nevertheless put on Moscow kolkhozes by the January 1933 plenum of the Central Committee. Kaganovich insisted on the purge of Utkin, the Efremov district secretary, at the MK bureau meeting with the MKK presidium; Utkin had failed to achieve the grain collection target for his district despite two warnings of the MK.[18] Utkin had already been dismissed from the district secretaryship by end of 1932, and a long article in *Rabochaya Moskva* underlined the political lessons of this case.[19] However, he was disgraced again in the MK February plenum because of his anti-party and 'liberal' attitude to 'kulak sabotage'. The district itself had to face a preliminary local purge. A huge population exodus followed, and agricultural work slowed down.[20] The Utkin case was a warning signal for district leaders who were tardy in preparing for the spring sowing campaign.

The February plenum of the MK decided to mobilise a further 2000 party workers for the countryside, and on 11 March the first 400 were sent.[21] It is striking that even MK bureau members were mobilised, and were requested to work in the kolkhoz for a period of ten days. The MK also sent 48 leading officials and 100 instructors to the district committees for the spring campaign.[22] This action was also repeated in May on a smaller scale. Additionally, people were mobilised from the district committee staff, about 270 being despatched initially.

Ryazan' district committee alone mobilised some 300 people for the kolkhozes.[23] *Shefstvo*, the patronage by a given factory of a certain kolkhoz or village soviet, was another important means of influence. The MK secretariat, in its decision of 7 April 1933, stressed that this important work was being carried out badly, and decided to abolish patronage by particular factories in favour of institutionalised patronage cells, subordinate to the district soviets.[24]

Other Moscow organisations were also involved. The drivers' union gorkom provided 400 tractor drivers and 70 mechanics. Even the military had to send surplus horses to the fields. Propagandists were mobilised by the MK culture and propaganda department under the direction of Kogan.[25]

From the point of view of political organisation, the kolkhoz system improved after the spring campaign of 1933, as was shown by the resolution of the joint MK and MGK plenum in July 'On practical measures for strengthening kolkhozes'.[26] The proportion of kolkhoz households reached about 65 per cent in 1933 against 55 per cent at the end of 1932. Some 21 000 kolkhozes were organised by then, usually small.

There had been 2271 party cells in 1932; this increased to 2924 cells at the beginning of 1933 in Moscow region.[27] The number of communists in the countryside in 1932 was said to be 42 035. However this figure may be exaggerated so far as the kolkhoznik-communists are concerned. Even after the despatch of 2000 communists in 1933, there were only 25 000 communists in the kolkhoz system, and few of these turned out to be genuine peasants. To make the best use of the small numbers of communists, the role of Komsomol nuclei groups and single communists was increased by the 15 June 1933 Central Committee decision. Even after that only 18.9 per cent of Moscow kolkhozes were under the control of Communist organisations. As many as 9500 kolkhozes, nearly half of the total, had no communists at all. Communist secretaries of rural and kolkhoz cells were to be re-educated during the winter in Moscow, Tula and elsewhere. The politotdely provided courses for the lower party apparatchiki. The 1000 largest kolkhozes were specially registered by the MK in order to maintain contact with these key groups.

The MK also paid considerable attention to the sovkhozes. About 70–100 sovkhoz directors were educated on 6–month courses. Kovalev, head of the Moscow regional agricultural department, was responsible for the preparation of managers and officials; while the MK orginstr department was to despatch 50 Party workers to the sovkhoz system. Trade unions also sent their officials to the sovkhozes.[28]

9.2 PARTY LEADERSHIP OF CAMPAIGNS

The grain collection campaign for the 1933 harvest, the year following the famine, and the simultaneous livestock campaign, will serve to illustrate the role of the party in the endeavour to improve the performance of agriculture and subordinate it to the interests of the state.

(a) The Grain Collection of 1933

At the beginning of 1933, the authorities introduced the new compulsory-delivery system of collection. In the summer of 1933, when procurement and delivery of grain were delayed by the sovkhozes, secretary Mikhailov despatched some 50 Party members in consultation with the Central Committee. An MK bureau decision of 28 August 'On the progress of harvesting and grain delivery' revealed the serious concern of the Moscow leaders with this problem in relation to kolkhozes as well as sovkhozes.[29] Workers were allocated to districts lagging behind in threshing or collection. Where grain deliveries were badly delayed, the MK bureau members themselves were despatched to the districts. Ten 'firm workers' were also mobilised and sent to delivery points. The responsibility for preparing grain warehouses and the appropriate staff was placed upon Kaminsky and the head of the MK cadres department. False receipts were to be investigated by Redens, OGPU head, and show trials were to be organised as required.[30]

At the same time, the oblispolkom chairman and Kaganovich both stressed that labour discipline must be tightened.[31] They also sent an Appeal to district committee secretaries, chairmen of raiispolkoms and heads of politotdely, criticising the delays in the oat harvest and the passive attitude of the local authorities towards the anti-kulak struggle. Following previous practice, each district had to report how directives had been implemented, and each district committee secretary, together with Nikolaev, the plenipotentiary of the state procurement commission, were made responsible for grain delivery.

While the party gave top priority to the grain collections, the sowing campaign had received rather less attention in Moscow, in contrast to the situation in the south, where it presented a severe trial for both the regional leadership and the population. In preparation for the spring sowing of 1933, at the end of January, the MK bureau issued a decision on the accumulation of horse fodder; those who neglected horses were to be prosecuted in show trials.[32] On 9 May, when the spring sowing was at its peak, the joint bureau of the MK and MGK sent an extraordinary telegram to the local authorities. The individual farms were not neglected. Certain district committee secretaries were directed to pay special attention to the sowing campaign, and some 100 Party workers were mobilised to ensure that sowing took place. Daily reports on potato sowing had to be sent to Moscow.

In the midst of the 1933 harvest campaign, the MK bureau had to turn its attention to the winter sowing for the 1934 harvest, and approved the sowing plan for winter wheat. The bureau stressed the need to finish threshing by August, following which the seed stock was to be collected.[33] 'Special workers' concerned with the seed collection were sent to 22 districts by Moscow and the MK cadres department.

Much attention was also paid to virgin land cultivation. The MK plenum of July 1932 proposed to bring some 150 000 hectares into cultivation.[34] The result of this plan is not known to the present author, but a year later in July 1933 the joint MK and MGK bureau also decided to cultivate the same amount of virgin land.[35] Every district committee had to reported on the plan achievement every five days. Substantial incentives were promised for work on virgin land.

Repair and supply of machinery was another important if far less successful part of the agricultural campaigns. At the end of February 1933, the MK bureau called for the production of potato-planting machines in two engineering enterprises.[36] This proposal was not carried out. In April 1933, the MK criticised the Laptev district and the brigade which it had sent there to strengthen leadership in the agricultural machinery factory.[37] Similar decisions were taken about another factory which manufactured potato-planters, Ryazsel'mash.

The above evidence indicates the rather low priority attached to the repair and supply of agricultural machines and tools. Central supplies were extremely limited. The MK leadership sought to solve this problem from local resources, and in March 1933 its bureau requested Mospromtrest to mobilise the artisan (kustar') industry for this purpose.[38] Tula and other district committees were asked to tackle the problem by organising handicraft industry for dealing with horse shoes and other items. But the supply and repair of machinery remained inadequate.

(b) Livestock

Livestock was disastrously affected in the whole period 1930–33 following forced collectivisation. In Moscow there was a substantial decrease in the number of horses and cows.[39] At a national level, the Central Committee condemned the forced confiscation or 'socialisation' of cattle in March

1932. After the decision to prohibit forced 'socialisation', leading district officials were sent to the countryside to promulgate it; the authorities claimed that 'kulaks' were agitating against Soviet power and taking advantage of the situation following the forced 'socialisation' of poultry and other livestock.[40]

In August 1933, a joint decision of Party and government resolved to assist cow-less kolkhozes. This was supplemented by a decision at MK level to carry out the central directives; the MK was particularly concerned with encouraging the development of sovkhozes which specialised in pig farms.[41]

In the MK apparatus, it was secretary Mikhailov who was placed in charge of livestock. He supervised the construction of a pig-raising sovkhoz, headed the commission on the payment for this sovkhoz, and selected the politotdely workers.[42] The MK itself twice in 1933 ordered that Mikhailov should check the implementation of the decision on aid to cow-less kolkhozes.

This decision offered one million calves to the 12 regions or republics where the number of cows had particularly declined.[43] Moscow was instructed to buy 80 000 calves by the end of 1933. Following the central decision, the MK bureau in its decision of 28 August gave a detailed instruction for the purchase of cows.[44] But two months later an MK secretariat decision showed that this plan was not observed.[45] In Epifan district, for example, calves were not bought; the district committee bureau failed to discuss the MK or even the Central Committee decisions. The laggard district committees were warned and Mikhailov himself was required to reinforce control over them. Still by the end of 1933 a third of the plan remained unfulfilled. Nevertheless, a further purchase of 125 000 calves was planned in Moscow.[46]

A central directive at the beginning of 1932 directed attention to pig-raising.[47] In September 1933 Moscow claimed that pig-raising sovkhozes under the supply commissariat had been relatively successful, and took further steps to develop this system. To construct 30 pig-raising sovkhozes, personal responsibility was placed on nine district secretaries and on the directors of those sovkhozes.[48] The MK permitted the use of some 300 railway freightcars to carry timber and other construction materials for this purpose. Kolchinskii, plenipotentiary of the supply commissariat in Moscow, was to specialise in fodder supply for the sovkhozes.[49] Other sovkhozes were requested to release fodder reserves on the advice of MOZO (Kovalev), Kolchinskii, and the OGPU representative (Redens).

The importance of this project can be inferred from the circumstance that Mikoyan, the People's Commissar for Trade, sent 288 tractors for these sovkhozes, while the plenipotentiary of the People's Commissariat of Heavy Industry in Moscow (Manfred) was instructed to provide tractor repair facilities. On the Party side, Mikhailov and Statsevich (the MK cadres department) appointed within a month 30 Party workers as heads of sovkhoz politotdely; Statsevich also had to select 30 directors for these sovkhozes and 50 other workers from among graduates of communist higher education institutions.[50] The MK secretariat ratified the list of these appointments, and the whole project was controlled by Mikhailov.

But, in contrast with Leningrad, Moscow remained especially weak in pig-raising, and in 1933 pig numbers increased by only three per cent.

Meanwhile, preparation to shelter and feed livestock in the winter was another preoccupation of the Moscow Party apparatchiki. Each district committee secretary as well as the chairman of district ispolkom was reminded about construction for the winter.[51] Less important construction sites were halted so as to concentrate on preparations for the winter.

9.3 *POLITOTDELY* AND AGRICULTURAL CONTROL

The *politotdely* of the MTS and sovkhozes were introduced at the January joint plenum of the Central Committee and Control Commission 1933, (see Chapter 3). This was an extraordinary organising measure by the central authorities to cope with the disastrous situation in the countryside, especially in the Ukraine, North Caucasus and Lower Volga.[52] In Moscow, where the relative weight of agriculture was still very low and the 1932–33 rural crisis somewhat muted, the impact of the politotdely on its local agriculture was less. But Moscow was the most important source for politotdely workers, together with Leningrad and the Red Army. The main personnel sent to the kolkhozes in the Ukraine and North Caucasus were from Moscow, and were selected by the new Central Committee department of agriculture, headed by L. M. Kaganovich.

Moscow Party workers sent to rural areas of the USSR amounted to 2768 by the end of 1933, out of a total of 12 000 workers in the MTS. As many as 38.2 per cent of the heads of the politotdely (949 persons) and 23.1 per cent of the deputy heads of politotdely responsible for mass Party work came from Moscow.[53]

Those recruited for politotdely were probably drawn mainly from the city and the factories of Moscow region. Frunze district committee alone provided 327 heads of politotdely and 250 other officials, while Stalin district committee contributed 52 workers.[54] In the case of the Frunze district, the proportion of students and higher education graduates was large; about one third of those sent to politotdely were recruited from them, probably from higher communist agricultural institutions. The MK and MGK undoubtedly sent their most energetic workers to the rural areas.

In the Moscow rural areas the politotdely were also established. The Moscow regional committee sent some 400 workers to the Moscow region itself, to work in MTS and kolkhozes.[55] 58 politotdely were initially established in the Moscow region, manned by people screened in February 1933.[56] The screening was carried out by an MK commission, which probably included secretary Mikhailov, and the head of the MK cadres department. This was the practice followed for the politotdely of the pig sovkhozes, as established by an MK bureau decision of September 1933.[57]

The politotdely in the Moscow region had several important functions. The first was the negative one of removing 'alien and useless persons' from kolkhoz leadership positions. In some 50 politotdely, 1600 so-called 'kulaks' or 'alien' leading officials were purged from their posts and a further 3400 were dismissed as 'useless'.[58] As many as 34.2 per cent of Moscow kolkhoz chairmen were dismissed, mainly those held responsible for the poor condition of the horses, or who had failed to sow on time, or hampered early sowing. Kolkhoz officials were described as 'kulaks' when they were reluctant to begin work at dawn, or objected to night threshing work. Others were said to have spread rumours of an 'anti-state' character (for example, that politotdely held all the storehouse keys and only 10–15 per cent of the grain was left to the kolkhozniks').[59] In other words, those who were slow to follow the official line were likely to be labelled as 'alien' or 'kulaks'.

Second, the politotdely reshuffled the leading MTS apparatus personnel. Of 5400 MTS staff under the jurisdiction of 50 politotdely, 1276 were dismissed.[60] Almost half of the heads of production sections (*proizvodstvennye uchastki*), accountants and warehouse keepers were removed, and about 15 per cent of tractor drivers were dismissed. Their posts were filled by activists or promoted workers (*vydvizhentsy*). The task of strengthening labour discipline and reinforcing work brigades was naturally emphasised, and attempts were made to organise shock workers.[61]

Thirdly, the politotdely had to reorganise the Party apparatus in these districts where MTS were operating. The Moscow Party organisation was very thinly spread; communists in Moscow kolkhoz agriculture were relatively few, and the problem of Party organisation was complicated by the relatively small size of the typical Moscow kolkhoz.

Agricultural Policy

Even after the reorganisation of the Party by the decision of 15 June 1933, which temporarily increased the number of communists and related organisations in the countryside, there were only 18.9 per cent Party organisation for every 100 of the kolkhozes in the Moscow region, compared with the national average of 41.1.[62] Only about 10 per cent of kolkhozes had cells or candidate groups, and formal Party cells were to be found in only 5.3 per cent of kolkhozes (the national average was 17.9 per cent).[63] In Moscow, there were only 4.2 Party cells per MTS, as against 6.2 nationally. The number of kolkhozes with no communists at all amounted to 57.4 per cent, against a national level of 37.6 per cent.[64] These kolkhozes were regarded by Kaganovich as hostile kolkhoz. Communist strength was also weak in Leningrad and other grain-consumption areas.

The Moscow Party leadership sought to improve this situation. In the intensifying crisis of 1933, the February plenum of the MK decided to sent 2000 Party workers to the rural campaign, some 400 as early as March plus another 268 be mobilised on the recommendation of the MK department of agitation and mass and of the district committee.[65] In all, more than 4000 people were despatched from Moscow to the surrounding countryside.[66]

However, the number was evidently insufficient to reinforce the rural Party organisation and only highlighted the weakness of the available forces. Moscow's best forces were sent to the south of the USSR, with Moscow itself only occupying a marginal place in the rural anxieties of the central leaders.

The effectiveness of the pressure of both the politotdely and the normal channels in influencing kolkhozes and kolkhozniks is open to doubt. On the one hand the Party forcefully pressurised peasants to join the kolkhozes, and on the other it purged those kolkhozniks who were regarded as 'kulaks' or saboteurs, even those who were former poor peasants or middle peasants. When kolkhoz members acted to preserve their harvests or distribute them among themselves at a time of shortage and threat of hunger, this was ascribed to 'anti-socialist or anti-state' influence by 'kulaks'.

This situation caused complicated reactions on the part of peasants. After partial exodus from kolkhozes in 1932, they again turned to kolkhozes by 1933, probably as a result of the pressure from above. Some 50 000 petitioned to join the kolkhozes, including some who were 'kulaks' or had been previously punished.[67] In turn, there were cases where 'kulak' leadership was blamed for preventing poor and middle peasants joining the kolkhozes, as in Egor'evsk district.[68] In Chernskii, the kolkhoz administration was alleged to have built up stocks or distributed them in favour of kolkhoz members at the cost of state collection.[69] The MK secretariat in its decision in January 1933 requested the district committees to make correct distributions.

The balance between the pressure from above and the reaction of the rural administration was also difficult to maintain. The MK secretariat in April 1933 warned against the abuse of haphazardly purging kolkhozniks so as to create the impression that right amount of tension was maintained in the spring sowing campaign. There were cases, as in one kolkhoz of the Pronsk district, where poor peasants were expelled.[70] This decision called for a strengthening of the district commissions which investigated appeals by those expelled from kolkhozes. The most extreme case was found in the '10th Anniversary of October' which was said to be dominated by 'kulaks'.[71] Their failure to fulfil the plan was regarded as due to 'wreckers'. Despite the warning from the local paper, the local authority neglected to take proper action. The district secretary was investigated because of his relationship with 'kulaks', and cadre workers were despatched from obkom level.

The introduction of politotdely resulted in clashes with the already long-established district committees (raikoms). The politotdely sought to reorganise the lower Party apparatus of kolkhoz cells, which had been the responsibility of the district committees.[72]

The January 1933 plenum of the Central Committee called for collaboration between the district and the MTS, but in practice the relationship deteriorated when the politotdely dismissed rural secretaries who were on the nomenklatura of the district committee. In the Krasnokholm district of Moscow region, the first secretary, Ginderman, attributed the delay in spring sowing and the poor execution of the MTS contract to the politotdely.[73] He was accused of hindering the summoning of rural secretaries to a conference convened by the politotdely, and interfering with communication between the secretaries and the politotdely. Every Moscow raikom where MTS politotdely had been established was ordered to discuss the lessons of Krasnokholm district at joint meetings of district committee bureau and politotdely. This was one of several manifestations of rivalry between the two structures.

A Central Committee decision of 15 June 1933 formally settled the case in favour of politotdely over district committees in rural Party matters.[74] Rural Party organisations, hitherto grouped and controlled on a territorial basis, were to be regrouped on the production principle. Scarce Party members were to be deployed in the form of candidate groups or Party-Komsomol groups. The number of rural communist organisations increased by subdivision, and more than doubled nationally. But even after this reorganisation, as we have seen, the density of party organisation in

Moscow kolkhozes was thin: 5.3 kolkhoz cells per 100 kolkhozes, 6.0 candidate groups, 7.6 Party-Komsomol groups, making a total of only 18.9 communist-associated organisations per 100 kolkhozes.[75]

The proportion of communists in each sector of the kolkhoz hierarchy deserves analysis. Communist kolkhoz chairmen accounted for 28.6 per cent in Moscow (44.0 per cent for the USSR as a whole). The average proportion of communists in book-keeping, tractor operation, and warehouse keeping was two thirds of the national average. Only the proportion of communist heads of the 'commodity' farms (*tovarnye fermy*) was above average in Moscow. Despite the sending of Party activists into the kolkhozes and countryside in 1933, the number of rural communists remained small. This was partly compensated by the mobilisation of non-party activists in rural areas. About 8.4 non-party activists were involved per communist in Moscow, against a national level of 5.2.[76] The number of activists per MTS was also above average in Moscow. Judging from the numbers of activists mobilised by communists the Moscow kolkhoz had more support from a minority of active peasants than the all-Union average.

The success of the politotdely as perceived by the Moscow leaders accelerated the change in the Party apparatus from the 'functional' principle to the 'production' principle. Kaganovich proposed to the XVIIth Party Congress in January 1934 that the politotdel principle should be generally followed in the Party machine. The normal size of the politotdely (four persons) was increased by the addition of the editor of the politotdel newspaper and an organiser for women by decision of the MK and MGK joint plenum of July 1933.

Agricultural policy in Moscow had certain specific features. Moscow was not intended to produce for other regions; at most, it was meant to provide for the consumers within the region. Accordingly, the policy directed against 'kulak sabotage' was not applied as directly and as severely as in the critical North Caucasus, Lower Volga and Ukrainian regions. In Moscow the kolkhozniks felt the effects of the 'kulak' problem and the famine to only a moderate degree. All the same, Moscow was the power base of Kaganovich, who was the inspiration of the hard-line policy of 1932–33, and Moscow workers and students were mobilised and sent to the countryside to cope with the serious agricultural situation.

10 Management of the Municipal Economy

The term municipal economy (*gorodskoe khozyaistvo*) refers to the urban services necessary for city life. In the Statute on City Soviets promulgated in 1933, the following functions came into the category of communal services and municipal economy: housing, organisation of social facilities, city planning, management of local enterprises, electrification and use of other forms of energy, city transport, water supply, land utilisation, fire prevention, and the production of building materials.[1]

The resolution of the June 1931 Party plenum on Moscow was almost certainly the first document in which Soviet strategy for city construction was formulated.[2] Needless to say, Soviet leaders were strong advocates of central planning and government; there was little room for the idea of independent or autonomous local government which would decide on the main issues concerning city management. This centralising tendency was extremely strong in the First Five-Year Plan period, when the Stalinist political system and the centrally-planned economy emerged.

Paradoxically, the central planning system itself caused a vacuum which local leaders had to fill. The central authorities were preoccupied with national projects, and the municipal economy was regarded as residual. Moscow leaders therefore had to develop their own initiatives to cope with local problems, and to mobilise their own resources and ideas, sometimes without central direction. Independent solutions had to be worked out without benefit of precedent. It is not accidental that the initial measures for the Moscow resolution on the municipal economy adopted by the June plenum were initiated and worked out in the MK and Mossoviet.[3] Moscow experience became a sort of model for other cities, although the results were not always so convincing.

Local Party and soviet leaders were the key people in the municipal economy. Khrushchev and Bulganin both played major roles here. Other high city officials also assumed responsible tasks. By the decision of the MK bureau of January 1933, for example, the task of setting up targets for each trust of the municipal economy was given to 'Filatov's commission'.

helped by secretary Ruben.[4] The result of this consultation was reported to the joint plenum of the MK, MGK, and Mossoviet, with the prior consent of Bulganin and Khrushchev.

The same procedure was followed by the regional level municipal economy, though its relative weight was much smaller. The overall plan was developed by the 'Gei commission,' formed by the MK bureau decision of 4 January 1933, and consisting of the regional soviet chairman (Kaminsky), Guberman from the planning commission, and important city secretaries from Kalinin and other towns as well as the plenipotentiary of the MK in the Sub-Moscow coalfield.[5] This commission decided, for example, to extend tramway transport in Tula and Kalinin, and to develop water supply and sewage in the region.

In this chapter the relatively substantial autonomy exercised by the Moscow Party and soviets in these matters is illustrated with reference to various aspects of the municipal economy.

10.1 MOSCOW CITY PLANNING

An advantage in principle for a socialist state is the greater feasibility of comprehensive city planning, than in the case of a capitalist city, according to Socialist theory. As early as 1920, Mossoviet began to develop Moscow city planning, although virtually nothing happened in those years of decline and scarcity.[6] Towards the end of the 1920s the future shape of Moscow was visualised and designed, by several different planners, sometimes very imaginatively, sometimes fantastically. Some radicals called for the total dismemberment of Moscow.[7] The less radical, like Prof. Ladovskii, said that Moscow should be the city of the industrial proletariat, and were opposed by Semenov and Iofan, who claimed that 'Moscow is not Magnitogorsk'.[8]

Prior to the June plenum foreign experts were also invited to take part in the discussion. Le Corbusier and others proposed a 'broad-acre city.' The projects of Ladovskii and Le Corbusier were rejected as 'urbanism' and 'dis-urbanism' respectively by the conservative authorities.[9]

The 1931 June plenum, pointing to the lack of planning in Moscow city construction, emphasised the need for a 'scientifically based plan'.[10] This was followed by a local decision on practical measures to develop the municipal economy which suggested that a 'special commission' for city planning be set up.[11] Following this, Mossoviet organised a Committee on Architecture and Planning with Khvesin (deputy chairman of Mossoviet) as chairman. In Mossoviet, the architecture and planning administration (APU), was primarily engaged in land requisition, although it was also collecting information on various aspects of city life, and was interested in general planning. A commission on artistic design for Moscow was also set up, including the famous theatre director Meierkhol'd and the film director Eisenstein.[12] But these arrangements lacked both political authority and effective power. The APU was particularly weak in controlling the development of the city and economy.[13]

By mid-1933 the APU had drawn up a long-term plan, the General Plan (Genplan) of Moscow, and detailed work was based on the Genplan. Khrushchev, Bulganin and Khvesin convened several experts' meetings at that time, culminating in a general experts' meeting on the Genplan in June 1933 organised by the MGK secretariat.[14]

But this did not satisfy Kaganovich. Some architects were critical towards the plan of destroying 'Sukharev Tower' – a symbol of Old Russian buildings, and even sent a letter to Stalin himself in August. Kaganovich was alarmed by the 'Severe class struggle' among the architecture and planning system, and urged 'communist-architects' to react to it. And on his initiative there followed a reorganisation of the planning system. In September 1933, an MGK bureau and Mossoviet presidium decision noted the unsatisfactory work of the APU, and decided to establish three separate departments for design, city planning and land-allocation. The first had ten design offices for main streets and areas; one notable design office, led by Professors Iofan and Shchuko, drew up plans for the abortive Palace of Soviets and the Lenin Library.[15]

For comprehensive decision-making in city construction and planning, ARPLAN was set up. This was a permanent commission of the MGK and Mossoviet for architecture and planning, and able to control all departments and design offices.[16] Its members included Party and soviet leaders like Kaganovich, Khrushchev, Kaminsky and Bulganin, as well as department heads. Seven famous architects also attended, including Zholtovskii and Iofan. This body was in practice under the auspices of Kaganovich, and he involved himself in the most specific details.[17] Stalin took a personal interest in the remaking of Moscow. Gosplan now advocated a 10-year plan, rather than the 15–20-year plan originally intended, and the new plan was presented to a Politburo meeting in July 1934, and was eventually ratified as a government and Party decision in 1935.[18] But, as time went on, this system of city planning turned out to be largely nominal; individual planning projects proceeded without the approval of the Moscow soviet.

10.2 WATER SUPPLY

Water supply was one of the main concerns of the city leaders. The daily consumption rose from 29 million vedro (1 *vedro* = 12.3 litres) in 1931 to 39 million by the end of 1933; a consumption of 60 million was anticipated for 1935. Water shortages were frequent, and the newspapers were full of reports about water cuts.[19] The June 1931 plenum decided to construct the Moscow-Volga Canal to change and improve the supply pattern drastically; until its completion in 1937, the conventional system had to be modified to cope with increasing demand.

A decision of the MGK bureau in October 1931 required the secretariat to collaborate with Filatov and Bulganin on this question.[20] Bulganin, in his turn, convened a specialists' meeting on the pipeline problem, and appealed to the government to import those pipeline materials in short supply. He also sought to obtain from the government construction commission the necessary materials for the Rublev water supply installation.

The Rublev installation was the main construction project aimed at water-supply improvement in 1932–33. But its completion was delayed.[21] Shternberg, the Mossoviet deputy chairman who was mainly responsible for this question, was instructed by the MK bureau to take necessary measures with the approval of the secretariat. These measures seem to have produced some results: an MGK decision 15 months later remarked in the considerable benefits resulting from the building of this installation. The Moscow leadership still complained of 'lack of vigilance' in the matter of water supplies, however, and the Moscow water-supply trust (Mosvodoprovod) was instructed to take concrete measures in 1934.[22]

The crucial means of resolving this problem was the Moscow-Volga Canal. The Central Committee plenum decision on Moscow in 1931 planned to connect the two rivers so as to double Moscow's water supply by 1935. One version claims that this idea was initiated by Stalin.[23] Whatever the authenticity of this claim, the project was first considered in a Politburo commission in June 1931, involving the MK, Gosplan, and the Peoples' Commissariat of Water Transport (NK Vod).[24] In March 1932 the Canal was included by the STO in the category of national 'shock' work.[25] It was to be three times as large as the Moscow-White Sea Canal. By the end of 1932 construction was entrusted to the OGPU, and the experience of the Moscow White Sea Canal was used, as well as many of its workers.[26]

Although actual construction did not begin until mid-1932, the Moskanalstroi trust was organised and L. I. Kogan, who used to be head of the White sea canal construction, became its head. Three plans were presented for consideration; in its decree of June 1932, Sovnarkom adopted the Dmitrovskii plan, the least expensive, and set the completion date at November 1934.[27] The project was nominally financed by Mossoviet, but the fact that Gosplan, NK Tyazhprom and other peoples' commissariats were instructed to co-operate shows its national significance.[28]

The MGK played an important role in carrying out the plan. On 27 August 1932 the MGK secretariat adopted a detailed decision on the construction, assigning tasks to the relevant institutions and officials.[29] Bulganin, for example, was responsible for securing the necessary building materials from STO. The details of the plan required preliminary work by specialists before it was presented for approval by the MGK and Mossoviet. The MGK cadres department was responsible for selecting leading officials of Moskanalstroi, and Kogan, with its approval, presented a list of the managers of work sectors and construction sites (*uchastki*). Each construction site set up Party cells and a special Party organiser was appointed for the Moskanalstroi project as a whole. Secretary Ruben and Bulganin were assigned the task of persuading the Central Committee to purchase foreign machinery. The labour mobilisation question was somewhat complex. The above-mentioned decision of August 1932 prescribed that 'twenty or thirty thousand workers' were to begin the earthworks by the autumn of 1932.[30] The mobilisation was probably carried out by NK Trud (Peoples' Commissariat of Labour). The responsibility for workers' supplies was undertaken by Mikoyan himself as People's Commissar for Supplies.

The amount of work undertaken by convicted labour, and the numbers involved are not known.[31] Some officials as well as prisoners used for the Baltic-White Sea Canal almost certainly began to work on this new project. Lord Simon, who visited Moscow, observed the highly-controlled nature of this work.[32] According to a British observer, an OGPU official S. G. Firin, who had worked in the White Sea Canal camps, suggested that 81 000 were engaged in this work in 1935, of whom nine-tenths were prisoners.[33] The project was not completed until 1937.[34] It provides an example of a highly centralised project carried out with the strong support of the local Party and soviet.

10.3 HOUSING POLICY

Of 56 790 houses and housing blocs in Moscow city in 1933 about 70 per cent were wooden and 86 per cent two-storey or smaller.[35] The housing situation, already poor in the 1920s, deteriorated sharply in the First Five-year Plan period. The poor housing situation was due to the population explosion from 2.3 million to 3.7 million in 1933, together with the damaging effect of the priority enjoyed by industrial building.[36] The Central Committee plenum resolution about Moscow in June 1931 envisaged the building of accommodation for at least a million people in three years, but this was not carried out.[37] One year after the plenum, only 80 000 workers and employees had received new housing. Khrushchev claimed that 1 164 000 square metres were built for 275 000 people between 1931 and 1933, less than 30 per cent of the June 1931 target.[38] The 'standard' quality was extremely low, as was acknowledged by the MK bureau and Mossoviet presidium decision on the housing problem in September 1933. Despite the instruction to build high-quality, architecturally respectable buildings, dormitory-barrack types of building were constructed.[39] The average area of accommodation per head for the population as a whole diminished from the low figure of 5.9 square metres in 1928 to a mere 4.3 in 1933.

To keep housing from falling even below this level, considerable efforts were made in the difficult years of 1932–33. From 1927/28 onwards some 400–500 000 square metres were built every year, and in 1932 a peak of 592 000 square metres was reached.

Moscow dwellings were built under three main auspices: municipal organisations like Mossoviet (regional housing); co-operative associations; and enterprises and institutions. Between 1931 and 1934 as much as three quarters of the new floor space was financed by enterprises or institutions; NK Tyazhprom was the most important organiser in this field.[40]

The Mossoviet and the district soviets were supposed to play a significant role in implementation of the housing policy, even in the case of enterprise housing. The February 1932 decision of the MGK secretariat indicates the role and responsibility of the Mossoviet in this area.[41] According to this decision, the allocation of sites for housing was made in the name of the Mossoviet, and the approval of the Party secretariat was also required. Chairman Bulganin's job was to find materials and manpower resources. Details of construction were supposed to be the responsibility of Khvesin, a deputy chairman of Mossoviet, and of the head of the projects department. The specified type of housing bloc was over-idealistic. It had to be of at least five storeys, and decorated in colour inside. Half of the flats were to be 3-room, 35 per cent 4-room, and 15 per cent 2-room. Worker-settlement barrack-type designs were supposed to be excluded, although in practice they were not.

Some emphasis was also placed on regional housing from 1932 onwards. In the textile areas, about 140 000 square metres were planned by the MK bureau decision of June 1932.[42] The main responsibilities were placed on the cotton-textile and other trusts. However, in this case, buildings were to be less than three storeys because of financial constraints. In Kalinin city, for example, a mere 9600 square metres were expected to be built. In the Sub-Moscow coal area, housing was also planned by the MK bureau decision of March 1932, which allocated resources.[43] There were as many as 100 communists and Komsomol members occupied with this question, and five of them were attached MK bureau for Sub-Moscow to prepare for the construction season. Experts were sent via the labour department.

In 1933 economic difficulties halted many of these plans and hampered housing construction generally. Although 890 housing blocks were planned for 1933, only 40 per cent had been built by August, and half of these were of a 'simplified' type. About 70 per cent of the dwellings were built for enterprises and institutions and 20 per cent for Mossoviet. Enterprises were primarily concerned with the amount of housing available irrespective of quality, and this led to a further deterioration of housing standards. Mossoviet had little influence on the construction standards of commissariats and enterprises, even when they were grossly violated. Even barracks for the builders, intended as temporary, ended up as permanent 'tenant co-operatives.' In real terms, 1933 construction in Moscow city was only half that of the previous year. This created many problems.[44] Nor was there much progress in 1934.

Co-operatives were responsible for one tenth of housing construction in Moscow city, but building in this category was tightly controlled by the central authorities. In Gosplan the 'Mezhlauk committee' set the limit of 1933 construction at some 12 million roubles, and infringement of this limit was prohibited by the MGK secretariat in April 1933.[45] Superfluous dwellings built in this category were to be handed over to the Peoples' Commissariats, the transfers being made by a commission headed by Konstantinopol'skii of the Mossoviet construction department.[46] Moscow housing construction was thus dominated by the People's Commissariats, especially those for industry. Regional housing construction formed a small proportion of the total, and both it and co-operative housing were strongly limited by the central authorities. The design schemes of MK and Mossviet looked good on paper, but had little influence in practice.

(a) Utilisation and Management of Housing Stock

Here the local Party and soviet authorities were of great importance. The general pattern of subordinates was similar to that for house construction. In Moscow, as elsewhere, housing was managed by enterprises and institutions, co-operatives, and by local soviets like Mossoviet.

The ZhAKT (*zhilishchno-arendnoe ko-operativnoe tovarishchestvo*), or house leasing co-operative association, was an organisation intended to improve housing conditions as well as administer rented dwellings. It covered some 47 per cent of housing, and Mossoviet housing trusts (*domtresty*) were in charge of 15–17 per cent. The remainder was the responsibility of RZhSKT (workers' house-building co-operative associations) and other categories. The contrast with house construction is striking. While most new housing was provided by the commissariats, most existing housing stocks were under direct municipal control.[47]

The official policy for housing management was to hand over much of the housing stock to ZhAKT. In March 1933 the MK decided to 'decentralise' house management in the form of ZhAKT. Many housing blocks were transferred to ZhAKT from the state stock and from the other soviets; Mossoviet and the district soviets would directly control less than 35 per cent of houses.[48]

Priority and privilege were accorded to certain categories of officials and workers in the allocation of scarce housing space. The OGPU, the Red Army and diplomatic organisations were accorded the right to reserve their own quotas. Those mobilised in the procurement campaign in the Moscow and other regions could also reserve their space. The militia was allotted about 10 per cent of space evacuated as a consequence of the introduction of internal passports.[49] Special consideration was given to participants of the Revolution and Civil War. Special housing was built for specialists after policy towards them changed in 1931; the Central Committee decided to build ten blocks of houses in March 1932 and this was endorsed by the MGK bureau in January 1933.[50]

The extremely limited available space and the increasing population brought major problems and abuses. The behaviour of the Mossoviet department of housing was so scandalous that stricter control was introduced over it at the end of 1932. It transpired that high officials of this department had abused their position; the head and other officials of the department were living in good apartments that had been allocated to workers.[51] A joint meeting of the MGK bureau, Mossoviet presidium and the presidium of the MGKK took a severe attitude towards the officials involved. City procurator Filippov was asked to bring the most severe charges, while the MGK was to check the cells of institutions that were involved. District-level housing departments were also investigated, and more centralised control over housing stock followed.

Considerable tension developed about the right to housing in 1932–33. A decree prohibited dismissed workers from continuing to use factory-controlled accommodation. This was part of the campaign to tighten labour discipline and reduce absenteeism.[52] With the introduction of the passport system in January 1933, the exchange of flats and rooms was suspended; offers of accommodation were to be handled directly by the Mossoviet housing department.[53] Strict control over the exchange of flats between people living in different cities was also introduced as a method of stemming the population influx. This centralising tendency was endorsed by a Mossoviet decision of March 1933, which made clear that neither the housing administrations (upravdom) nor the district executive committees had any authority over the allocation of accommodation. Those who violated this were threatened with punishment according to the criminal code.[54]

This situation raised the question of control, especially Party control, over the ZhAKT. The introduction of passports necessitated tighter housing management. Newspaper articles refered to 'class struggle within the ZhAKT' and claimed that communists were opposed by 'Kolchakites' or 'nobles,' who were threatened with losing their food rationing and their right to live in Moscow.[55] The party strongly emphasised the role of the comrades' courts in controlling the ZhAKT and the need to elect reliable people to them.[56] The use of the savage decree 'On the protection of socialist property' as a tool for protecting housing was mentioned. When the exchange of apartments was resumed, possession of a passport became a prerequisite for obtaining accommodation.

At that time, municipalised dwellings were managed either by trusts subordinated to Moszhiltrest (Moscow housing trust), or by the ZhAKT, which directly controlled houses by concluding contracts with Mossoviet. The general policy from 1931 onwards was to decentralise the management system in favour of the ZhAKT. The trusts controlled 3.34 million square metres and the ZhAKT 7.27 million. On the whole, the trust's blocks of flats were well equipped and large; some were over five storeys, exceeded 10 000 square metres, and had central heating, gas, baths and lifts. Well-built houses over 5000 square metres (numbering 190 in 1933) were directly controlled by Moszhiltrest as the property of Mossoviet.[57] Less well-equipped houses within the trust system (688 blocks with 1000–5000 square metres each) were controlled by the district housing trust as district property. The occupants were not the formal administrators in the trusts, but merely organised the council of co-operation and social control, which helped the housing administration.

Dwellings managed by the ZhAKT, responsible for about 47 per cent of all space in 1933, were on the whole small and poorly-equipped. There were 13 857 under the ZhAKT in 1933 with 1 500 000 residents. Among them, only 1750 were above 1000 square metres, while almost half were wooden houses with less than 300 squaremetres. 250–300 ZhAKT were integrated into podraizhilsoyuzy (sub-district housing unions); these, in turn, were subordinated to Mosgorzhilsoyuz (Moscow city housing union).[58]

Despite the decentralising policy of the housing management, things at first remained very complicated. The system was simplified in August 1933. An MGK bureau decision eliminated the intermediate institutions between ZhAKT and upravdom of the block of flats on the one hand, and Moszhiltrest or Mosgorzhilsoyuz on the other.[59] Both organisations cut their staffs. Party control mechanisms were instituted; the head and deputy head of Moszhiltrest, and the chairman and deputy chairman of Mosgorzhilsoyuz, were put on the nomenklatura of the MGK secretariat; their assistants and inspectors were included in the nomenklatura of the MGK department.[60] Subsequently the districts followed the same procedure. The administrative head of a first-category ZhAKT, for example, was put on the nomenklatura of the district committee cadres department.

The repair of houses and dormitory-barracks was another important activity. At the June 1931 plenum of the Central Committee, a new impetus for repairs was provided, about 10 000 were repaired in 1931 and 15 000 in 1932.[61] But the authorities tended to neglect repair, especially in the case of barracks. In August 1933 the Moscow leaders suddenly began to deal with this problem. Bulganin and Konstantinopol'skii (deputy chairman of Mossoviet for construction), together with two or three members of the presidium, were allocated to the repair problem. The deputy chairman for transport was also mobilised. The MGK bureau warned that delay in work might warrant sanctions.[62] The Mossoviet presidium appointed a special commission, headed by city procurator Filippov, to investigate the question of repairs to central heating in houses.[63]

In November 1933 the MGK bureau, and then the MK itself, again warned about the delay of repair work. Both the sanctions of the control commission, and the severe second purge by the 'chistka' commission headed by Filatov, were on the horizon. So far as the region was concerned, lagging districts were listed, and the party secretaries warned. MK plenipotentiaries were to be despatched. Several officials were sent to court in one district.[64]

Harsh sanctions could not compensate for the basic shortage of housing space. More fundamental policies should have been followed; but they were not. One decree in 1934 on the improvement of housing construction admitted that it did not 'correspond with the rising cultural level and demands of the broader toiling masses'.[65] Bulganin insisted on building accommodation for approximately 900 000 people in the Second Five-Year

Plan, two and a half times more than the area actually built in 1928–32.[66] However, even this plan was never intended to increase the area per head (5 square metres), although quality was intended to improve. The new plan was not immediately fulfilled; in 1934 the construction level was about the same as in the previous year. Even in 1935, Moscow leaders had still failed to make a major change. A rather sympathetic voice from Britain noted:

> In fact, the rate of building in the USSR has been incomparably slower than in the UK . . . It is clear, therefore, that Moscow has not yet begun to make any serious effort to overtake the terrific shortage of houses which exists.[67]

10.4 CITY TRANSPORT

The Central Committee decision of June 1931 also proposed to expand city transport services. The construction of the Metro was regarded as the principal means of solving the problem, and was widely publicised as a national project. Meanwhile the general policy was to reduce the proportion of trams in favour of buses, and also to introduce trolley buses.

(a) Tram Traffic

Tramways were the biggest enterprise in the Moscow municipal economy, employing some 80 per cent of all municipal workers.[68] But they were slow; they were inevitably overcrowded; and they hindered other traffic. Lack of supplies and poor labour discipline over a number of years added to these difficulties. It therefore seemed rational to reduce their relative importance. The proportion of trams was very high; 2200 trams were in use in 1932, ten times the number of buses.[69] Kaganovich rightly believed that trams would remain the 'most important' means of transport at the end of the Second Five-Year Plan.[70]

As this was an already established means of transport, it aroused no political questions. The Mossoviet appointed a commission under the chairmanship of Bulganin, including many specialists in various areas.[71] It was the Mossoviet presidium, rather than the MGK, which requested the central authorities to provide materials and facilities. Tram transport was under the control of the Mossoviet transport department headed by Gende-Rote, and the Party played a fairly small role. The tramway section of Mossoviet was itself restricted to a consultative function. Mostramtrest, headed by Denisov at that time, had about 1400 officials. The reorganisation of the trust, carried out in 1933, involved increasing the responsibility and authority of the depots at the expense of the trust. The number of trust officials declined by 75 per cent; but it is not clear how far, if at all, the reorganisation reduced the total number of officials, including those in the depots.[72]

The quality of the labour force was a frequent matter of complaint at this time. At the beginning of 1933, the poor state of labour discipline was strongly stressed. In one depot, the foreman was dismissed and sent to court because he only sacked 17 out of 111 absentees.[73] The labour situation was a major factor in the slow tempo of repair and operational work.[74] An important decision by the MK, MGK, and presidium of Mossoviet in January 1933 approved measures to provide incentives to engineers and workers. But the poor work continued. An MGK decision in mid-November 1933 insisted that the Mossoviet should to present a plan for tram repair.[75] But this was followed by joint plenums of the MK and MGK which continued to complain about the slow pace of the reorganisation.[76]

The underlying trouble was the huge pressure on the tram network: the number of passengers doubled in 1930–34, and supplies were short.[77] Despite the endeavours of Bulganin and others to supply materials and resources, all the trams had defects of one kind or another.

Mossoviet also changed the city transport fare system, with the aim of reducing the flow of public transport vehicles into the city centre and reducing the financial burden of the net work. The Soviet may have taken this step without a central directive.[78] A Mossoviet and MGK decision of January 1933 asked the financial department and the tramway trust to examine the latter's financial plan.[79] In September 1933 a joint session of the tramway and finance sections of Mossoviet decided to abandon the flat-rate system in accordance with the report it received.[80] The Mossoviet plenum approved this conclusion, which was supported by Khrushchev and Bulganin mainly with the objective of reducing traffic volume.

(b) **Trolley Buses**

While tramway transport received little attention from the Moscow Party, a strong initiative was taken by the MGK in relation to trolley bus services. They were not mentioned in the Central Committee's 1931 decision; the innovation was probably the work of the MGK at secretary level in mid-1933, as Khrushchev himself later recalled.[81] Kaganovich was also an enthusiast in this matter, and he directed Bulganin to devote all his Moscow Party conference speech about city transport to this novel system.[82]

On 25 June 1933 the MGK bureau, after discussion, insisted that the Moscow tram trust should initiate a trial trolley-bus route.[83] The strong

Party concern for this project was clear. The plan and its implementation by the tram trust were to be approved by the MGK secretariat. The MGK bureau decided that the trial route was to be established along the Leningrad Highway.[84] The innovation proved very successful.[85] In November 1933 the MGK bureau planned to produce 10 trolley buses in 1933, 30 by the spring of 1934 and 150 by the end of 1934.

The production plan, allocated among several factories, was supervised by Khrushchev, Bulganin and one of the district secretaries, and they were also responsible for materials supply. The equipment of the routes was to be planned by Gende-Rote, Mel'bard (city planning) and Denisov. The Mossoviet decided to open a 7.3-kilometre line, and that a plan for further extension should be agreed by the MGK secretariat in December 1933.[86] The second five-year plan stated that as many as 750 trolley buses were to be completed by the end of the plan in 1937; and the Genplan, as promulgated in 1934, even planned that 1000 trolley buses would replace the trams.[87]

While the introduction of trolley buses was apparently largely undertaken on the initiative of the Moscow Party, in this, as in other innovations, the Politburo also played an active part. Khrushchev, for example, claimed that Stalin personally intervened because he was convinced that the trolley buses would overturn on the slope at the top of Gorky street.

(c) Horse Transport

Horse transport was a diminishing but not negligible sector. Bulganin at the Party conference in 1934 indicated that one fifth of goods traffic would be handled by 20 000 horses in the near future, although the proportion might diminish in time.[88] Horse transport was generally undervalued by economic organisations, who regarded it as obsolescent, and this tendency was reflected in the poor care of horses in this year of shortages and famine. The number of horses fell by about 15 per cent between 1932 and 1933, and was 90 per cent that of 1928.[89] Food and care were lacking, and sanitation was poorly organised. The carriers' scandalous attitude towards their beasts aroused public attention, and the Mossoviet in March 1933 sent 300 section activists (*sektsionery*) and delegates as voluntary inspectors to check the carriers.[90]

To cope with shortages of fodder and other supplies, the authorities ordered oblsnab (regional supply departments) to set up a special fodder group. Gende-Rote was requested to reorganise new sovkhozes for this, and to acquire horses from other regions. Automatic rockers (*avtokachiki*) for improving loading densities were introduced; this was recommended by the MGK secretariat.[91] Each raisoviet was instructed to set up a transport department, mainly responsible for horse transport. A thousand horses were allocated to serve the daily needs of the population.

The motor bus was another important means of transport, and its proportionate share was growing; there were 120 buses in 1931 and 350 in 1934. It seldom posed serious problems, apart from the poor and irregular service, for which Gende-Rote and other officials were criticised.[92]

The local authorities also played an important role in maintaining the roads. The June 1931 plenum resolution specified that old cobbled road surfaces should be replaced by an improved coating of asphalt and other materials. This task was carried out quite speedily, as was noted by the August 1933 joint plenum of the MGK and Mossoviet.[93] But the covering was sometimes of poor quality and uneven, and tram traffic sometimes damaged the carriageway. In 1933 the level of work was poor. The August 1933 decision of the joint plenum prohibited any work which might damage the improved surface or the changing of tram rails without Mossoviet permission. About 3 per cent of roads were covered by the improved surface in 1928, 18.3 per cent in 1932, and 45 per cent in 1937.[94]

10.5 BUILDING THE METRO

A Metro is one of the most outstanding features in several Russian cities. The Moscow Metro was the first. Plans had first been made in the nineteenth century, and after the Revolution the German firm Siemens-Bau prepared a plan.[95] A plan for Metro construction in the suburbs was also considered, and was hotly discussed prior to the June 1931 plenum. Critics like Prof. Obravtsov and the officials of the regional planning agency (*oblplan*) argued that it would be too expensive and proposed instead to introduce suburban railway lines into the city centre.[96]

But the June plenum approved the proposal to build a Metro. Kaganovich criticised the sceptics as leftist phrasemongers, although he never rejected the possibility of connecting electrified suburban lines with the Metro.[97]

The construction of the Metro was intended to ease Moscow transport problems, and as a major project to demonstrate the industrial power of the Soviet Union. It also had a national defence function, as was frankly stated in a newspaper article.[98] It was therefore accorded all-Union significance;[99] and the government decision of May 1932 stated that it was a 'shock' project with high priority.

In 1932 it was financed centrally from the state budget on the instructions of the STO. In 1933, 110 million roubles were included in the Moscow city control figures.[100] In 1934 it was again totally financed by the state budget; the expenditure of 340 million roubles had the 'support of Stalin'.[101] On the supply side, Metrostroi, the constructing trust, was treated as of first priority; 539 factories provided materials and products.[102]

The local authorities were closely involved in the whole construction. Following the June 1931 plenum, the gorispolkom and Mossoviet were instructed to organise 'a special commission with the best specialists invited' to discuss the possibility of starting the construction at the beginning of 1932.[103] In September 1931 the Metrostroi trust was formed. Its chairman Rotert had worked with the Dneprostroi project, and its deputy chairman Abakumov had worked in the Donbass.[104] The MGK cadres department was responsible for recruiting officials and engineers, as well as workers. The participation of foreign consultants was encouraged. In November 1931 there was some discussion about whether suburban railway lines should be coordinated with the project, but the MK bureau finally settled the question in favour of keeping Metro construction independent, probably as a result of the study of foreign experience by a Mossoviet commission under Academician I. M. Gubkin.[105]

The work began at the beginning of 1932. An MK bureau decision of December 1931 specified that seven lines would be built with a total length of 58.4 km. Two lines would be finished in 1933. On 8 April 1932 a Central Committee decision endorsed this.[106] However, when it became clear that the plan was behind schedule the Central Committee, in its decision 'On the construction of the Moscow Metro' modified the plan on the advice of experts; the number of lines was increased to ten, and the completion of the first line was postponed from January to December 1934.[107]

In the Moscow hierarchy, it is not surprising that Kaganovich was generally responsible for the project. With characteristic enthusiasm, he insisted in July 1933 on bringing forward the initial completion date of the Metro from December to 7 November 1934.[108]

To make the more complicated decisions, the MGK and Mossoviet sometimes formed special commissions. For example, when Kaganovich proposed to change the course of the Arbat line, a special commission was appointed, including geological and other experts.[109] In the autumn of 1933 the MGK and Mossoviet also formed a standing commission on architecture and planning, including Kaganovich, Khrushchev, Bulganin and eight architectural experts.

It is not clear who was controlling the Party apparatus in relation to Metro. Donenko, MK transport secretary, and Voropaev, MGK secretary, probably supervised the process, but Khrushchev was clearly involved throughout.[110]

The number of Party members working for Metrostroi rose rapidly from eleven in the beginning to 1700 in June 1933. The Metrostroi Party organisation was directly controlled by the MGK; Starostin, MGK candidate and Sokol'niki district committee secretary, was appointed partorg in Metrostroi in 1934, and Matusov was elected secretary of the Metrostroi Party organisation.[111]

One important question in the Metro construction was the involvement of experts and specialists in the decision-making process. The MGK decision of December 1931 prescribed that the construction plan would be drawn up by Metrostroi, with foreign experts participating. Technical help was also to be given by the all-Union scientific-technical association (VSNITO) and by the veteran Soviet planner and electrical engineer Krzhizhanovskii.[112]

The construction of the Metro gave rise to major technical problems. Whether the Metro should be an open-cut (cut-and-cover) or deep-cut tunnel was much debated. The MGK bureau stated that this should be decided by the terrain, the method being confirmed by the Mossoviet presidium, but it also stressed that street traffic movement should be safeguarded.[113] This conclusion was endorsed by the Central Committee decision of March 1932. On the whole, Metrostroi, headed by Rotert and backed by foreign experts, preferred the open-cut system, which was cheaper and easier although inconvenient for the population. But a group of experts led by the 'red expert' V. L. Makovskii advocated a deep tunnel of a modified London style; and Kaganovich and Khrushchev supported this proposal.[114] The controversy was taken to the Politburo, and Stalin supported the deep tunnel, rejecting Rotert's report.[115] By mid-May of 1932 the MGK and Mossoviet had also decided in favour of the deep-cut variant, although foreign experts were still sceptical.

A serious bottleneck in construction was the recruitment of building workers. By February 1933, when construction was well under way, about 12 000 were working. This was still not enough, and a mobilisation campaign was organised. At the end of July 1933 there was a meeting of Metrostroi held on Kaganovich's suggestion, at which Rotert made a report before 2000 communists and 1500 Komsomol members.[116] Komsomol members were strongly encouraged to participate in the project, and 2500 members were mobilised by September 1933. It was intended to mobilise up to 10 000, and workers' schools (*rabfaks*) were set up to train young workers.[117] Khrushchev, who had worked in the Ukraine mines, strongly supported this campaign.

The number of building workers remained insufficient, and a commission headed by Drizul of the MGK cadres department, and including Abakumov and the Komsomol leader was required to mobilise 20 000 workers by the end of 1933.[118] By the end of 1933 27 000 were at work, including 5000 employees and 2500 engineers and technicians.[119] In the early months of 1934, numbers continued to rise, and the total employed amounted to 75 000 in May 1934; this included 10 000 Komsomol members, kolkhozniks from the western and central black-earth regions and from the Tartar and Bashkir republics, and workers from Magnitogorsk and Chelyabinsk.[120]

One constraint on worker recruitment was the poor living conditions. In 1933 houses and dormitory-barracks had been prepared for 11 000, but this was obviously not enough, even though construction of accommodation took up one fifth of total investment.[121] Wages were another problem. By the end of 1931 the wages of Metrostroi workers had been put on a level with those of Moscow industrial workers.[122] But a *Vechernyaya Moskva* commentator related the delays in construction to lack of incentives and premiums.[123] The May 1933 decision on the Donbass coal industry strongly criticised the equalisation of wages, and favoured the use of a progressive piece-rate system.[124] This system influenced wage requirements in Metrostroi, but only three mines adopted progressive payments. At the end of 1933, the MK, MGK and Mossoviet decision about Metrostroi had a section on wages which again recommended the use of bonus and premium systems; engineers, technicians and foremen could receive 20 per cent premiums for good work.[125]

In view of all the difficulties, the project was not completed on time. The deadline of November 1934 proposed by Kaganovich had been endorsed by the MK and MGK joint decision of December 1933. But it turned out to be too optimistic and was cancelled in 1934 on the authority of Molotov and Khrushchev.[126]

Thus the municipal economy of Moscow had both specific and general features. Specific in the sense that Moscow was the metropolis of the USSR, with substantial political power, and resources to manage the city which exceeded those of any other city. At the same time, it became a general model for city construction and reconstruction. Such subjects as housing management, city planning, transport, gas and energy supply, would one day be on the agendas of Soviet municipal officials in less importants towns, which at this time lacked resources for any substantial development. In this sense, Moscow was certainly a 'laboratory' for urban politics in the USSR, in which central power and local activity and initiative both played a part.

11 Supply and Shortage

11.1 THE STRUGGLE FOR SUPPLIES

The first half of the 1930s was a time of great shortages in Moscow, like everywhere else in the USSR. The struggle for supplies, and particularly for food, was a major preoccupation of its authorities. The situation had become evident from the start of the First Five-Year Plan; food rationing was introduced from the end of 1928. Private trade, which accounted for 18.8 per cent of commodity turnover at that time, was totally eliminated in the 1930s.[1] A more discriminatory rationing system was introduced from the autumn of 1930; classes of the population, areas, and institutions were categorised according to their importance. Cities like Tula and important factories were included in the first List (*spisok* 1), and Moscow city itself was even more privileged.[2] In spite of this priority, the real wages of Moscow workers were very low, and fell to perhaps half of what they were in the NEP period, even though nominal wages rose rapidly.[3] Kaganovich admitted to 'difficulty' in supply, living conditions and commodities, and at the beginning of 1932 even commented that 'We can never underestimate the difficulties'.[4]

There were several reasons for the shortages, and for their culmination in the crisis of 1932–33. There was over-investment in favour of heavy industry, which created problems for light industry. Grain and food collection was disrupted by the rural turmoil and by the weak organisation of kolkhozes and sovkhozes. Harvests were poor after 1930, and collection quotas bore heavily on the kolkhozniks, especially in the south of the USSR. The position was further disturbed from 1931 onwards by the threatening international situation, amounting almost to a war scare, in both east and west, with first Japan and then Hitler's Germany both obliging the USSR to develop the military potential of the economy.[5] All these factors resulted in shortages and eventually in severe famine in the Ukraine, North Caucasus, Lower Volga, and other areas.[6]

In spite of the privileged position of Moscow, a major new series of measures had to be adopted to secure supplies for the workers. From 1931 onwards, the authorities adopted a new pre-emptive approach to consumption and trade in the cities.

After Stalin's June 1931 speech at the economic managers' conference, which stressed productivity as against equality, the Central Committee directed its attention to a differentiated supply system, aimed at stimulating the workers' economic interest at this time of shortages.[7] A series of decisions on consumer co-operatives and worker's supply in the middle of 1931 marked the end of the egalitarian policy of supply, and vigorously enforced the supply of essential goods and food through the ZRK (*zakrytye rabochie ko-operativy*, or closed workers' co-operatives). ZRK were organised from the end of 1931, and by January 1932 MSPO had 171 of them, covering half the city's population.[8]

By the beginning of 1932, when food shortages became more serious, the authorities emphasised the need to introduce a 'decentralised supply system' that is, supply based on efforts, at their own expense, of enterprises and factories. This was an implicit admission of the failure of the 'central supply system'. Rudzutak at the February meeting of the Central Control Commission proposed setting up 'supply bases' inside factories.[9] This implied measures to secure part of the workers' food independently of the centralised supply system. On the positive side, factories were managing fruit and vegetable gardens, rabbit farms, pig farms, and fish farms. These measures were strongly pressed for by Stalin, and were directed at the industrial regions, including Moscow, Leningrad and Ivanovo.[10] The leadership was keenly and anxiously aware of workers' grievances which had culminated in the spring 1932 Ivanovo workers' strike.[11] In May 1932 the ban on kolkhoz trade at market prices was lifted.[12]

But the situation continued to deteriorate sharply, contrary to the expectation of the authorities. By the autumn of 1932, severe action was being taken against kolkhozniks who were allegedly influenced by 'kulak sabotage'. This was followed by further emphasis on the selective distribution of food as well as a tightening of control over urban labour. The rationing system and the internal passport system were used as controlling measures to concentrate food supplies.

Local Party mechanisms were directly and far-reachingly involved in supply questions; policies had to be evolved and carried out mainly by using local resources and initiative. Secretary Davidson specialised in this field, and the second secretaries Ryndin and especially Khrushchev played an important role. The secretariat was closely involved in planning, checking and mobilising.[13] In the soviets, the supply department was the key institution and the object of considerable Party concern. The consumer co-operatives MOSPO and MSPO also played major parts; at this time the head of MOSPO was an MK bureau member.

In the following account, I first consider the various initiatives launched in 1932–33 to supplement the basic supplies received from the centre, and then part placed by the kolkhoz market. These were the new elements in

Supply and Shortage 127

the supply system; while they were part of a national campaign, the local party and soviet organisations were closely involved in their realisation. I then turn to the changes in the central state rationing system.

11.2 EMERGENCY SUPPLIES: RABBITS, FISH, AND VEGETABLES

(a) Rabbits

Among the numerous measures adopted to ease the supply situation, rabbit farms, in which Stalin was strongly interested, were prominent in Moscow.[14] In the Moscow suburbs a rabbit institute was established, and *Pravda* launched a rabbit-breeding campaign. A Central Committee decision of 8 May 1932 specified that 360 000 rabbits should be bred by the end of 1932 in Moscow city and region.[15] The ZRK were responsible for raising them on a voluntary basis, depending on local resources.

In its turn, the MGK bureau submitted in May a plan to raise 220 000 rabbits for workers' supply. About 100 factories were to raise 100 000, half of them being the responsibility of the ZRK.[16] Hospitals, and even the OGPU, were also assigned quotas. The Institute of Rabbits was to provide short courses to train about 500 brigade-leaders (*brigadiry*) to take charge of rabbit farmers. Bulganin was responsible for obtaining financial support for this campaign, and the management of the campaign was entrusted to Trainin, 'plenipotentiary for rabbits' of the Moscow oblispolkom and later of the Mossoviet presidium.[17] About 150 Komsomol members were mobilised and put at his disposal. In every district, one member from the raiispolkom presidium was assigned to this task. A rabbit exhibition was held in Moscow.

Serp i Molot and the other Moscow factories responded enthusiastically. But the implementation of these plans was fraught with difficulties. The MK plenum in June noted that the campaign had so far been carried out 'impermissibly slowly'.[18] In Bauman district no rabbit plenipotentiary had been appointed. Trainin was criticised about lack of supervision.[19]

This decision apparently had some effect. By October 1932 the planned number was exceeded in Moscow.[20] However, in the terrible winter of 1932–33 rabbit raising posed serious problems of fodder and manpower. In the Elektrosvet factory the farm director and others were arrested because their rabbits had died of cold.[21] A people's judge was criticised in the press because he had given only 18-month sentences to those who had allegedly harmed rabbits, and it was suggested that the decree on 'socialist property' might be applied.[22] By spring 1933 as many as 430 000 rabbits had been bred in Moscow, but many turned out to be infertile. At this time the closing down of rabbit farms was made a criminal offence.[23]

Subsequently, an MK bureau decision of October 1933 'On the development of rabbit-raising in Moscow and the industrial centres of the region' made it clear that well-established rabbit farms were not being developed in Moscow; the number of rabbits had diminished to 300 000 because of disease and fodder shortage.[24] The decision again stressed the importance of increasing the number of rabbits. Instead of the plenipotentiary system, a rabbit inspectorate was to be established within the ispolkom and Mossoviet. These measures had little long-term effect. The rabbit campaign had assisted the food crisis in the worst years, but played little part in subsequent developments.

(b) **Fish Farming**

Another way of developing a 'decentralised' supply system in the face of shortages was fish raising in ponds, rivers and lakes. *Pravda* had referred to the vastness of fish resources which contrasted with the poor results of the Moscow fish trust (Mosryb) in 1931.[25] But, in spite of these strictures, in May 1932 the Central Committee commended the 'initiative of the Moscow and Leningrad obkoms' in fishery development.[26]

The campaign for fisheries reached its height in the summer of 1933, following an unpublished Central Committee decision on Moscow fish farms.[27] In the Moscow Party Ryndin and Davidson took charge of the fish campaign, the former in a supervisory capacity. Peters, chairman of the MKK, was chairman of the fishery development commission; this included Ryndin and Davidson and was attended by several MK and MGK bureau members, including Red Army and politotdel representatives.[28]

An MGK secretariat decision on the Moscow fisheries illustrates how the Party organisations were involved in this process.[29] The secretariat set out the arrangements for its campaign. Malenkov was to select a Party organiser. The Mosryb trust was to arrange accommodation for the workers. The soviet labour department was to recruit carpenters. The agricultural department was to arrange for the supply of motors and the supply department for footwear for the fishery workers. Mosgormashtrest was to prepare winches. Five days later, the MGK secretariat despatched plenipotentiaries to the fisheries. The distribution and sale of the catch were assigned to Mosrybtrest and Soyuzrybsbyt, under the leadership of the regional supply department. The leadership redeployed officials from the trusts, despatching them to the sites. The MK and MGK cadres departments selected workers to check and control the work for the season. Several gorkom secretaries of the region, and officials of various institutions, were also sent to the sites to check preparations.

Following the autumn season, the joint MK and MGK bureau entrusted the Peters commission with discussing and formulating practical ways of developing the region's fisheries.[30] But the results of these measures are not precisely known.

(c) Production of Vegetables

The Moscow authorities paid special attention to vegetable supplies. Unlike grain and other products, procurement, transport, storing and distribution of vegetables were mainly a local Party task. Two MK and MGK plenums were devoted to this question, and particularly to potatoes, a major source of nourishment, on which Khrushchev made a lengthy report to a joint MK and MGK plenum in July 1933.[31] The local authorities had the exacting task of organising the provision to a growing city population of a diminishing supply.

Workers' farms were established in an attempt to increase supplies. On 20 February 1932 the MK bureau planned that the average size of farms in Moscow would be ten times as large in 1932 than in 1931.[32] Secretary Davidson was in complete charge of planning, seed collection, and even of the preparation of seed clamps. Seed was particularly strictly controlled: approval of MGK secretariat was required before seed could be released.

The ZRK of each factory organised workers' farms on a 'voluntary' principle; those who worked on the farms in their spare time were entitled to payment in kind. Sovkhozes were allocated to large factory ZRKs. In the case of MSPO and the vegetable trust, Davidson was again responsible for allotting each piece of land to ZRKs, with the approval of the secretariat. The MGK cadre department selected experts for the vegetable trust.[33]

Few reports were published on the practical results of all this activity. A quarter of the vegetables were obtained by this system, so it was evidently a useful auxiliary source of supplies.

(d) Procurement and Transport of Vegetables

Most vegetables were obtained not through workers farms but from the kolkhozes, sovkhozes and individual peasants of the Moscow region. About 80 per cent of vegetables consumed in Moscow city were produced in the region itself. They were primarily obtained by MOSPO, and other agencies like Mosnarpit and Soyuzprodovoshch played an auxiliary role. The main task of the Party in relation to vegetables was the supervision and enforcement of the vegetable procurement campaign. In 1932, the MGK Party bureau sent out 20 plenipotentiaries of the STO procurement commission on the campaign together with 200 workers.[34] The MK plenum instructed the cadres department to send a further 200 workers and Komsomol members. In September 1932 the MK secretariat decision on the potato harvest gave detailed instructions to the districts, and the district committees were instructed to organise themselves accordingly.[35] In the 1933 campaign, to co-ordinate the various activities, Khoroshilkin was appointed to the new post of plenipotentiary for vegetables of the Mossoviet. The Komispol (the soviet's implementation control agency), which was headed by Bulganin, checked the implementation of the campaign.[36]

At the district level, personal responsibility for the success of the procurements was laid on the district committee secretary and the district soviet chairman.[37] The severity of the campaign is indicated by the threats to send to court or purge from the Party any kolkhoz or sovkhoz leaders who failed to meet the procurement plan. Factory workers attached to the farms could also face Party or judicial inquiries.

Given the chronic transport difficulties of this period, the mobilisation of transport for vegetables was another difficult task. The gorispolkom Party fraction was instructed to mobilise vehicles belonging to the city, and the secretariat had to intervene to obtain other road vehicles and railway cars to move potatoes. The district committees had to prepare warehouses.[38] In 1933 the problem of transport and storage became more serious, partly because of the increased shortage of transport and partly because of the increased potato volume. A deputy chairman of oblispolkom and relevant transport department officials were given very detailed instructions. Komsomol members were mobilised for potato transport and storage, and some additional auxiliary rail lines and warehouses were even constructed.

It was also necessary to enlarge the storage capacity for vegetables. In 1932 Mossoviet and MOSPO were supposed to provide large increase of storehouse capacity.[39] In 1933 a more detailed storage plan was prepared.

Each district organisation, and institutions like Metrostroi, had to provide storage space for vegetables. In some combines, workers were sent to court because of delays in building storage space. District committees and soviets agreed that storekeepers should be recruited.[40] Deputy chairmen of raisoviets were made responsible for storing vegetables on their own territories.

The Moscow press and the local decrees passed at that time provide striking examples of the pressure on the responsible officials to carry out the various aspects of these campaigns. Thus the MGK secretariat purged the head of the Mosnarpit trust because his control over vegetables was weak.[41] In Khrushchev's name, the secretariat claimed that the Mosnarpit special trust had worked badly; those responsible were put on trial.[42] A special MKK troika imposed sanctions on the manager of a combine who failed to keep his vegetables in a good state. In this combine the ZRK chairman was sent to a penal labour camp because repair work on storehouses had been slow.[43] A plenipotentiary who had been sent to the badly-hit famine area of the Lower Volga was criticised because he failed to secure watermelons as planned.[44]

Those who failed to store and distribute vegetables properly once they had been collected were also penalised. Party sanctions or judicial proceedings were the main weapons used to combat inefficiency. In January 1932 the head of the city supply department was sent to trial with others in connection with the cabbage shortage.[45] The ZRK chairman of a factory was dismissed and purged from the Party because 20 tons of potatoes went rotten, and such cases were quite frequent at this time. The city procuracy was ordered to check potato storage in January 1933, and some 15 people were punished under the criminal code.[46] The Mossoviet presidium heard the MKK's report and proposed to the chairman of the procuracy that a show trial be organised of 'those who violated the law concerning potatoes'.[47]

In the winter of 1933 the MGK bureau paid even more attention to potato preservation. Davidson and Khoroshilkin were charged with responsibility for decentralised storage, which they shared with the factories responsible for the storehouses. Workers patrolled the warehouses throughout the winter. Potato preservation figured on the agenda of almost every meeting of the MGK bureau.[48] According to Khrushchev, the MGK bureau and secretariat discussed vegetables and potatoes on 161 occasions in two years, compared to 62 occasions for grain.[49] Newspapers were filled with reports on these matters.[50] The crucial role of the Moscow Party in securing these supplies was thus evident.

11.3 THE ROLE OF THE FREE (*KOLKHOZ*) MARKET

The Central Committee and Sovnarkom decrees of May 1932 reducing grain and meat procurements, and enabling kolkhoz peasants to sell their products at market prices in the city market, was a frank recognition that state and co-operative trade had failed to supply enough to meet the needs of the masses.[51] In July 1932, a decision of the MK and MGK joint bureau called on every district committee and soviet, together with the city health department, to prepare the market places and take measures against thieves and hooligans. In order to establish these places into model markets as soon as possible, MK and MGK bureau members, including Kaminsky himself, were mobilised and sent to each market.[52] According to Kaganovich, these bureau members were endowed with 'full powers'. The development of the market was discussed at a special conference of the leaders (*rukovoditeli*) of the markets and the officials mobilised to organise this activity.[53]

To encourage an inflow of agricultural products, a 50-verst (1 verst = 1.07 kilometres) zone round the city was exempted from the state procurement and 'kontraktatsiya' system, except of course in the case of grain.[54] The MGK mass agitation department was instructed to organise special help from factories to kolkhozes within 50–100 kilometres of the city. The effects of these measures were to be reported at the bureau meetings at the end of July.

To organise this trade, a kolkhoz trade sector was established in the Mossoviet supply department. City and raiispolkoms also instituted kolkhoz and sovkhoz trade sections. At each market, a special council was organised, including nearby factories and associated kolkhozes. Each district committee sent a special agitator. Even doctors were mobilised.[55] Within the city, a total of 51 markets were planned, and in fact 44 opened by July 1932, including 18 new markets; local authorities, however, were dissatisfied with the slow increase.

In spite of these developments, the whole kolkhoz market policy lacked clearly stated objectives. In July 1932, Kaganovich made an inconsistent report to the MK plenum. Although he advocated the improvement of kolkhoz trade and a better inflow of products, he simultaneously emphasised the dangers of a free market. It is also noteworthy that in the published version of his speech he quoted Stalin's words on the protection of socialist and kolkhoz property.[56] The celebrated decree on socialist property, written by Stalin himself, was issued a month later, on 7 August. This had an adverse effect on kolkhoz trade development.

The decree 'On the struggle with speculation' of 22 August also placed constraints on the kolkhoz market.[57] This decree noted that speculation had increased since the inauguration of a free market system. Prior to this decree, speculators and second-hand dealers had been watched by the militia, the courts and the financial agencies, as was mentioned in the MK June plenum. Trading agencies which had bought goods from them were to be punished according to criminal law.[58] By the new decree, the OGPU and the local soviets could send 'speculators and resellers' to concentration camps for five to ten years. The September 1932 plenum of the Central Committee struck a balance in the wording of its resolution between the development of 'kolkhoz trade' and the struggle with 'speculators'.[59] However, in practice the balance shifted towards tighter control over the markets.

What Stalin termed 'the negative side of kolkhoz trade' became all the more serious in the deepening crisis which culminated in the southern famine in the winter and spring of 1932–33. Although Moscow was called an 'oasis' in times of shortage, the situation of the markets became uncomfortable. The alleged thriving of 'speculators' in the Sukharevka market led to its closure in November 1932. Incidentally, the symbolic tower of this site was destroyed earlier in spring 1934.[60] More than 1000 'speculators' fled to other markets. Similar pressure was exerted on other markets. At the Tishinsk market about 36 per cent of traders were fined and about a further 10 per cent punished in other ways.[61] Three markets were declared to be abnormal, presumably because the prices were so high and a Mossoviet special commission was appointed to improve them in January 1933. In March the supply department sent 65 officials to the markets, and the Arbat and three other markets were treated as models for the remaining 40. After some hesitation, hand-to-hand trade (*torgovlya s ruk*) was allowed in most markets. The militia, headed by Vul, was instructed to keep 'speculators' under control.[62]

Kolkhoz trade was important not simply as a source of food but also as a channel for supplying necessities and industrial products for the villages. As many as 344 markets were organised in the region. However, consumer retail trade in the village was insufficient, and goods were sold indiscriminately.[63]

The percentage of kolkhoz trade commodities in total personal consumption was as follows, according to Moscow city data for 1932: potatoes 15 per cent, vegetables 31.1, fruit 13.6, meat 9.0, milk 59.3, eggs 59.1.[64] Kolkhoz trade thus occupied an indispensable place in Moscow food supplies.

The gradual normalisation of the trade in this market can be seen in Figures 11.1 and 11.2.

134   *Moscow: History, Geography, and Society*

FIGURE 11.1   *Cost of 1kg of beef in the Bazaar, 1932–33*

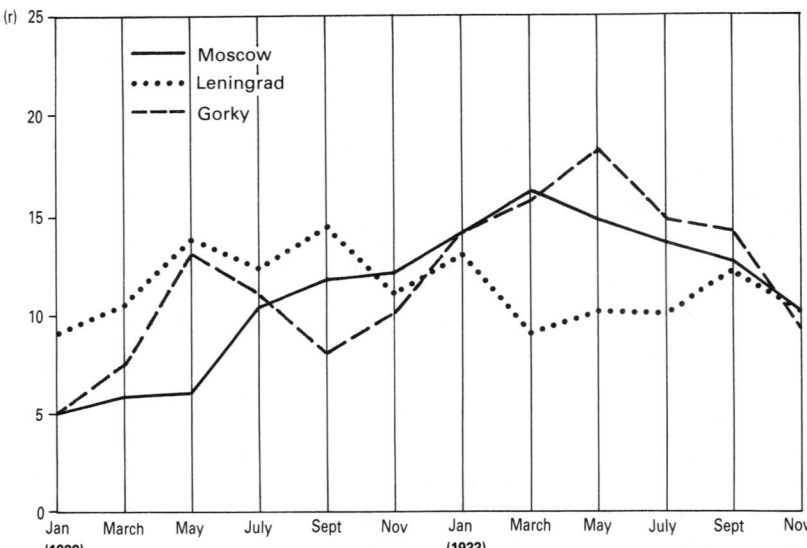

Calculated from *Kilkhoznaya Torgovlya* (1934), pp. 12–14.

Sale of grain on the kolkhoz market was strictly forbidden until the completion of state procurement. In Moscow region the collection plan in 1933 was more or less achieved on 1 December 1933, in contrast to 1932, when there had been serious problems. One day after, on 2 December, grain sales on the market were already being reported.[65]

11.4 FACTORY SUPPLY AND RATIONING

While the supply of food to the Moscow population was supplemented by the various methods and products described in sections 11.1–11.3, the core of the supply system was the official ration. The most important development in the official system in the period of acute shortages was the Central Committee and Sovnarkom decree at the end of 1932 increasing managers' rights over workers' provisioning; the attempt to improve the rationing system was directly related to the supply mechanism at factory level.[66] The trade system at this time was divided into two, state and co-operative trade, but the general trend was to increase

Supply and Shortage

the proportion of state trade, and the strictness of control. The selective supply system for important factories was strengthened as a result of the decree: ZRK of the first-category factories were reorganised into ORS (*otdely rabochego snabzheniya*, or workers' supply departments). These were subordinated to the managers, and lost their formal co-operative character. Under the new system, goods and food were supplied to the workers through the ORS system in exchange for ration coupons. While bread could be purchased in other shops, those who were not connected with factories or institutions suffered severe deprivation. Although some commercial shops ('Mikoyan shops') were revived in 1933, their prices were high and their goods were scarce.[67]

There were 461 ORS organised by the end of 1933 in Moscow city.[68] The ORS was a kind of factory department, and its head was a deputy manager with the function of specialising in workers' supply. In the factories concerned, shops, and auxiliary farming and the former ZRK management were all transferred to the ORS. In Moscow 84 factories, a quarter of the total, were classified in this first category, including many of the largest factories. The ORS covered about 950 000 people in the city and 500 000 in the region.[69] Enterprises in the second category retained

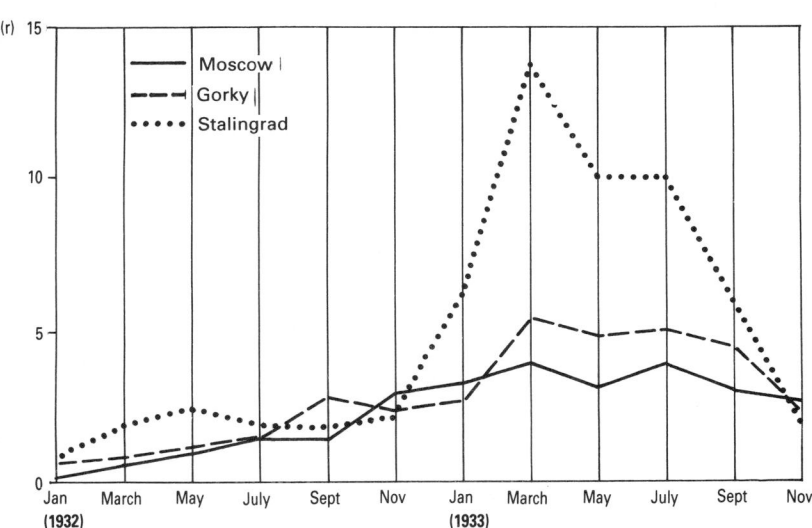

FIGURE 11.2 *Cost of 1kg of rye bread in the Bazaar, 1932–33*

Calculated from *Kilkhoznaya Torgovlya* (1934), pp. 12–17.
Stalingrad was the area where the famine hit most seriously.

the ZRK as formally co-operative organisations, but they also tended to become dependent on the manager of the factory.

In Moscow city, an MGK bureau decision of 9 December 1932 initially replaced the ZRK system by the ORS in 35 factories.[70] Secretary Davidson was placed in charge of this operation, together with Drizul, the head of the cadres department who was responsible for selecting the heads of the ORS. The ORS heads were listed in the MGK secretariat nomenklatura. In the transferred factories, goods and food were supplied by NK Snab, the supply commissariat, although they were also able to obtain some decentralised supply through local supply agencies. These privileged factories had high priority.

The ORS, like the ZRK and the co-operatives, were subordinate to the city supply department, which was a branch of NK Snab. In 1933 it included seven sectors: kolkhoz trade; fruit and vegetables; kolkhozes (dealing with decentralised procurement); goods and warehouses; workers' supply; grain; and a sector to check implementation.[71] The ration-book administration of Mossoviet, together with the raiispolkoms, were responsible for distributing and regulating coupons through enterprise managements. At the beginning of 1933 the entire system of rationing was working badly. Even the new system of first-category ORS was poorly organised; it was described as 'unsatisfactory' in an important factory like Serp i molot.[72]

The introduction of internal passports at the beginning of 1933 led to a reduction of in the number of bread coupons. According to a report from the British embassy, about 300 000 persons lost the right to obtain bread coupons.[73] The supply situation in Moscow remained poor, even though it was a top-priority location and its residents were meant to have twice as much of such foods as sugar than other residents in the region. Even in the case of bread, a new mechanised bakery was being built in 1933, but could hardly meet the pressing demand.

The authorities were watching keenly for speculation with scarce commodities in the kolkhoz markets, and especially for co-operative associations or ZRK selling rationed goods at market prices. In one tram depot the ZRK sold butter on a commercial basis instead of at the official price. The MSPO presidium reacted mildly to this, treating it merely as a violation of price regulations. The MGK secretariat annulled this decision. Legal proceedings were then taken on grounds of 'speculation', and severe sanctions followed.[74]

The authorities also devoted a great deal of attention to distribution of goods at the site or shop level. The MK secretariat severely reprimanded one district committee secretary when the bread ration norm was reduced from 800 to 600 grams per day without notice.[75] In Kalinin city there were complaints of groats and butter shortages in some factories. In this case those responsible were sent to the MKK for investigation, and the regional supply department imposed penalties on their subordinates. Even Kalygina, gorkom secretary and MK bureau member, was warned.

Probably one of the most extreme cases related to the shortages was that of the Elektrokombinat at the end of 1932. According to a report of February 1933 to the MGK bureau, a thousand workers were unable to get sugar for a month, because some was stolen and some was given to sovkhoz workers not entitled to received a ration.[76] In this case the deputy manager responsible was purged from the Party and dismissed, the ZRK head was sent to court, and the factory troika was reprimanded. Three months corrective labour was imposed on the district people's judge, who was said to have been 'soft' and reluctant to apply the severe decree 'On the protection of socialist property'. The MGK bureau warned the city procurator and chairman of the city court to be more stern and active in the case of the theft of food. But equal deprivation was caused in the combine when some 800 workers failed to obtain passports on the grounds that they were 'kulaks' or 'whiteguards'.[77]

All these measures to strengthen the rationing system, and all the efforts of the Moscow Party, failed to improve the situation fundamentally. In the winter of 1932–33 Moscow workers experienced the most severe conditions since the end of the Civil War. This was more or less admitted by Moscow leaders. Khrushchev for example stated that: 'We have shortages of services for the workers, caused by the difficulties of development. All the toiling masses know this.'[78] But the real picture was hardly presented at all in the press.

11.5 PUBLIC CATERNG

In August 1931 the Party Central Committee decided to set up glavnarpit, the main administration for public catering, as an agency for organising a public catering system in cities; this was a measure to cope with shortages.[79] This institution integrated the public catering system of the cities, which had previously been under the consumer co-operatives which had recently come into the control of NK Snab.

In Moscow Mosnarpit was mainly responsible for public catering in Moscow, and other systems like the ORS and other co-operatives were less significant.[80] By July 1933 about 65.5 per cent of the population, or

2 027 000, were fed by public catering. This was the highest proportion in the USSR.[81] But in Moscow this did not represent a fundamental change, as public catering already provided for some 1 800 000 people in 1928.[82]

The public catering system was poorly organised. The oblispolkom presidium criticised the poor quality of the catering trust under MOSPO in March 1932. Public catering facilities in the large factories were also criticised as being in a miserable condition. An MK secretariat decision in September 1932 instructed each trust of MOSPO to plan the improvement of dining-room and other facilities; the trade unions were to interest themselves in this, together with the district committee bureaux and district control commissions.[83] A member of each district committee bureau was placed in charge.

The public catering system of the textile industry received lower priority, and was particularly poor. The MGK secretariat decided to subsidise the dishes provided so as to improve the quality of textile workers' food.[84] A small commission headed by the chairman of Moscow trade union council was to report to the MK on the use made of this subvention.

All these organisational measures failed to bring about a major improvement in public catering, because the core of the problem was the poor supply of food. Mosnarpit operated about 120 public catering establishments in heavy industry, 240 in light industry, and 125 for students, but only 20 of them were described as acceptable. There were many newspaper reports at this time about poor menus. 'Kulak' disturbances about the poor quality of the food were also reported in Stalin district, and there were even five death sentences for alleged sabotage in July 1933.[85]

To tighten control over the cadres in the public catering system, the MGK secretariat took greater responsibility for dining-room managers in August 1933. The head and deputy-head of factory dining rooms serving more than 1000 dishes daily were to be hired or fired by direct decision of the MGK secretariat, although Mosnarpit could recommend candidates.[86] Heads of smaller dining rooms were to be listed on the nomenklatura of the district committee. Simultaneously a commission of the cadres and mass agitation departments of the MGK and Mosnarpit checked the books of dining rooms and heads of buffets. This attempt to control the catering system through tight control of its personnel reflected the existence at this period of serious tension over food supply.

So far as shortages and supplies are concerned, Moscow was in a special position, as a huge consumption area with limited food-producing capacity. The advantage of being the metropolis enabled Moscow to overcome its disadvantageous position in food production. Food was obtained at the expense of the agricultural regions, where in the worst months of 1933 people were starving to death in large numbers. But supply was still very limited in Moscow. Great efforts had to be exerted to get the best out of a bad situation. Although there was no joy in city life at this time, at least it was more secure than rural life.

12 Conclusions

As elsewhere in the Soviet Union, Moscow went through a great transformation in 1931–34, a change which was the product both of destruction and construction. In the city of Moscow, some of the old buildings and churches were demolished. The Nepmen and other private economic activity disappeared, while factories were built for heavy industry and new schools appeared. There was a significant demographic change. The influx of rural population into the cities and workers' settlements drastically changed the face of city life. It was not just a simple 'urbanisation', and there is some truth in Moshe Lewin's term 'ruralisation of the city'.[1] In this transformation, confusion, compulsion and heroism all made their contribution.

The development pattern of Moscow reflected these changes in Soviet society, although there were also particularities. The Moscow region, especially in the south, was predominantly agricultural, and was faced with the process and the consequences of rapid collectivisation. The city of Moscow and its outskirts was meantime witnessing the construction of new factories. The great industrialisation drive changed the face of the cities, including Moscow, which had an exceptionally high proportion of industry.

At the same time, Moscow was the metropolis, and this meant that there were specific characteristics in its local and regional politics. It was not merely a rural region or a newly industrialised city, but the very centre of the socialist state. In conditions of shortage, and even famine in some regions, Moscow was privileged in terms of political power and supplies. Its dignitaries, men like Khrushchev and even lesser officials, might even be invited into Stalin's dining room . . .

There were also special features on the industrial side. The proportion of agriculture was somewhat marginal, and the 'kulak problem' not all that pressing. In this area the coercion that was applied to rural areas, especially in the south of the country, played only a small role. As urbanisation was at a high level, industrial or urban issues were especially important in the region's politics and government, a circumstance that somewhat complicated Moscow's local politics.

Several dimensions have to be distinguished. The first concerns Party-soviet relations. In this connection the observation of Professor Merle

Fainsod, based on his research on the agrarian Smolensk region, bears repetition. Some thirty years ago he emphasised that a distinct demarcation between Party and soviet power never existed in the Soviet Union, and that there were 'overlapping, duplication, and parallel functions between them'.[2] He even asserted that the secretariat 'intervened constantly to direct, scold, and prod the administrative organs' subject to its supervision.[3]

The experience discussed in this book differs to some extent from the Smolensk model. Relationships were much more complex in Moscow. Four aspects deserve special mention. *First, the Party structure, and especially the secretariat and the department system, was based on the 'functional' principle at this time and never corresponded directly with the soviet structure.* Role differentiation developed within the Party bureaucracy, however, and the production-branch principle was advanced well before any other region or national republic adopted it. Moscow Party secretaries and instructors were more specialised in their allotted tasks. With these more complex relationships at city level there was a mutual penetration of political cultures that was much more noticeable than in the rural areas.

In other words, Party leadership in the soviet and in other matters was more sophisticated than elsewhere. It is true that Kaganovich introduced highly bureaucratic and administrative methods of control in the form of politotdels but it only confused the administration and did not have a long-term impact. The soviet functioned more autonomously, and the Party secretariat had few channels of approach to the daily routines of the ispolkom *'pyaterka'*, apart from the fact that Bulganin might in those days have attended the secretariat meetings. This may perhaps be true of the soviets of all important cities, but no other city possessed the same degree of autonomy as Moscow.

Related to this was the Party's role in regional politics. It is certain that there were many cases in which the Party played an essential role. Possibly it all depended on the policy areas; in agriculture, especially, the local Party organisation had to act as a direct agent in conducting the campaigns, for no other institution knew how to deal with the new kolkhoz type of agriculture. The decision of the joint bureau of the MK and MGK in May 1933 about the sowing process is worth citing in this connection:

> Entrust Kaminsky [chairman of oblispolkom, the regional executive committee] to prepare by tomorrow for acknowledgement by the secretariat of the MK a draft of the obligatory decision of the oblispolkom presidium on the reinforcing of sowing by individual

peasants . . . in the decision, which must be published in all district newspapers no later than the 14th, and be posted in all villages, there must be instructions on practical measures for strengthening the 'group of ten householders' [*devyatdvorka*], organising work teams, as well as placing precise responsibility on the chairman, members of the village soviet, and plenipotentiaries of the commune for the sowing process in the individual sectors as settled by the oblispolkom.[4]

The resolution also warned the district committee secretaries about delays in sowing crops. This indicates the extent to which the Party controlled the agricultural areas through the channel of soviets. It was in practice the local Party organs which dominated agricultural work, including the detail of its campaign. This parallels what Fainsod observed in Smolensk politics.

However, this degree of direct involvement on the part of the local Party organisations was not so common in other policy areas. In industry, while in light industry the Party's role was more apparent than in heavy industry, the role of the economic commissariats was generally huge, and the role of the MK or MGK secretariat was limited. The Party played the part, rather, of a broker or co-ordinator, as described in Chapter 7. In education and 'law and order', despite the principle of 'dual subordination', horizontal control (by the oblispolkom or Mossoviet and their corresponding Party organisations) was minimal. Here, the Party organisation was a secondary part of the system. The more Soviet society was urbanised and industrialised, the less became the direct involvement of the role of the party organisation. This was not a simple process, and it was only clearly visible at that time in such an avant-garde city as Moscow.

The role of Party control through the nomenklatura should not be exaggerated in this context. It is hard to visualise soviet officials being promoted or demoted by the arbitrary decision of the Party apparatus or the will of Party bosses. Instead, the soviet bureaucracy could nominate officials for the approval of the Party organisation. Many a young Party member was being trained as a red specialist or soviet official. Though qualitative data are lacking, there were differences of sub-culture among Party apparatchiki and soviet officials. Under Stalin's new conciliatory line towards specialists after 1931 the regime had to coexist with the officials, although suffering occurred in some cases, as in the Metro-Vickers case.

The MGK and MK doubtlessly supervised soviet organisations quite carefully. Important departments were watched, as in the case of the regional finance department, which the MGK criticised because of the shortfall of state revenue. Its heads were warned and they had to make monthly reports on the out-turn of the budget, item by item and giving reasons for any non-fulfilment.[5]

As already noted, the dominant role of the Party meant neither its arbitrary intervention (which, however, could happen) nor the total subordination of the soviet to the Party. But this limitation should not be exaggerated. From an institutional point of view, it was the MK and MGK bureaux which preceded decisions by the Mossoviet and oblispolkom. In other words, the supremacy of Party over soviet (the 'highest organ on its territory') signified the procedure by which a decision was taken. The Party bureau was the final place where decisions were made, of the Party members in the soviet (the Party fraction in the soviet) proposed the approval of a given policy. Without its sanction no important plan or decision could be implemented. This was a universal pattern in Soviet government.

This leads to the *second point concerning Moscow politics, the relationship between the Party and specialists or 'technocrats'*. Governing large cities, controlling big industries, needs special knowledge and qualifications which rural leaders did not need at that time. Leaders of other small cities might have to possess this know-how, but Moscow officials had consciously to acquire it because of the level of urbanisation. That could be the reason why the bureau had to consult with specialists, or organise commissions with the involvement of related institutions before policy was formulated. The Mossoviet and MGK decisions were often taken in the framework of a commission. Some bold architects such as Zholtovskii and Schusev had even gone so far as to send letters of warning to Stalin and Kaganovich, to try to prevent the destruction of the Sukharev Towers, an event which finally occurred in the spring of 1934.[6]

This is related to the other dimension presented by Moscow politics, the role of the Party in production. In this sphere, the Party's image wavered between intervention or isolationism towards management. However, the stress in Moscow was on reliance on managers. It is characteristic that Kaganovich emphasised *edinonachalie*, or one-man management, in the Moscow city committee in May 1932. This tendency is more apparent than in the rural areas, where intervention dominated the scene, especially in 1932.

The third aspect of Moscow politics which has been stressed in this book is the relationship between the 'centre' and the 'locality' in different policy areas. The period 1931–34 was the peak of centralisation, and even small matters were settled 'from above'. The methods adopted by the Party for industrialisation and collectivisation required this. Few areas remained where local initiative was taken; even the 'decentralisation' of supply was decided at the upper level. Nevertheless the municipal economy was an area where local initiative and orientation had considerable leverage. Housing and other functions were in fact motivated 'from below'. The fact that Moscow was the capital may have lessened, to some degree, these possibilities; in fact Stalin did intervene in many matters, from rabbit-raising to the design of the Moskva Hotel. But these matters were locally initiated, as was the case in the June 1931 plenum decision on the municipal economy itself. Also, to some extent, light industry needed local initiative and resources; that is why the MK had to pay attention to the needs of textile workers. This was also true of the energy problem; because energy was short, it had to develop its own resources, as for example in the case of peat.

Fourthly and finally, the relationship between the regime and the masses was very complex, and this book has not attempted to analyse this fully. There were contradictions in the lives of the masses. On the one hand, shortages were the direct result of collectivisation and industrialisation. Real wages were far below the NEP level. Living conditions were desperate because of urbanisation, although passportisation cut the inflow of rural population. Textile workers were not docile citizens and produced some kind of *volynka*, a go-slow kind of resistance quite common at that time, which resulted in some improvement of conditions even though repression followed. The policy towards specialists softened after 1931, and the Metro-Vickers case was not important to the Stalinist system in general. Many a young worker got a chance of promotion. For the peasants and kolkhozniks, whose conditions worsened, there was upward mobility for those able to enter the technical higher-education system or find a job in a city or factory.

There was a curious mixture in the Moscow of 1931–34. There was a Metro and there were horse-carts, there was compulsion and there was education, there were district central heating and barrack-type accommodation, there were kolkhozniks and there were specialists, there were destruction of the architectural heritage and creation of apartment blocks. The Moscow city leaders, and notably Kaganovich, Khrushchev, Bulganin and Malenkov, faced new tasks of city management, tasks which no other city management, nor regional and republic leaders, so fully experienced.

It is interesting that the Moscow leadership group had a remarkable survival rate in the Great Purge, and it may be asked whether it was mere coincidence that some of them, including Khrushchev and Bulganin, became the post-Stalin leaders of the USSR just as Soviet society as a whole was becoming as urbanised as Moscow Region had been in 1931.

Notes

1 Moscow: History, Geography, and Society

1. *Bol'shaya Sovetskaya Entsiklopediya, 1–izd.*, M. (1938) t. 40, p. 334.
2. D. Koenker, *Moscow Workers and the 1917 Revolution* (Princeton, 1981); also D. Koenker, 'Urban Families, Working-class Youth Groups and the 1917 Revolution in Moscow', in D. L. Ransel (ed), *The Family in Imperial Russia* (Urbana, 1978), pp. 280–304.
3. S. Cohen, *Bukharin and the Bolshevik Revolution* (London, 1973), p. 51–55.
4. N. Shimotomai, *Rodokumiai Ronso* (Trade union controversy 1920–1921), M. A. thesis submitted to Tokyo university in 1973.
5. *Bol'shaya Sovetskaya Entsiklopediya, 1–izd.*, t. 40 (1938) p. 360.
6. N. Shimotomai,'Defeat of the Right Opposition in Moscow Party organization: 1928' in *Japanese Slavic and East European Studies*, No. 4 (1983) p. 20.
7. N. Shimotomai, *Sovieto seizi to Rodokumiai* (Soviet Politics and Trade Unions) (Tokyo, 1982).
8. R. W. Davies, *The Socialist Offensive: the Collectivisation of Soviet Agriculture* (London, 1980).
9. *Izvestiya TsK KPSS*, No. 9 (1989) p.116.
10. *Sbornik deistvuyushchikh vazhneishikh postanoblenii prezidiuma Moskovskogo soveta RK i KD za isklyucheniem obyazatel'nikh postanoblenii 1923–34gg.* (1934), p. 294. (Hereafter *Sbornik deistvuyushchikh . . .*)
11. A. N. Gasilovskii, *Moskva* (1932), p. 42,
12. W. Chamberlin, *Russia's Iron Age* (London, 1935), p. 124.
13. *Administrativno-territorial'noe delenie Soyuza SSR* (1931), pp. 28–41.
14. *Propagandist*, No. 11–12 (1931) p. 2.
15. Ibid., No. 4 (1933) p. 43.
16. *Moskva v tsifrakh* (1934), p. 7–11.
17. *Bol'shaya Sovetskaya Entsiklopediya*, t. 38, pp. 425–32; *Atlas Moskovskoi oblasti* (1934), p. 16.
18. *Atlas Moskovskoi oblasti* (1934), pp. 54–5.
19. L. M. Kaganovich, *Za sotsialisticheskuyu rekonstruktsiyu Moskvy i gorodov SSSR* (1931), p. 70.
20. *Ekonomiko-statisticheskii spravochnik po raionam Moskovskoi oblasti*, ch.1, vyp. 2 (1934) p. 49.
21. *Moskva v tsifrakh* (1934), p. 13.
22. Ibid., p. 51.
23. *Sbornik deistvuyushchikh.*, p. 40.

24. *Moskva v tsifrakh*, p. 87.
25. *Istoricheskie zapiski*, No. 92 (1973) p. 34.
26. V. I. Kuz'min, *V bor'be za sotsialisticheskuyu rekonstruktsiyu 1926 –1937* (1976), p. 119.
27. W. Chamberlin, *ibid.*, p. 125.
28. *Istoriya rabochikh Moskvy* (1983), p. 245.
29. *Moskva v tsifrakh*, p. 91.
30. *Istoriya rabochikh Moskvy* (1983), p. 217.
31. *Rabochii klass v upravlenii gosudarstvom 1926–37* (1968), pp. 47, 51.
32. TsGAOR SS f. 2287, ot. 1, op. No. 1, sv. 36, d. 381.
33. *Kollektivizatsiya sel'skogo khozyaistva Tsentral'nogo promyshlennogo raiona 1927–37* (Ryazan, (1970), pp. 460, 488.
34. Ibid., pp. 542, 590.
35. I. Ya. Trifonov, *Likvidatsiya ekspluatatorskikh klassov SSSR* (1975) p. 2
36. V. Kuz'min, *V bor'be za sotsialisticheskuyu rekonstruktsiyu 1926–37* (1976), p. 119.
37. L. Kaganovich, *Za sotsialisticheskuyu rekonstruktsiyu Moskvy i gorodov SSSR, pererabotannaya stenogramma doklada na iyun'skom plenume TsK VKP(b)* (1931), p. 15.
38. *KPSS v rezolyutsiyakh i resheniyakh,s'ezdov, konferentsii i plenumov TsK*, t. 4 (1971) p. 545.
39. L. Kaganovich, *Za sotsialisticheskuyu rekonstruktsiyu*, p. 10–44.
40. *Moskovskii sovet 1931–34* (1934), p. 84–92.
41. L. Kaganovich, *Za sotsialisticheskuyu rekonstruktsiyu . . .* , p. 66; *KPSS v rezolyutsiyakh.*, t. 5 (1971) p. 554.
42. *KPSS v rezolyutsiyakh.*, t. 4, p. 549.
43. *Rabochaya Moskva*, 1 June 1931.
44. *Rabochaya Moskva*, 6 June 1931.
45. *Rabochaya Moskva*, p. 21, 25 June 1931.

2 Moscow Party Organisation and Membership

1. T. H. Rigby, *Communist Party Membership in the USSR* (Princeton, 1968), p. 52.
2. S. Fitzpatrick, *Education and Social Mobility in the Soviet Union 1921–34* (Cambridge, 1979).
3. *Pravda*, 28 January 1932.
4. *Sbornik vazhneishikh postanoblenii MK i MGK(b)* (1934), p. 549. (Hereafter *Sbornik.*)
5. *Pravda*, 10 December 1932. There were also reported those who were dropped out from the party in the first half of 1932. Their number amounted to 31 000, though their precise number in Moscow is uncertain (*Partiinoe stroitel'stvo*, No. 21 (1932) p. 47).
6. *Partiinoe stroitel'stvo*, No. 21 (1932) p. 50–51.

7. *Propagandist*, organ of the MK culture and propaganda department, No. 6 (1932) p. 56.
8. Ibid.
9. A. Getty, *Origins of the Great Purges, the Soviet Communist Party Reconsidered, 1933–38* (Cambridge, 1985)
10. *Acta Slavica Iaponica*, t. 1 (Sapporo, 1983) pp. 48–50.
11. *Spravochnik partiinogo rabotnika*, vyp. 8, 1934, p. 292.
12. *Acta Slavica Iaponica*, t. 1, (1983) 50; t. 4 (1986) pp. 1–34; Rigby, *ibid.*, p. 202; A. Getty, *ibid.*, pp. 48–52. My version differs from that of Getty. He underestimates the political implications of the 1933 purge, because he fails to analyze the agricultural crisis in 1932–33, particularly in the south of the USSR.
13. V. K. Palishko, *Rost i ukreplenie partiinikh ryadov v usloviyakh stroitel'stva i upravlenie sotsializma* (1979), p. 60.
14. *Vechernyaya Moskva*, 14 January 1934.
15. *Vechernyaya Moskva*, 31 May 1933.
16. *Vechernyaya Moskva*, 5 July, 14 August 1933.
17. *Rabochaya Moskva*, 5 September 1933.
18. Ibid.
19. *Sbornik.*, p. 537.
20. *Rabochaya Moskva*, 5 September 1933; *Sbornik.*, pp. 538–40.
21. *Materialy k otchetu Stalinskogo raikoma i RKK VKP(b)* (1934), p. 50–51. (Hereafter *Materialy.*)
22. *IV Moskovskaya oblastnaya i III gorodskaya konferentsii VKP(b)* (1934), p. 296.
23. *Ot pobedy k pobede:materaly k otchetu RK VKP(b) 13 part. konf. Frunzenskoi raiona*, 1934, 114. (Hereafter *Ot pobedy k pobede*).
24. *Ot pobedy k pobede* (1934), p. 116.
25. *Ot pobedy k pobede*, p. 117.
26. *Rabochaya Moskva*, 3 March 1932; *Znamya*, No. 9. (1989) pp. 6–12.
27. *Acta Slavica Iaponica*, t. 1 (1983) p. 51; *KPSS v rezolyutsiyakh i resheniyakh, s"ezdov, konferentsii i plenumov TsK*, t .5 (1971) p. 90. (Hereafter *KPSS v rezolyutsiyakh.*, t. 5 (1971).
28. *IV Moskovskaya oblastnaya i III gorodskaya konferentsii VKP (b)* (1934), p. 490.
29. Ibid., p. 490; *Materialy*, p. 130.
30. *Vechernyaya Moskva*, 5 December 1933.
31. *IV Moskovskaya oblastnaya i III gorodskaya konferentsii VKP (b)* (1934), p. 364.
32. *XVII s'ezd VKP(b)* (1934), p. 287.
33. *IV Moskovskaya oblastnaya i III gorodskaya konferentsii VKP (b)* (1934), p. 300.
34. *XVII s'ezd VKP(b)* (1934), p. 286.
35. *Materialy.*, pp. 49–50.
36. Rigby, *ibid.*, p. 196.
37. Getty, *ibid.*, chapters 1, 2.

38. *IV Moskovskaya oblastnaya i III gorodskaya konferentsii VKP (b)* (1934), p. 295.
39. *IV Moskovskaya oblastnaya i III gorodskaya konferentsii VKP (b)* (1934), p. 489.
40. *IV Moskovskaya oblastnaya i III gorodskaya konferentsii VKP (b)* (1934), p. 488
41. *IV Moskovskaya oblastnaya i III gorodskaya konferentsii VKP (b)* (1934), p. 489.
42. Reasons for purging and their percentages are as follows:
    1. Opportunistic deviation, distortion of the class line: 965 investigated and 33.2 per cent purged.
    2. Violation of party and labour discipline, non-implementation of party directives: 10 904 investigated and 24 per cent expelled.
    3. Connection with 'alien' elements: 2 085 investigated and 70.1 per cent expelled.
    4. Abuse of position, waste and so on: 4103 investigated, 54.7 per cent expelled.
    5. Suppression of self-criticism, violation of VI party democracy: 406 investigated and 17.8 per cent expelled (*Moskovskaya oblastnaya i III gorodskaya konferentsii VKP (b)* (1934), p. 489).
43. Khrushchev rather cunningly showed the reduction of the communist ranks from the 1932 level (some 22 500) to the 1934 level (according to him, some 11 700 – which turned out to be wrong), bypassing the increase in 1932–33, and thus gave the impression that the reduction was rather minor. He also mitigated the reduction by mentioning the impact of the dispatch of *politotdel* workers who were sent from Moscow, some 3 000 (*IV Moskovskaya oblastnaya i III gorodskaya konferentsii VKP (b)* (1934), p. 294–95.)
44. *Ot pobedy k pobede*, p. 40.
45. *Moskovskaya gorodskaya i Moskovskaya oblastnaya organizatsiya KPSS v tsifrakh* (1972), p. 29.
46. *Ocherki istorii Kalininskoi organizatsii KPSS* (1971), p. 390.
47. *Propagandist*, No. 17 (1932) p. 10–11.
48. *Propagandist*, No. 17 (1932) p. 11.
49. *Spravochnik partiinogo rabotnika*, vyp. 8 (1934) p. 607–08.
50. *Sbornik.*, p. 573. Secretary Gei was apparently specialising in cultural affairs.
51. *Vechernyaya Moskva*, 15 July 1934.
52. *Sbornik.*, p. 512; *Ocherki istorii Ryazanskoi organizatsii KPSS* (1974), p. 268. In Ryazan some 700 attended in 1933/34.
53. *Propagandist*, No. 19–20 (1932) p. 1–3. This system also existed in Kalinin as well (*Ocherki istorii Kalininskoi.*, p. 390).
54. *Ocherki istorii Moskovskoi organizatsii KPSS*, kn. 2 (1983) p. 483.
55. *Sbornik.*, pp. 512, 572.
56. *Sbornik.*, p. 569.

57. *Sbornik.*, p. 571.
58. *Ocherki istorii Ryazanskoi organizatsii KPSS* (1974), p. 268; *Ocherki istorii Kalininskoi organizatsii KPSS* (1971), p. 390.
59. *Propagandist*, No. 10 (1932) p. 19.
60. *Materialy.*, 1934, p. 139. In Stalin raion 150–200 cell secretaries were being taught (*Materialy.*, p. 56).
61. *Ocherki istorii Moskovskoi.* (1983), p. 483.
62. *Spravochnik partiinogo rabotnika*, vyp. 8 (1934) p. 322; *Ocherki istorii Moskovskoi.* (1983), p. 483.
63. *Materialy.* (1934), p. 139.
64. On the educational level of these insitutions, see the curriculum in *Propagandist*, No. 19, 1933, 40 and other issues. For example, the Marx-Leninist circle on party education studied N. N. Popov's, V. G. Knorin's and E. M. Yaroslavskii's texts.
65. *Sbornik.*, p. 485.
66. *Sbornik.*, p. 480.
67. *Sbornik.*, p. 473.
68. The Programme-methodological bureau of the department of culture and propaganda issued various text books and pamphlets.
69. *Sbornik.*, p. 487.
70. J.Barber, *Soviet Historians in Crisis 1928–32* (London, 1981), pp. 126–35.

3 Decision Making in the Party

1. N. Shimotomai, 'Defeat of the Right Opposition in Moscow: 1928' in *Japanese Slavic and East European Studies*, vol. 4 (1983), p. 15–34. Incidentally, these Moscow 'Right' oppositionists were rehabilitated by the Gorbachev campaign for the rethinking of the past. On Uglanov see *Moskovskaya Pravda*, 12 February 1989 (information given by T. Colton); *Izvestiya TsK KPSS*, No. 2, 1990, pp. 116–26; on Ryutin, *Krasnaya zvezda*, 23 July 1988; *Izvestiya TsK KPSS*, No. 3, 1990, pp. 150–78.
2. N. Shimotomai,'A Note on the Kuban Affair' in *Acta Slavica Iaponica*, tom 1, Sapporo (1983), p. 15–34.
3. *Moskovskaya gorodskaya i Moskovskaya oblastnaya organizatsiya KPSS v tsifrakh* (1972), p. 78
4. *Rabochaya Moskva*, 5 August 1933.
5. *Pravda*, 31 January 1932; *Vechernyaya Moskva*, 26 January 1934.
6. *Rabochaya Moskva*, 26 January 1934.
7. *Vechernyaya Moskva*, 26 January 1934; Pravda, 16 May 1932.
8. *Sbornik.*, pp. 19, 77, 152, 185, 415.
9. *Bol'shaya Sovetskaya Entsiklopediya*, 3–izd. (1975), t. 22, p. 451. Reportedly Kaganovich was not a punctual participant in the MK buro (*Byulleten' oppozitsii*, No. 32 (1932) p. 33).
10. *Sbornik.*, pp. 62, 117, 189, 395, 590.

11. *Sbornik.*, pp. 185, 213, 230. Mikhailov mainly worked in the Moscow party orgainization after 1918, though he also worked in Central Asia (*Rabochaya Moskva*, 8 June 1933).
12. *Sbornik.*, pp. 102, 415, 572.
13. *Rabochaya Moskva*, 8 June 1933. N. E. Donenko had worked in the Party Central Committee orgraspred in 1923 before he moved to the Far East and Ukraine in the NEP.
14. *Sbornik.*, pp. 18–20; *Khrushchev Remembers* (Penguin ed., Harmondsworth, 1971), p. 90; R. Medvedev, *All Stalin's Men* (1983), p. 125. He also initiated the adoption of new machines for plastering (*Moskovskii sovet:otchet o rabote* (1934), p. 134); *Znamya*, No. 9 (1989) p. 3–39.
15. *Sbornik.*, pp. 369, 376, 395.
16. Kogan was also an old Bolshevik since 1905. He had worked on the Moscow railway since 1908 (*Rabochaya Moskva*, 8 June 1933).
17. *Sbornik.*, pp. 295, 366, 569.
18. *Sbornik.*, pp. 13, 16, 19, 315.
19. M. Fainsod, *Smolensk under Soviet Rule* (London, 1958), p. 67.
20. *Sbornik.*, pp. 69, 97, 135, 151, 581.
21. *Sbornik.*, pp. 10, 74, 181, 184, 214, 220, 176, 414.
22. *Sbornik.*, pp. 13, 16, 19, 20, 276, 295, 299, 308, 326, 384, 465.
23. *Sbornik.*, pp. 395, 568.
24. *Sbornik.*, pp. 13, 403.
25. *IV Moskovskaya oblastnaya i III gorodskaya konferentsii VKP(b)* (1934), p. 265.
26. M. Fainsod, *Smolensk under Soviet Rule* (London, 1958), esp. chap. 3.
27. *Sbornik.*, p. 328.
28. Incidentally, the MK Secretariat decided that the railway procuracy should organize a show trial (*pokazatel'nui sud*) of those who had disturbed the normal operations of transport on August 1932 (*Sbornik.*, p. 170).
29. For example, G. Malenkov and his department (Org.-instructors department) were instructed to strengthen the party cadres and the result of this was checked by Mikhailov. There were also another decision on this topic: this was that if some institutions took part in the next bureau meeting 'without preparation' and could not present their case and could not answer essential questions on the result, 'they were to be purged from the bureau meeting' (*Sbornik.*, p. 184; *IV Moskovskaya III oblastnaya i gorodskaya konferentsii VKP(b)* (1934), p. 237).
30. *Rabochaya Moskva*, 6 May 1933. The Far Eastern obkom's work plan also clearly indicates that the bureau and Secretariat sessions took place every ten days respectively (*Tikhookeanskaya Pravda*, 17 October 1932).
31. The composition of the commissions was as follows:
    1. On the issue of the migration of the chemical factory:

Khrushchev, Guberman (planning commission) and Agranov (OGPU).
2. On the establishment of a trust for consumer goods: Kaminsky, Mikhailov, Egorov, Agranov and representatives of the supply departments and industry co-operatives.
3. On the dairy factory: Ryndin, Mikhailov, Kaminsky, Davidson, and representatives from the supply department, Union of Milk, and Mosfood trust.
4. On accommodation and municipal construction planning: Gei, Kaminsky, Guberman, Kalygina, Sedel'nikov (gorkom) and another four important raikom secretaries, the financial department of the oblast as well as the plenipotentiary of the MK on the sub-Moscow coal mining areas.
5. On the construction, planning and municipal economy of the Sub-Moscow coal mining areas: Ryndin, Malenkov, the plenipotentiary of the MK in this area, the representative of Moscow coal trust.
6. On education investment: Gei, Guberman, and fraction of oblispolkom.
7. On the completion of economic planning for 1933: Kaminsky, Guberman.
32. *Sbornik.*, pp. 13–18.
33. Other tasks were assigned to the MGK bureau members: three raikom secretaries were to control the leather industry; and Khrushchev, Bulganin and Filatov (city control commission) and others were instructed to develop city construction (*Sbornik.*, pp. 18–20).
34. It was decided to discuss the textile industry in every bureau meeting at that time (*Sbornik.*, p. 151).
35. *Sbornik.*, p. 584.
36. *Stroitel'stvo Moskvy*, No. 2 (1932) p. 27; *Spravochnik partiinogo rabotnika*, vyp. 8 (1934) p. 204; *Sbornik.*, p. 272.
37. *IV Moskovskaya oblastnaya i III gorodskaya konferentsii VKP(b)* (1934), p. 68. Margolin, secretary of Stalin raikom, had worked in Kiev in the 1920s and moved to the Promakademiya in 1928–29 with Khrushchev. He was appointed secretary of Dnepropetrovsk obkom in 1937 before he was finally disgraced (*Vostochno-Sibirskaya Pravda*, 21 March 1937).
38. *IV Moskovskaya oblastnaya i III gorodskaya konferentsii VKP(b)* (1934), p. 561.
39. Ibid., p. 186.
40. *XVII s'ezd VKP (b)* (1934) p. 6.
41. See note 29.
42. *IV Moskovskaya oblastnaya i III gorodskaya konferentsii VKP(b)* (1934), p. 31. In the case of Khar'kov gorkom, Ukraine, the Secretariat made some 36 decisions out of 85 by the 'opros' method (*Partiinoe stroitel'stvo*, No. 11 (1935) p. 21).
43. From the *Sbornik*.

44. *Sbornik.*, pp. 308, 403–04. In 1931, Bulganin was also a member of the MGK Secretariat and it is likely that he or the Mossoviet secretary attended the Secretariat meeting.
45. *IV Moskovskaya oblastnaya i III gorodskaya konferentsii VKP(b)*, 1934, p. 313. The size of the MK is not known. Incidentally, the total number of officials of the Leningrad obkom and gorkom was 296 and 239 in 1933 and 1934 respectively (*Byulleten' V ob'edinennoi oblastnoi i III gorodskoi Leningradskoi konferentsii*, No. 6 (1934) p. 9).
46. Fainsod, *ibid.* (1958), p. 112. The Perm gorkom in the Urals had 57 officials, though the established number was 19 (*Partiinoe stroitel'stvo*, No. 15 (1934) p. 40).
47. L. M. Kaganovich, *O vnutripartiinoi rabote i otdelakh rukovodzhashchikh partiinikh organov* (1934), p. 13.
48. *Spravochnik partiinogo stroitel'stva*, vyp. 7, ch. 1 (1930), pp. 169–71.
49. *Byulleten' Moskovskogo obkoma VKP (b)*, No. 1 (1930) p. 4.
50. *Partiinoe stroitel'stvo*, No. 13–14 (1933) p. 40.
51. *Partiinoe stroitel'stvo*, No. 22 (1932) p. 26; No. 13–14 (1933) p. 40.
52. *Sbornik.*, pp. 542, 544.
53. *Partiinoe stroitel'stvo*, No. 15 (1933) p. 11.
54. *IV Moskovskaya oblastnaya i III gorodskaya konferentsii VKP(b)* (1934), p. 311.
55. *ibid.*, p. 311.
56. *Sbornik.*, pp. 214, 234, 368. There was organized,for instance,a commission under his chairmanship with six persons, including the deputy head,on the selection of 500 active members to be sent to the kolkhoz. Incidentally, a deputy head was instituted only in this department (*Byulleten' Moskovskogo obkoma VKP(b)*, No. 1 (1930) p. 4).
57. *Sbornik.*, p. 542.
58. *Sbornik.*, p. 148.
59. *Sbornik.*, pp. 165, 293, 295, 369, 393.
60. *Sbornik.*, p. 121.
61. Barber, pp. 125, 174.
62. *Sbornik.*, pp. 570–72.
63. *Sbornik.*, p. 439.
64. *Sbornik.*, pp. 97, 185.
65. *Sbornik.*, p. 564.
66. *Spravochnik partiinogo rabotnika*, vyp. 7, ch. 2 (1930), p. 170.
67. *Sbornik.*, p. 356.
68. *Sbornik.*, p. 369.
69. *Sbornik.*, p. 586.
70. *Sbornik.*, pp. 398–99.
71. *Sbornik.*, p. 324.
72. *Sbornik.*, p. 166.
73. *Sbornik.*, p, 12; *Sbornik.*, p. 180. A typical example of this is shown in the decision of the MK on the Moscow-Donbass railway on April 1933.
74. *XVII s' ezd VKP*(b) (1934) p. 19

75. Ibid., p. 561.
76. *Vechernyaya Moskva*, 5 March 1934.
77. L. Kaganovich, *O vnutripartiinoi rabote* (1934), p. 8.
78. *VI Moskovskaya.*, pp. 295, 511.
79. *Spravochnik partiinogo rabotnika*, vyp. 9 (1935) p. 113.
80. *Vechernyaya Moskva*, 5 March 1934.
81. *Partiinoe stroitel'stvo*, No. 7 (1935) p. 48.

4 The Party at District Level

1. *Sbornik deistvuyushchikh.*, pp. 5–7.
2. *Atlas Moskovskoi oblasti* (1934).
3. *Seikei Hogaku*, No. 21 (1983) p. 156.
4. *IV Moskovskaya oblastnaya i III gorodskaya konferentsii VKP (b)* (1934), p. 262.
5. *Sbornik.*, p. 524.
6. This was true in the Central Black Earth region where the oblast bureau's first meeting after the congress ratified the all the raikom secretaries, though relevant data on Moscow was unobtainable to the author. See note 3.
7. See my article, 'Defeat of the Right Opposition in the Moscow Party Organization: 1928', in *Japanese Slavic and East European Studies*, vol. 4 (1983) pp. 15–34; S. F. Cohen, *Bukharin and the Bolshevik Revolution* (London, 1973), pp. 286–87.
8. *Rabochaya Moskva*, 8 June 1933.
9. *IV Moskovskaya oblastnaya i III gorodskaya konferentsii VKP (b)* (1934), p. 261.
10. *Ibid.*, p. 328.
11. *Sbornik.*, p. 570.
12. *IV Moskovskaya oblastnaya i III gorodskaya konferentsii VKP (b)* (1934), p. 530.
13. *Sbornik.*, p. 552.
14. *Sbornik.*, p. 555.
15. *Partiinoe stroitel'stvo*, No. 15 (1933) p. 2.
16. *Spravochnik partiinogo rabotnika*, vyp. 8 (1934) pp. 288–89; *Acta Slavica Iaponica*, tom 4 (1986) p. 23, pp. 28–9.
17. *Sbornik.*, p. 550.
18. *Partiinoe stroitel'stvo*, No. 13–14 (1933) p. 64.
19. *Partiinoe stroitel'stvo*, No. 15 (1933) p. 9.
20. Ibid.
21. Ibid. p. 15; *IV Moskovskaya oblastnaya i III gorodskaya konferentsiya VKP (b) (1934), p. 311.*
22. *Partiinoe stroitel'stvo*, No. 16 (1934) p. 19.
23. *Sbornik.*, p. 543.
24. *IV Moskovskaya oblastnaya i III gorodskaya konferentsii VKP (b)* (1934), p. 302.

25. *Sbornik.*, p. 50–52.
26. *Sbornik.*, p. 550.
27. *Ot pobedy k pobede* (1934), p. 10–35; *Ot Khamovnikov k Frunzenskomu raionu 1917–32* (1932), p. 4. The number of working class in this raion is uncertain. The statistical hand book gives some 98 800 in 1933 (*Moskva v tsifrakh* (1934) p. 18). *Rabochaya Moskva*, 21 March, 1933.
28. *Ot pobedy k pobede*, p. 133; These VUZ and VTUZ amounted 20 in this raion (*Ot Khamovnikov*, p. 5).
29. *Moskva v tsifrakh*, p. 12.
30. *Ibid.*, p. 39.
31. *Ibid.*, p. 121.
32. *Ot pobedy.*, p. 119. In 1932 there were 24 000 members (*Ot Kamovnikov.*, p. 9).
33. *Materialy k otchetu Stalinskogo raikoma i RKK VKP(b)* (1934), p. 50. A newspaper gives the total number of Communists as 23 000 in 1933 in this raion, which seems a little overstated (*Rabochaya Moskva*, 15 August 1933). Still, considering the small population of this raion, the relative weight of communists is higher in the Stalin raion.
34. *Ot pobedy.*, p. 120.
35. *Ibid.*, p. 40.
36. On the raion party conference see *Pravda*, pp. 9–15, January 1932; *Pravda*, 14–15, January 1934.
37. *Rabochaya Moskva*, 17 March 1933. Karpov had been chairman of the same raion ispolkom in 1931. Karpov was coopted to the MGK bureau in April 1932, but was demoted to candidate status by the reduction of membership in 1934.
38. *Vechernyaya Moskva*, 15 January 1934; *IV Moskovskaya oblastnaya i III gorodskaya konferentsii VKP (b)* (1934), p. 626.
39. Stalin raikom had 33 party-members on its staff, which was regarded as excessive (*Rabochaya Moskva*, 15 August 1932).
40. In the Stalin raikom Secretariat, 31 out of 41 questions were decided by the opros method in one protokol (*Rabochaya Moskva*, 15 August 1932; 24, 27 March 1933).
41. *Materialy.*, p. 114.
42. *Vsya Moskva* (1936), p. 74–75. The number of instructors before 1934 was small: about 10 (*Rabochaya Moskva*, 15 August 1932). In 1936 Frunze raion had instructors specializing in higher education, whilst Stalin raion had energy, machine building and wood-working, which the former lacked.
43. *Ot pobedy.*, p. 126.
44. *Ibid.*, p. 127.
45. *Materialy.*, p. 56. The unfication of shop cells may have increased the role of shop secretaries;in the 'Gigant' combinat 140 cells were reduced to 53.
46. *Materialy.*, p. 5.

47. *IV Moskovskaya oblastnaya i III gorodskaya konferentsii VKP (b)* (1934), p. 296.
48. *Ot pobedy.*, pp. 38–39. There were 71 enterprises in 1932, 38 of which were large scale (*Ot Khamovnikov.*, p. 20).
49. *Materialy.*, p. 113.
50. *Ibid.*
51. *Spravochnik sovetskogo rabotnika* (1937), p. 37–44.
52. *Materialy.*, p. 64–65.
53. *Sbornik deistvuyushchikh.*, p. 49–60.
54. T. Colton, 'Moscow: Urban politics and policy under Stalin', *Occasional Paper of the Kennan Institute* (1982), p. 11–12.
55. E. D. Simon, *Moscow in the Making* (London, 1937), p. 31.
56. *Rabochaya Moskva*, 8 February 1932.

5 The Governmental Process in Moscow

1. *Spravochnik partiinogo rabotnika*, vyp. 8 (1934), p. 201.
2. *Spravochnik sovetskogo rabotnika* (1937), p. 51.
3. *Sbornik deistvuyushchikh* (1934), p. 30–31.
4. *Rabochaya Moskva*, 26 February 1931; 29 February 1931.
5. N. M. Aleshchenko, *Moskovskii sovet v 1917–41 gg.* (1976), p. 57.
6. *Rabochaya Moskva*, 1 March 1931. Kaminsky was the second secretary of the MK from February 1931. This appointment suggests that the chairman of the ispolkom was no lower than the second secretary of the corresponding party organisation.
7. *Sbornik.*, pp. 425–27.
8. *Sbornik.*, p. 426.
9. *Sbornik.*, pp. 12, 16, 19, 20, 276, 299, 300, 308, 315, 326, 331, 384, 405.
10. Bulganin kept the Secretariat of the MGK membership as well as bureau membership in 1931 (*Rabochaya Moskva*, 27 February 1931).
11. Bulganin had been a chekist in Nizhnii-Novgorod (Gorky) in the civil war, and he might have got acquainted with Kaganovich, who had been the first secretary there. No wonder that some independent observer saw Bulganin as a rising star, whilst Khrushchev was only a bureau member in 1931 (*Bol'shaya Sovetskaya Entsiklopediya*, 2–izd., t. 6 (1951) p. 260; *Sotsialisticheskii vestnik.*, No. 20 (1932). p. 34)
12. Aleshchenko, *op. cit.*, p. 357.
13. *Sbornik.*, p. 426.
14. *Rabochaya Moskva*, 28 December 1931; *Sbornik.*, pp. 11, 63, 70, 74, 81, 94, 367, 14.
15. *Sbornik.*, pp. 14, 128, 276, 313; *Vechernyaya Moskva*, 4 March, 1933.
16. *Rabochaya Moskva*, 29 February 1932; 12 August 1932, 17 March, 1933. This department was called as Secretariat of the presidum of Mossovet. One secretary was responsible for supervising the newspaper *Vechernyaya Moskva* (*Sbornik deistvuyushchikh.*, 295).

17. *Sbornik.*, p. 426.
18. According to the statute of the city soviet,there should have been at least such departments as municipal construction, finance, supply, education, health, social insurance as well as the organisation and planning commission, inspectors of the national records,in the presidium of each city soviet. The last three were added by the change of structure in 1933. There were also departments like RKI, road construction or car-road transport (*Spravochnik sovetskogo rabotnika.* (1937), p. 47.
19. *Vechernyaya Moskva*, 17 March 1933.
20. *Sbornik deistvuyushchikh.* pp. 9–13.
21. *Ibid.*, pp. 15–17.
22. *Ibid.*, pp. 18–26.
23. According to the decision on oblispolkom organisation department, which was regarded as a model for the other soviets, it mainly dealt with cadres, information, administrative distinction, and rationalisation of apparatus (*Spravochnik sovetskogo rabotnika* (1937), p. 75.).
24. *Sovetskoe stroitel'stvo*, No. 13 (1932) p. 62.
25. *Spravochnik sovetskogo rabotnika* (1937), p. 79.
26. Vechernyaya Moskva, 3 January 1933. This body mobilized and sent some 1800 personnel of the labour department to the 300–400 issue points.
27. *Vechernyaya Moskva*, 4, 15 January 1933.
28. *Vechernyaya Moskva*, 9 March 1933.
29. *Vechernyaya Moskva*, 13 October 1933.
30. The transport department, for instance, offered a hundred vehicles to carry them.
31. *Materialy k otchetu Stalinskogo raikoma i RKK VKP(b)* (1934), p. 81.
32. *Sbornik deistvuyushchikh.*, p. 13.
33. *Spravochnik sovetskogo rabotnika* (1937), p. 44.
34. Some sections like fruit and vegetables, or public catering, were probably short-lived, though 'the problem of waifs' survived in Moscow (*Sovetskoe stroitel'stvo*, No. 12 (1932) p. 116).
35. *Moskovskii sovet:otchet o rabote 1931–34* (1934), pp. 248–55.
36. The energy section was occupied with the economic use of energy, whilst the section on revolutionary legality was concerned with the complaints or appeals of the masses to the effect that some were sent to court. The health section checked 108 barracks,whilst the industrial section mobilized tenants' organisations to collect 4300 tons of scrap-iron. However, high turn-over of the heads was one of the reason for the weak activity (*Vechernyaya Moskva*, 13, 14 September 1933; *Sbornik deistvuyushchikh.* p. 222.
37. *Vechernyaya Moskva*, 17 April 1933.
38. *Vechernyaya Moskva*, 16 March 1933.
39. *Sovetskoe stroitel'stvo*, No. 6 (1933) p. 95.
40. *Vechernyaya Moskva*, 22 February 1933.

41. *Materialy Moskovskogo oblastnogo soveshchaniya planovykh rabotnikov*, 25–28 yuniya (1931) pp. 33, 46.
42. *Sbornik.*, p. 48; *Vechernyaya Moskva*, 1 December 1933.
43. The process by which the oblplan for 1932 was drafted was prescribed by the Sovnarkom directives as follows: each raiplan (district level planning agency) and gorplan present their outline by June. Enterprises and Kolkhozes make their own counterplan, and make necessary correction upon receiving directives. Oblplan, based on the decision of the oblispolkom, sets limits and gives directives to each raion and the city by 1st September. Raiplan and Gorplan present their plans to the oblplan by 20 September. At that time each department and economic organisation also present their plans. The oblplan, in its turn, presents the economic plans for Moscow oblast 1932 to the oblispolkom by 1st September (*Materialy Moskovskogo oblastnogo*, (1931) 15–16).
44. *Rabochaya Moskva*, 2 September 1932.
45. *Sbornik.*, pp. 13–17.
46. *Sbornik.*, p. 13.
47. *Sbornik.*, p. 13.
48. *Sbornik.*, pp. 13–14.
49. This resulted in the decision by which the Mossoviet set up the trust 'Univerprom' in May 1933 (*Moskovskii sovet* (1934), p. 40).
50. *Sbornik.*, p. 14.
51. *Sbornik.*, p. 13.
52. *Sbornik.*, p. 15.
53. *Sbornik.*, p. 15.
54. *Sbornik.*, p. 16.
55. *Sbornik.*, p. 18.
56. *Sbornik.*, p. 18.
57. *Sbornik.*, p. 20.
58. *Sbornik.*, p. 19. Also this bureau instructed Romanov, financial department to prepare the draft of the 1933 budget for the next MGK meeting.
59. *Sbornik.*, p. 17, 75.
60. *Sbornik.*, p. 20.
61. *Sbornik.*, p. 20.
62. *Sbornik.*, p. 52.

6 The Party and Social Problems

1. *Sbornik.*, p. 14.
2. *XVII Konferentsii VKP(b), sten. otchet* (1932), pp. 145, 146, 162 and so on.
3. *SZ*, No. 62 (1932) p. 360; *Propagandist*, No. 21 (1932) p. 1.
4. *SZ*, No. 65 (1932) p. 375.
5. *Moskovskii sovet*, p. 225.
6. *Sbornik.*, p. 585.

7. *Vechernyaya Moskva*, 10 February 1933, *Sbornik deistvuyushchikh.*, pp. 288–91.
8. *Sbornik.*, p. 585.
9. *Sbornik.*, p. 403.
10. On the rabbit-raising campaign, the newspaper launched another movement against those who failed to take care of them (*Vechernyaya Moskva*, 23 January 1933). Watching over the meat warehouses was another concern of the Moscow leaders and one procurator of Proletarii district was criticized because only a few people were sent to the court or procuracy in this district (*Vechernyaya Moskva*, 30 January 1933).
11. *Moskovskii sovet.*, pp. 323–24.
12. *Sbornik.*, p. 317.
13. *Vechernyaya Moskva*, 5 February 1933.
14. Fainsod., *ibid.*, p. 187; *Acta Slavica Iaponica*, t. 1 (1983) p. 55; t. 4 (1986) 12.
15. SZ, No. 40 (1933) p. 239. This date coincides with the news of alleged collision of OGPU with the Politburo over the Metro Vickers affair (Fo. 371, 17426, p. 121, the British Embassy source was a well-informed Lithuanian minister).
16. *Sbornik.*, p. 586.
17. *Sbornik.*, p. 586.
18. *Sbornik.*, p. 586.
19. *Sbornik.*, p. 587.
20. *Sbornik.*, p. 590.
21. SZ, No. 84 (1932) p. 516.
22. SZ, No. 3 (1933) p. 22.
23. *Moskovskii sovet*, p. 226.
24. *Sbornik deistvuyushchikh.*, p. 161.
25. *Vechernyaya Moskva*, 15 February 1933.
26. *Vechernyaya Moskva*, 3 January 1933.
27. *Sbornik.*, 13; Fo 371, 17426, 11.
28. *Vechernyaya Moskva*, 18 February 1933; Fo 371, 17426, p. 24.
29. *Vechernyaya Moskva*, 8 May 1933.
30. E. Simon (ed.), *Moscow in the Making* (1937), p. 137.
31. *Vo glave kul'turnogo stroitel'stva*, kn.1 (1983), p. 101; *Moskva v tsifrakh.* (1934), p. 220.
32. *Sbornik.*, pp. 455–57.
33. *Vechernyaya Moskva*, 7 March 1933.
34. *Vechernyaya Moskva*, 11 March, 5 April 1933.
35. *Vo glave kul'turnogo stroitel'stva* (1983), p. 181.
36. *Ibid.*, p. 181.
37. *Ot pobedy k pobede: materialy k otchety RK VKP(b) 13 part. konf. Frunzenskogo raiona* (1934), p. 70.
38. *Sbornik.*, p. 469.
39. A. Smith, *I Was a Soviet Worker* (London, n.d.), p. 106.
40. *Sbornik.*, p. 461.

Notes to pp. 70–76   159

41. *Vechernyaya Moskva*, 5 February 1932.
42. *SU*, No. 7 (1933), p. 21.
43. *Vechernyaya Moskva*, 16 February 1933.
44. *Ibid.*
45. *Vechernyaya Moskva*, 27 February 1933.
46. *Vechernyaya Moskva*, 15 March 1933
47. *Vechernyaya Moskva*, 19 May 1933.
48. *Vechernyaya Moskva*, 27 May 1933.
49. *Vechernyaya Moskva*, 4 June 1933.
50. *Vechernyaya Moskva*, 31 May 1933.
51. *Vechernyaya Moskva*, 3 July 1933.
52. *IV Moskovskaya oblastnaya i III gorodskaya konferentsii VKP (b)* (1934), p. 486.
53. *SZ*, No. 32 (1935) p. 252.
54. *Vsya Moskva* (1936), pp. 2, 37.

7 Industry in Moscow

1. *Pravda*, 28 January 1932.
2. *Moskovskii sovet rabochikh krest'yanskikh i krasnoarmeiskikh deputatov, Otchet o rabote* (1934), pp. 36–42. (Hereafter, *Otchet o rabote*).
3. *Sbornik.* (1934), p. 72.
4. *Sbornik postanovlenii i prikazov po promyshlennosti*, No. 46 (1931) p. 763–68.
5. N. Davydova, A. Ponomarev, *Velikii podvig* (1970), p. 96.
6. Davydova, *ibid.*, p. 155.
7. Industrializatsiya SSSR 1929–32 (1970), p. 610.
8. See Chapter 3.
9. *Sbornik.*, p. 117.
10. *Sbornik.*, p. 117.
11. *Sbornik.*, p. 110.
12. *Sbornik.*, p. 112.
13. *Sbornik.*, p. 130.
14. *Sbornik.*, p. 123.
15. *Sbornik.*, p. 130.
16. *Rabochaya Moskva*, 6, 12 April 1933.
17. *Sbornik.*, p. 117.
18. *Sbornik.*, p. 117.
19. *Sbornik.*, p. 127.
20. *Sbornik.*, p. 119.
21. *Sbornik.*, p. 124.
22. *Sbornik.*, p. 130.
23. *Sbornik.*, p. 118.
24. N. Davydova, A. Ponomarev, *Velikii podvig* (1970), p. 166.
25. *Vechernyaya Moskva*, 19 September 1933.
26. *Rabochaya Moskva*, 2, 8 January 1932.

27. *Rabochaya Moskva*, 17 April, 9 May 1933.
28. *Sbornik.*, p. 62.
29. *Sbornik.*, p. 69.
30. *Pravda*, 29 February, 1 March 1932.
31. *Sbornik.*, p. 112. On the personality of Tevosyan, see A. Bek, *Novoe naznachenie*, 1987. Also G. Popov's fine review article in *Nauka i zhizni'*, No. 4 (1987).
32. Davydova, *ibid.*, pp. 168, 201.
33. *Rabochaya Moskva*, 5 March 1933.
34. *Sbornik.*, p. 151.
35. *Rabochaya Moskva*, 6 April 1933.
36. *IV Moskovskaya oblastnaya i III gorodskaya konferentsii VKP (b)* (1934), p. 212. This criticism was repeated in the Moscow party conference of 1934, when the Second Five Year Plan was modified slightly in favour of the light industry.
37. *Sbornik.*, p. 36.
38. *Rabochaya Moskva*, 3 September 1932.
39. *Propagandist*, No. 21-22 (1933) p. 62.
40. *Sbornik.*, p. 131.
41. A *Pravda* article on 29 April 1932, indirectly indicated the serious problem in Ivanovo Voznesensk by mentioning the supply problem as well as the parasitic mood of a 'significant' part of the Ivanovo party workers. On the 1925 strike movement here, see Nobuo Shimotomai, *Sovieto seiji to rodokumiai* (Soviet Politics and Trade Unions), (Tokyo University Press, 1982), Chapter 2.
42. British Public Record Office, Fo. 371, 16322, p. 185. Another telegram from the same source on 22 August 1932 reported that more than one hundred communists were reprimanded in this region because they stood by the workers in labour conflicts (Fo. 371, 16322, p. 238. See also A. Ciliga, *The Russian Enigma* (1979 reprint), p. 45).
43. *Sbornik.*, p. 151.
44. *Propagandist*, No. 12 (1932) p. 60.
45. *Sbornik.*, pp. 131-50.
46. *Sbornik.*, pp. 134.
47. *Sbornik.*, pp. 498.
48. *Sbornik.*, pp. 149, 512.
49. *Sbornik.*, p. 149; *Spravochnik partiinogo rabotnika*, vyp. 8 (1934), p. 331.
50. *Ibid.*, p. 668.
51. *Sbornik.*, p. 574.
52. *Sbornik.*, p. 512.
53. *Sbornik.*, p. 150.
54. *Sbornik.*, p. 149.
55. *Sbornik.*, p. 150.
56. *Sbornik.*, p. 512.
57. *Propagandist*, No. 21-22 (1933) p. 62.

Notes to pp. 81–89 161

58. *IV Moskovskaya oblastnaya i III gorodskaya konferentsii VKP (b)* (1934), p. 213.
59. *Sbornik.*, p. 131.
60. *KPSS v reszolyutsiyakh*, t. 5 (1971) p. 56.
61. *Rabochaya Moskva* 4 September 1933.
62. *Sbornik.*, p. 133
63. *Sbornik.*, p. 133.
64. *Sbornik.*, p. 137.
65. *Sbornik.*, p. 131.
66. *Sbornik.*, p. 154.
67. *Sbornik.*, p. 155.
68. *Sbornik.*, pp. 150–51.
69. *Sbornik.*, p. 146.
70. *Sbornik.*, p. 148.
71. *Materialy k otchetu VTsSPS IX s'ezdu profsoyuzov* (1932), p. 41.
72. *Sbornik.*, pp. 134–35.
73. *IV Moskovskaya oblastnaya i III gorodskaya konferentsii VKP (b)* (1934), p. 226: *Spravochnik partiinogo rabotnika*, vyp. 8 (1934) p. 215–25.
74. *Sbornik.*, pp. 136–38
75. *Sbornik.*, p. 141.
76. *Sbornik.*, p. 511.
77. *Sbornik.*, p. 444.
78. *IV Moskovskaya oblastnaya i III gorodskaya konferentsii VKP (b)* (1934), p. 236.

8 Transport and Energy

1. *SZ*, No. 31 (1932) p. 193.
2. *Sbornik vazhneishikh postanovlenii MK i MGK* (1934), p. 179.
3. *Sbornik.*, pp. 180–82.
4. *Sbornik.*, p. 182.
5. *Sbornik.*, p. 181.
6. *IV Moskovskaya oblastnaya i III gorodskaya konferentsii VKP (b)* (1934), p. 237. See Chapter 3, note 28.
7. *Sbornik.*, p. 185; *Rabochaya Mockva*, 30 October 1933.
8. *Sbornik.*, p. 185; *Rabochaya Mockva*, 30 October 1933.
9. *IV Moskovskaya oblastnaya i III gorodskaya konferentsii VKP (b)* (1934), p. 521.
10. *Sprabochnik partiinogo rabotnika*, vyp. 8 (1934) p. 517.
11. *Ibid.*
12. *Sbornik.*, p. 168.
13. *Sbornik.*, pp. 169–70.
14. *IV Moskovskaya oblastnaya i III gorodskaya konferentsii VKP (b)* (1934), p. 219.
15. *Spravochnik partiinogo.*, vyp. 8 (1934) p. 533.
16. *Vechernyaya Moskva*, 16 September 1933.

17. *Spravochnik partiinogo.*, vyp. 8, p. 534.
18. *IV Moskovskaya oblastnaya i III gorodskaya konferentsii VKP (b)* (1934), pp. 219–20.
19. *Ibid.*, p. 206.
20. *Otchet o rabote* (1934), p. 47.
21. *Sbornik deistvuyushchikh* (1934), p. 13.
22. *IV Moskovskaya oblastnaya i III gorodskaya konferentsii VKP (b)* (1934), p. 207.
23. Ibid, p. 476.
24. Ibid, p. 476.
25. *Sbornik.*, pp. 92–98.
26. *Sbornik.*, p. 95.
27. *Sbornik.*, p. 96.
28. *Sbornik.*, p. 565.
29. *Sbornik.*, p. 97.
30. *Otchet o rabote* (1934), p. 47.
31. Davydova, *Velikii podvig*, 1970.
32. *Rabochaya Moskva*, 14 April 1933. A. J. Cummings, *The Moscow Trial* (London, 1933).
33. *Acta Slavica Iaponica*, tom 1 (1983) p. 52; tom 4 (1986) p. 1–34.
34. *Rabochaya Moskva*, 3 March; 15 March 1933.
35. *SZ*, No. 17 (1933) p. 99.
36. *Vechernyaya Moskva*, 19 April 1933. See also Monkhouse's memoirs, A. Monkhouse, *Moscow 1911–33*, London 1933. He was the head of the Moscow branch of this company.
37. *IV Moskovskaya oblastnaya i III gorodskaya konferentsii VKP (b)* (1934), p. 207.
38. *Vechernyaya Moskva*, 19 April 1933.
39. See also Fo. 371, 17426 (1933) p. 143. According to a Lithuanian minister who had good sources of information, there was a fierce dispute between the OGPU collegium and the Politburo, which was apparently afraid of international repercussions from the affair. The Politburo sought to reduce the influence of OGPU. In fact, it was reorganized into the NKVD in 1934.
40. *Sbornik.*, p. 99.
41. *Rabochaya Moskva*, 5 August 1933.
42. *Otchet o rabote*, 1934, pp. 47–48; Monkhouse, *Moscow 1911–33* (London, 1933), pp. 195, 245, etc.
43. *Postanovlenie 7 plenuma MOK VKP(b): ob'edinennogo plenuma Moskovskogo oblastnogo i gorodskogo komiteta VKP (b)* (1931), p. 11.
44. *Otchet o rabote*, p. 52.
45. *IV Moskovskaya oblastnaya i III gorodskaya konferentsii VKP (b)* (1934), p. 552.
46. *Ibid.*, p. 415.
47. *Ibid.*, p. 265.

48. *Sbornik.*, p. 420.
49. *Ibid.*, p. 415.
50. *Otchet o rabote*, p. 53.
51. *Vechernyaya Moskva*, 9 December 1933.

9 Agricultural Policy

1. R .W .Davies, *The Socialist Offensive* (London, 1980), p. 202; *KPSS v rezoliutsiyakh. .* , t. 4 (1970) p. 384; *Ocherki istorii kollektivizatsii sel'skogo khozyaistva v soiuznikh respublikakh* (1963), pp. 35, 37, 44.
2. Davies, *ibid.*, p. 203.
3. Nobuo Shimotomai, 'Defeat of the Right Opposition in the Moscow Party Organization', *Japanese Slavic and East European Studies*, vol. 4 (1983) p. 33.
4. Kozlova, *ibid.*, p. 275.
5. *Sbornik.*, p. 198.
6. Kozlova, *ibid.*, p. 275; According to one official report, the level of collectivisation by the end of 1932 fell to 50 per cent, *IV Moskovskaya oblastnaya i III gorodskaya konferentsii VKP (b)* (1934), pp. 4, 251.
7. *Sbornik.*, p. 198–99.
8. *Sbornik.*, p. 200.
9. *Sbornik.*, p. 201.
10. *Sbornik.*, p. 201.
11. *Sbornik.*, pp. 201–2.
12. *Sbornik.*, pp. 202–03.
13. *Propagandist*, No. 19–20 (1932) p. 36.
14. *Sbornik.*, pp. 583–84.
15. *Sbornik.*, p. 552.
16. *SZ*, No. 79 (1932) pp. 773–74.
17. *Acta Slavica Iaponica*, t. 1 (1983) p. 39–56.
18. *Sbornik.*, p. 524: Roy Medvedev, *All Stalin's Men* (1983), p. 122.
19. *Rabochaya Moskva*, 24 December 1932.
20. *Rabochaya Moskva*, 17 March 1933.
21. *Sbornik.*, p. 527; *Acta Slavica Iaponica*, t. 4 (1986) p. 1–34.
22. *Rabochaya Moskva*, 4 April 1933; 22 May 1933.
23. *Ocherki istorii Ryazanskoi organizatsii KPSS* (1974), p. 279.
24. *Sbornik.*, p. 569.
25. *Sbornik.*, p. 569.
26. *Sbornik.*, pp. 527–29.
27. *Acta Slavica Iaponica*, t. 4 (1986) p. 20–25; *Pravda*, 28 January 1932; *Materialy o rabote politotdelov MTS za 1933 g.* (1934), p. 104; *IV Moskovskaya oblastnaya i III gorodskaya konferentsii VKP (b)* (1934), p. 260.
28. *Sbornik.*, p. 581.
29. *Sbornik.*, pp. 213–14.

30. *Sbornik.*, p. 214.
31. *Sbornik.*, p. 214.
32. *Sbornik.*, p. 218.
33. *Rabochaya Moskva*, 9 May 1933.
34. *Propagandist*, No. 19–20 (1932) p. 9.
35. *Sbornik.*, p. 223.
36. *Sbornik.*, p. 226.
37. *Sbornik.*, p. 225.
38. *Sbornik.*, p. 226.
39. *IV Moskovskaya oblastnaya i III gorodskaya konferentsii VKP (b)* (1934), p. 253.
40. *Sbornik.*, p. 232.
41. *SZ*, No. 52 (1933), art. 303; *Sbornik.*, pp. 233–36.
42. *Sbornik.*, pp. 228–30.
43. *SZ*, No. 52 (1933) art. 303.
44. *Sbornik.*, p. 236.
45. *Sbornik.*, p. 236.
46. *IV Moskovskaya oblastnaya i III gorodskaya konferentsii VKP (b)* (1934), p. 254.
47. *SZ*, No. 6 (1932) art. 303.
48. *Sbornik.*, p. 226.
49. *Sbornik.*, p. 228.
50. *Sbornik.*, p. 230.
51. *Sbornik.*, pp. 231–32.
52. See my article in *Acta Slavica Iaponica*, t. 4 (1986) pp. 1–34.
53. *Materialy o rabote politotdelov MTS za 1933 g.* (1934), p. 205.
54. See note 32.
55. *Materialy o rabote politotdelov MTS za 1933 g.* (1934), p. 3.
56. Kozlova, *K pobede kolkhoznogo stroya* (1971), p. 281.
57. *Sbornik.*, p. 230.
58. *Materialy o rabote politotdelov v Moskve* (1934), p. 11.
59. *Ibid.*, p. 14.
60. *Ibid.*, p. 17.
61. *Ibid.*, p. 30.
62. *Materialy o rabote politotdelov*, p. 105.
63. *Ibid.*, p. 105.
64. *Ibid.*, p. 106.
65. *Sbornik.*, p. 212.
66. *IV Moskovskaya oblastnaya i III gorodskaya konferentsii VKP (b)* (1934), p. 250.
67. *Sbornik.*, p. 205.
68. *Sbornik.*, p. 205.
69. *Sbornik.*, p. 207.
70. *Sbornik.*, p. 208.
71. *Sbornik.*, p. 212.
72. *Acta Slavica Iaponica*, t. 4 (1986) pp. 18–20.

73. *Sbornik.*, p. 554.
74. *Vazhneishie resheniya po sel'skomu khozyaistvu* (1935), p. 182
75. *Materialy o rabote politotdelov* (1934), pp. 103–06.
76. *Ibid.*, p. 122.

10 Management of the Municipal Economy

1. *Spravochnik partiinogo rabotnika*, vyp. 8 (1934), p. 204.
2. *Spravochnik sovetskogo rabotnika* (1937), p. 45.
3. *KPSS v rezolyutsiyakh.* . , t. 4 (1970) p. 549.
4. *Sbornik vazhneishikh.* . , p. 19. For example, this commission invited the representative of 'Mostramtrest', who gave indices of, for example, increasing tram utilization, introducing new cars, and building a new depot.
5. *Sbornik.*, p. 29.
6. Aleshchenko, *Moskovskii sovet v 1917–41g.* (1976), p. 491.
7. S. Fitzpatrick (ed.), *Cultural Revolution in Russia 1928–32*, (Bloomington, 1978), pp. 207–40.
8. *Stroitel'stvo Moskvy*, No. 7 (1932) p. 8; No. 8–9 (1932) p. 16.
9. M. F. Parkins, *City Planning in Soviet Russia* (London, 1953), p. 31.
10. *Spravochnik partiinogo.* . , p. 204.
11. *Sbornik.* . , p. 272.
12. *Stroitel'stvo Moskvy*, No. 2 (1932) p. 27; *Rabochaya Moskva*, 23 August, 1932.
13. *Sbornik.*, p. 293.
14. *Sbornik.*, p. 273.
15. *Sbornik deistvuyushchikh.* (1934), p. 25; *Izvestiya TsK KPSS*, No. 9 (1989) pp.110–12.
16. *Sbornik.*, p. 276.
17. *IV Moskovskaya oblastnaya i III gorodskaya konferentsii VKP (b)* (1934), p. 561.
18. E. Simon, *Moscow in the Making* (London, 1937), p. 45, pp. 189–97.
19. *Vecherynaya Moskva*, 18 January 1933.
20. *Sbornik.*, p. 296.
21. *Sbornik.* p. 298. Shternberg at that time reported to the MGK bureau every ten days on the progress of the construction. He was to devise a means of economizing water and leakage, the implementation of which was imposed on raion soviet chairmen.
22. *Sbornik.*, p. 299.
23. *Vechernyaya Moskva*, 17 September 1934.
24. *Rabochaya Moskva*, 10 December 1931.
25. *Rabochaya Moskva*, 27 March 1932.
26. *Propagandist*, No. 16 (1934) p. 30.
27. *Propagandist*, No. 7–8 (1933) p. 30; *Kanal imeni Moskvy, 50 let eksupluatatsii*, 1987.
28. *SZ*, No. 44 (1932) p. 263.

29. *Sbornik.*, p. 295.
30. *Sbornik.*, p. 295.
31. The completion of the Moscow-White Sea canal, which was a model for the Volga-Moscow canal, witnessed the release of 500 prisoners and reduced terms for some 60 000 prisoners in August 1933 (*Vechernyaya Moskva*, 5 August 1933).
32. L. Simon, *Moscow in the Making* (London, 1937), pp. 224–25.
33. W. Citrine, *I Search for Truth in Russia* (London, 1936), p. 80.
34. *Vechernyaya Moskva*, 6 June 1934.
35. *Sbornik.*, p. 28.
36. The neglect of housing in Moscow may be illustrated by the production of bricks. Whilst some 900 million bricks production was planned for 1933 in the city as a whole, only 5 per cent was for city housing construction (*Sbornik.*, p. 162–66).
37. *Spravochnik partiinogo rabotnika*, vyp. 8 (1934) p. 201.
38. *IV Moskovskaya oblastnaya i III gorodskaya konferentsii VKP (b)* (1934), p. 280.
39. *Sbornik.*, p. 273.
40. Although Kaganovich was pleased in 1931 by the fact that a worker's family who had lived in the basement now moved to a room of 15 square metres, they had to share this room with two or three families (*IV Moskovskaya oblastnaya i III gorodskaya konferentsii VKP (b)* (1934), p. 182).
41. *Sbornik.*, p. 314.
42. *Sbornik.*, p. 137.
43. *Sbornik.*, p. 317.
44. *Vechernyaya Moskva*, 4 March 1933.
45. *Sbornik.*, p. 318.
46. This body, including the head of the Cooperative Construction Union (Tokmachev) also compiled the list of cooperative construction (*Sbornik.*, p. 319).
47. *Sbornik deistvuyushchikh. .*, p. 64.
48. Kaganovich, *Za Sotsialisticheskuyu rekonstruktsiyu Moskvy i gorodov SSSR*, 1931, pp. 18–19, 98; *Rabochaya Moskva*, 25 March 1931.
49. *Sbornik deistvuyushchikh.*, p. 161.
50. *Spravochnik partiinogo rabotnika*, vyp. 8, p. 743; *Sbornik.*, p. 14.
51. *Sbornik.*, p. 318. This case was revealed when one worker appealed to the authorities. He was unable to move into a flat because it had been already alloted to an 'ex-trader', even though workers had priority.
52. *Spravochnik partiinogo rabotnika*, vyp. 8 (1934) p. 426.
53. *Vechernyaya Moskva*, 9 January 1933.
54. *Vechernyaya Moskva*, 21 March 1933.
55. *Vechernyaya Moskva*, 12 March 1933.
56. *Vechernyaya Moskva*, 1 September 1933.
57. *Sbornik.*, p. 320.

58. *Sbornik.*, p. 323.
59. *Rabochaya Moskva*, 16 October 1933. The published report omits the nomenklatura systen.
60. *Vechernyaya Moskva*, 1 September 1933.
61. *Spravochnik partiinogo rabotnika*, vyp. 8 (1934) p. 202. According to Bulganin, 700 houses out of 10 500 were on the verge of collapse (*Vechernyaya Moskva*, 22 February, 1933).
62. *Sbornik.*, p. 326.
63. *Vechernyaya Moskva*, 26 September 1933.
64. *Rabochaya Moskva*, 23 November 1933; *Sbornik.*, p. 329.
65. *SZ*, No. 23 (1934) p. 180.
66. *IV Moskovskaya oblastnaya i III gorodskaya konferentsii VKP (b)* (1934), p. 552.
67. Simon, *ibid.*, p. 167.
68. Aleshchenko, *ibid.*, p. 485.
69. *Sbornik.*, p. 247.
70. *IV Moskovskaya oblastnaya i III gorodskaya konferentsii VKP (b)* (1934), p. 555.
71. *Vechernyaya Moskva*, 9 August; 8 October 1933.
72. *Sbornik.*, p. 301.
73. *Vechernyaya Moskva*, 2, 15 February 1933.
74. *Ibid.*, 17 August 1933.
75. *Sbornik.*, p. 308; *Vechernyaya Moskva*, 13 December 1933.
76. *Ibid.*, 22 October 1933.
77. *Ibid.*, 13 November 1933.
78. Simon, *ibid.*, p. 18.
79. *Sbornik.*, p. 306.
80. *Sbornik.*, p. 306.
81. Crankshaw (ed.), *Khrushchev Remembers*, 1970, p. 63–4.
82. *IV Moskovskaya oblastnaya i III gorodskaya konferentsii VKP (b)* (1934), p. 554.
83. *Rabochaya Moskva*, 28 June 1933. The Yaroslavskii factory produced buses, whilst, 'Dinamo' and other trusts were ordered to prepare the electric systems.
84. *Rabochaya Moskva*, 10 October 1933.
85. *Rabochaya Moskva*, 23 November 1933.
86. *Sbornik.*, p. 308.
87. Simon, *ibid.*, p. 192.
88. *IV Moskovskaya oblastnaya i III gorodskaya konferentsii VKP (b)* (1934), p. 556.
89. *Sbornik.*, p. 309. *Vechernyaya Moskva* reported that more than ten per cent of horses got ill because of the shortage of fodder and insufficient care (*Vechernyaya Moskva*, 24 February 1933); *Moskva v tsifrakh* (1934), p. 140.
90. *Vechernyaya Moskva*, 16 March 1933.
91. *Sbornik.*, p. 267.

92. *IV Moskovskaya oblastnaya i III gorodskaya konferentsii VKP (b)* (1934), pp. 247, 555; *Vechernyaya Moskva*, 6 February, 1933.
93. *Sbornik.*, p. 267.
94. *Moskva v tsifrakh* (1934), p. 168; *Sbornik.*, p. 29.
95. L. Kaganovich, *Za sotsialisticheskuyu rekonstruktsiyu* (1931), p. 42; *Dni i gody Metrostroya* (1981), p. 29.
96. *Rabochaya Moskva*, 6 June 1931.
97. Kaganovich, *ibid.*, p. 43.
98. *Vechernyaya Moskva*, 7 January 1933.
99. *Vechernyaya Moskva*, 28 January 1933; *SZ*, No. 25 (1933) p. 279.
100. *Sbornik.*, p. 16.
101. *IV Moskovskaya oblastnaya i III gorodskaya konferentsii VKP (b)* (1934), p. 422.
102. *Dni i gody Metrostroya*, p. 74.
103. Kaganovich, *ibid.*, p. 110; *Rabochaya Moskva*, 21 June 1931; *Moskovskii sovet:otchet o rabote*, 34, p. 66.
104. *Vechernyaya Moskva*, 28 January 1933; *SZ*. No. 25 (1933) p. 279.
105. *Dni i gody* (1981), p. 42.
106. *Spravochnik partiinogo..*, vyp. 8, p. 743. This decision is not mentioned in *Ekonomicheskaya zhizn' SSSR: khronika sobytii i faktov*, kn.1, 1967.
107. *Spravochnik partiinogo.*, vyp. 8 (1934) p. 743–44; *Vechernyaya Moskva*, 9 April, 1933.
108. *Sbornik.*, p. 278; R. Medvedev, *All Stalin's Men* (1982), p. 125.
109. *Vechernyaya Moskva*, 16 July 1933.
110. *Vechernyaya Moskva*, 3 December 1933.
111. *Rabochaya Moskva*, 26 January 1934.
112. *Vechernyaya Moskva*, 28 January 1933.
113. *Sbornik.*, 277; *Spravochnik partiinogo*, vyp. 8 (1934) p. 743.
114. *Dni i gody*, p. 41–42.
115. *Vechernyaya Moskva*, 3 December 1933. Stalin allegedly criticized Rotert and Metro stroi on the grounds that economic considerations were not a technical matter but the concern of the government (*Khrushchev Remembers*, 1970, pp. 69–70).
116. *Vechernyaya Moskva*, 16 July 1933.
117. *Ibid.*, 1, 10 September 1933.
118. *Sbornik.*, p. 293.
119. *Vechernyaya Moskva*, 3 December 1933.
120. *Ibid.*, 3 April; 9 May 1934.
121. *Sbornik.*, p. 293; *Vechernyaya Moskva*, 27 January 1933.
122. *Sbornik.*, p. 278.
123. *Vechernyaya Moskva*, 14 July 1933.
124. *SZ*, No. 25 (1933) p. 147.
125. *Sbornik.*, 293.
126. *IV Moskovskaya oblastnaya i III gorodskaya konferentsii VKP (b)* (1934), pp. 279, 422, 561; *Vechernyaya Moskva*, 3 December, 1933.

11 Supply and Shortage

1. *Moskovskaya Oblast, Gos. Arkhiv. Okt. Rev. i Sots Str.* (Hereafter *GAMO*), f. 2287, op. 1, sv. 57, 26.
2. *Propagandist*, No. 1 (1930) p. 7.
3. S. M. Schwarz, *Labor in the Soviet Union* (London, 1953) pp. 152, 162; E. Zaleski, *Planning for Economic Growth in the Soviet Union, 1919–32* (Chapel Hill, 1971), p. 392; *Istoriya SSSR*, No. 3 (1974) p. 126.
4. *Rabochaya Moskva*, 17 March 1932. Some city workers put 'obeda' (food) by eliminating the first 'p' from the slogan 'pobeda' (victory). In Leningrad, some even cut the 'po' to the effect that 'beda' (misfortune) appeared in the May day slogan (Fo. 371, 16330, p. 274).
5. J. Haslam, *Soviet Foreign Policy, 1930–33* (1983).
6. See *Acta Slavica Iaponica*, t. 1, 1983, pp. 39–56.
7. Stalin, *Sochineniya*, t. 13 (1951) p. 51–80.
8. *GAMO* f. 2287, op. 1, sv. 51, p. 3.
9. *Pravda*, 9 February, 1932.
10. *Khrushchev Remembers*, vol. 1, (Harmondsworth: Penguin, 1971), p. 81.
11. See Chapter 7.
12. *Pravda*, 9 February 1932; *SZ*, No. 38 (1932) p. 233.
13. *Sbornik.*, pp. 369, 370, 376–77, 395, 401, 413.
14. *Khrushchev Remembers*, 81. See also, R. O. Urch, *The Rabbit King of Russia* (London, 1939), pp. 186–208.
15. *Spravochnik partiinogo rabotnika*, vyp. 8 (1934) p. 718; *Rabochaya Moskva*, 15 May, 1932.
16. *Sbornik*, pp. 379–85.
17. *Sbornik deistvuyoshchikh* (1934), p. 34.
18. *Rabochaya Moskva*, 24 May 1932; *Sbornik.*, p. 348.
19. *Sbornik.*, p. 386.
20. *SZ*, No. 77 (1932) p. 474.
21. *Vechernyaya Moskva*, 23 January 1933.
22. *Ibid.*, 5 February 1933
23. *Ibid.*, 28 April 1933.
24. *Rabochaya Moskva*, 21 October 1933; *Sbornik.*, p. 387–89.
25. *Pravda*, 17 May 1932.
26. *Pravda*, 23 February 1932. The activity of Mosryb was initiated by the September 1931 decision of MK. MK cadres department was responsible for selecting personnel, whilst one of the oblispolkom was responsible for controlling activity (*Rabochaya Moskva*, 8 September, 1931).
27. *Rabochaya Moskva*, 9 September 1933; *Sbornik.*, p. 390.
28. *Sbornik.*, p. 395.
29. *Sbornik.*, p. 392.
30. *Sbornik.*, p. 395.
31. *Rabochaya Moskva*, 5 July 1933.
32. *Rabochaya Moskva*, 5 July 1933.

33. *Rabochaya Moskva*, 5 July 1933.
34. *Rabochaya Moskva*, 18 May 1932; *Sbornik.*, p. 342.
35. *Sbornik.*, p. 193.
36. *Vechernyaya Moskva*, 31 July 1933.
37. *Rabochaya Moskva*, 5 July 1933; *Sbornik.*, p. 358.
38. *Rabochaya Moskva*, 5 July 1933; *Sbornik.*, p. 368.
39. *Vechernyaya Moskva*, 28 July 1933. In the case of potatoes, some 390 000 tons were to be held at raion level, whilst 160 000 tons were to be shared by all city organizations. In addition, 200 000 tons were to be stored in other industrialized cities of the region. For that purpose warehouses for 130 000 tons were to be secured in the city.
40. *Rabochaya Moskva*, 5 July 1933; *Sbornik.*, p. 364.
41. *Vechernyaya Moskva*, 31 July 1933.
42. *Vechernyaya Moskva*, 7 August 1933.
43. *Vechernyaya Moskva*, 21 September 1933.
44. *Vechernyaya Moskva*, 5 September 1933.
45. *Vechernyaya Moskva*, 19 February 1933.
46. *Vechernyaya Moskva*, 29 February 1933. For a real picture of supply in the 'Krasnyi bogatyr' factory, see *Vechernyaya Moskva*, 24 February, 1933.
47. *Vechernyaya Moskva*, 11 March 1933.
48. See *Rabochaya Moskva*, 17, 26 September; 10, 18 October; 23 November, 1933. Incidentally, the MK and MGK reported its agenda almost every week in 1933.
49. *IV Moskovskaya oblastnaya i III gorodskaya konferentsii VKP (b)* (1934), p. 283.
50. *Vechernyaya Moskva*, 2 November, 16 November 1933.
51. *SZ.*, No. 31 (1932) pp. 190, 193; No. 33 (1932) p. 195; No. 38 (1932) p. 233; and *Spravochnik sovetskogo rabotnika* (1937), p. 382.
52. *Propagandist*, No. 19–20 (1932) p. 14; *Rabochaya Moskva*, 27 July, 1932.
53. *Sbornik.*, p. 373; *Rabochaya Moskva*, 21 July 1932.
54. *Propagandist*, No. 19–20 (1932) p. 14.
55. *Sbornik.*, p. 375.
56. *Propagandist*, No. 19–20 (1932) p. 14; *SZ*, No. 62 (1932) p. 583–84; *Rabochaya Moskva*, 4 August 1932. It is strange that Kaganovich's report was not published until a month later.
57. *SZ.*, No. 65 (1932) p. 375.
58. *Rabochaya Moskva*, 5 July 1932; *Sbornik.*, p. 350.
59. *Vazhneishie resheniya* (1934), p. 54.
60. *Rabochaya Moskva*, 12 November 1932; 16 February 1933. On the destruction of the Sukharev Tower, see *Izvestiya TsK KPSS*, No. 9 (1989) pp. 109–16.
61. *Vechernyaya Moskva*, 3 January 1933.
62. *Sbornik deistvuyushchikh.*, p. 267.
63. *Vechernyaya Moskva*, 3 August 1933.
64. *GAMO*, f. 2287, ot. 1, op. 1, sv. 51, st. 53.

65. *Vechernyaya Moskva*, 3 December 1933; *Spravochnik partiinogo...*, vyp. 8 (1934) p. 645.
66. *SZ*, No. 80 (1932) p. 489.
67. Fo. 371, 17426, file 11, from W. Strang to Sir John Simon.
68. *Moskva v tsifrakh* (1934), p. 200.
69. *GAMO*, f. 2287, op. 1, sv. 51.
70. *Sbornik.*, p. 370.
71. *Vechernyaya Moskva*, 1 August 1932.
72. *Vechernyaya Moskva*, 9 January, 12 January, 7 February, 27 February, 16 May, 1933.
73. Fo. 371, 17251, p. 11 (Litvinov).
74. *Sbornik.*, p. 402.
75. *Sbornik.*, p. 405.
76. *Sbornik.*, p. 403.
77. *Vechernyaya Moskva*, 18 January 1933.
78. *Vechernyaya Moskva*, 23 February 1933.
79. *Spravochnik partiinogo rabotnika*, vyp. 8 (1934) p. 734–37.
80. *SZ*, No. 58 (1931) p. 375.
81. *Obshchestvennoe pitanie v SSSR* (1934), pp. 13, 88.
82. *Moskva v tsifrakh* (1934), p. 206.
83. *Sbornik.*, p. 396.
84. *Sbornik.*, p. 398.
85. *Vechernyaya Moskva*, 17, 19 July 1933.
86. *Sbornik.*, p. 398.

12 Conclusions

1. M. Lewin, *The Making of the Soviet System* (1985), p. 218.
2. M. Fainsod, *Smolensk under Soviet Rule* (1958), p. 93.
3. *Ibid*.
4. *Sbornik.*, 1934, p. 220. Agriculture was also an area where the leadership exercised strong ideological control over soviet institutions. In March 1931, the MK secretariat attacked the 'Right deviationists'of MOZO, the Agricultural department of the soviet (*Rabochaya Moskva*, 4 March, 1931.).
5. *Sbornik.*, p. 47.
6. *Izvestiya TsK KPSS*, No. 9 (1989) pp. 109-16.

Bibliography

1. Periodicals

Byulleten' Moskovskogo obkoma VKP(b)
Pravda
Izvestiya
Sbornik postanovlenii i prikazov po promyshlennosti
Sovetskoe stroitel'stvo
Rabochaya Moskva
Vechernyaya Moskva
Partiinoe stroitel'stvo
Propagandist (organ of the MK culture and propagandist department)
Sotsialisticheskii vestnik
Stroitel'stvo Moskvy
Za industrializatsiyu
Acta Slavica Iaponica (Sapporo, Japan)
Japanese Slavic and East European Studies (Kyoto, Japan)

2. Archives

Moskovskaya Oblast, Gos. Arkhiv. Okt. Rev. i Sots. Str. (GAMO), f. 2287, op. 1, sv. 57
British Record Office, Fo 371, 16322 and others.

3. Books in Russian

Place of publication is Moscow or Moscow-Leningrad, unless otherwise stated.

Administrativno-territorial'noe delenie soiuza SSR (1931).
Atlas Moskovskoi oblasti (1934).
N. M. Aleshchenko, *Moskovskii sovet v 1917–41 gg.* (1976).
Bol'shaya Sovetskaya Entsiklopediya, 1–izd., 1926–47.
IV Moskovskaya oblastnaya i III gorodskaya konferentsii VKP (b) (1934).
H. Davydova, A. Ponomarev, *Velikii podvig* (1970).
Dni i gody Metrostroya (1981).
Ekonomiko-statisticheskii spravochnik po raionam Moskovskoi oblasti (1934).
A. N. Gasilovskii, *Moskva* (1932).
Industrializatsiya SSSR 1929–32 gg. (1970).
Istoricheskie zapiski, No. 92 (1973).
Istoriya rabochikh Moskvy 1917–45 gg. (1983).
L. M. Kaganovich, *Za sotsialisticheskuyu rekonstruktsiyu Moskvy i gorodov*

Bibliography

SSSR (1931).
L. M. Kaganovich, *O vnutripartiinoi rabote i otdelakh rukovodyashchikh partiinikh organov* (1934).
Kanal imeni Moskvy. 50 let ekspluatatsii (1987).
Kolkhoznaya torgovlya (1934).
Kollektivizatsiya sel'skogokhozyaistva Tsentral'no go promyshlennogo raiona 1927-37 (Ryazan, 1971).
L. Kozlova, *K pobede kolkhoznogo stroya* (1971).
KPSS v rezolutsiyakh i resheniyakh s'ezdov, konferentsii i plenumov TsK VKP(b), t. 1-13 (1970-).
V. I. Kuz'min, *V bor'be za sotsialisticheskuyu rekonstruktsiyu 1926-37* (1976).
I. Yu. Trifonov, *Likvidatsiya ekspluatatorskikh klassov SSSR* (1975).
Materialy k otchetu Stalinskogo raikoma i RKK VKP(b) (1934).
Materialy k otchetu VTsSPS 9 s'ezdov profsoiuzov (1932).
Materialy Moskovskogo oblastnogo soveshchaniya planovykh rabotnikov 25-28 iyulya (1931).
Materialy o rabote politotdelov (1934).
Materialy o rabote politotdelov v Moskve (1934).
Moskva v tsifrakh (1934).
Moskovskaya gorodskaya i Moskovskaya oblastnaya organizatsiya KPSS v tsifrakh (1972).
Moskovskii sovet, otchet o rabote 1931-34 (1934).
Obshchestvennoe pitanie v SSSR (1934).
Ocherki istorii Kalininskoi organizatsii KPSS (1971).
Ocherki istorii kollektivizatsii sel'skogo khozyaistva vsesoiuznikh respublikakh (1963).
Ocherki istorii Moskovskoi organizatsii, kn. 2 (1983).
Ocherki istorii Ryazanskoi organizatsii KPSS (1974).
Ot pobedy k pobede, materialy k otchetu PK VKP(b) 13 part. konferentsiya Frunzenskogo raiona (1934).
Ot Khamovnikov k Frunzenskomu raionu 1917-32 (1932).
V. K. Palishko, *Rost i ukreplenie partiinikh ryadov v usloviyakh stroitel'stva i upravleniya sotsializma* (1979).
Postanovlenie 7 plenuma MOK VKP(b) (1931).
Rabochii klass v upravlenii gosudarstvom 1926-37 (1968).
Sbornik vazhneishikh postanovlenii MK i MGK (b) (1934).
Sbornik deistvuyushchikh vazhneishikh postanovlenii prezidiuma Moskovskogo soveta RK i KD za isklyucheniem obyazatel'nikh postanovlenii 1923-34 gg. (1934).
XVII konferentsiya VKP (b), stenograficheskii otchet (1932).
XVII s'ezd VKP (b), stenograficheskii otchet (1934).
Spravochnik partiinogo rabotnika, vyp. 7-9 (1929-35).
Spravochnik sovetskogo rabotnika (1937).
I. V. Stalin, *Sochineniya*, t. 13 (1951).
Vazhneishie resheniya po sel'skomu khozyaistvu (1935).

Vo glave kul'turnogo stroitel'stva (1983).
Vsya Moskva (1936).
A. Yakovlev, T *sel' zhizni* (1967).
A. Zimin, *Sotsializm i neostalinizm* (New York, 1981).

4. Books in English

J. Barber, *Soviet Historians in Crisis 1928–32* (London, 1981).
W. Chamberlin, *Russia's Iron Age* (London, 1935).
W. J. Chase, *Workers, Society, and the Soviet State* (Urbana and Chicago, 1987).
A. Ciliga, *The Russian Enigma* (London, 1940).
W. Citrine, *I Search for Truth in Russia* (London, 1936).
S. Cohen, *Bukharin and the Bolshevik Revolution* (London, 1973).
T. Colton, 'Moscow: Urban Politics and Policy under Stalin', *Occasional paper of the Kennan Institute* (Washington, 1982).
E. Crankshaw (ed.), *Khrushchev Remembers*, vol. 1–2 (London, 1971).
A. J. Cummings, *The Moscow Trial* (London, 1933).
R. W. Davies, *The Socialist Offensive: the Collectivisation of Soviet Agriculture* (London, 1980).
M. Fainsod, *Smolensk under Soviet Rule* (London, 1958).
S. Fitzpatrick (ed.), *Cultural Revolution in Russia 1928–32* (Bloomington, 1978).
S. Fitzpatrick, *Education and Social Mobility in the Soviet Union 1921–34 (Cambridge, 1979).*
A. Getty, *Origins of the Great Purges* (Cambridge, 1985).
J. Haslam, *Soviet Foreign Policy, 1930–33* (London, 1983).
P. Kneen, 'Higher Education and Cultural Revolution in the USSR', *CREES* (Univ. of Birmingham) unpublished SIPS *Discussion Papers*, No. 5, 1976.
D. Koenker, *Moscow Workers and the 1917 Revolution* (Princeton, 1981).
H. Kuromiya, *Stalin's Industrial Revolution* (Cambridge, 1988).
M. Lewin, *The Making of the Soviet System* (London, 1985).
R. Medvedev, *All Stalin's Men* (Oxford, 1982).
A. Monkhouse, *Moscow 1911–33* (London, 1933).
M. F. Parkins, *City Planning in Soviet Russia* (London, 1953).
E. A. Rees, *State Control in Soviet Russia* (London, 1987).
T. H. Rigby, *Communist Party Membership in the USSR* (Princeton, 1968).
R. Sakwa, *Soviet Communists in Power*, (London, 1988).
E. Simon, *Moscow in the Making* (London, 1937).
A. Smith, *I was a Soviet Worker* (London, n.d.).
D. Thorniley, *The Rise and Fall of the Soviet Rural Communist Party, 1927–39* (London, 1988).

Name Index

Abakumov, E. T.   122, 123
Agranov, Y. S.   28, 150n   158n
Andreasyan, N. V.   30
Andreev, A. A.   73

Babshikin   51
Badaev, A. E.   2
Bauman, K. Y.   x, 4, 9, 27, 78
Bodrov, A. M.   74
Bubnov, A. S.   69
Bukharin, N. I.   2, 27, 78
Bukharin   30
Bulganin, N. A.   29, 32, 35, 36, 53, 55, 56, 57, 62, 63, 73, 90, 108, 109, 110, 111, 112, 113, 117, 119, 120, 127, 130, 141, 151n   155n
  and Kaganovich   73, 155n
  and Khrushchev   62, 63, 108, 109, 110, 119, 120, 155n
Brezanovsky   57

Davidson, R. E.   32, 62, 126, 127, 129, 131, 136, 144, 151n
Denisov   118, 120
Donenko, N. E.   31, 76, 88, 122, 150n
Dubyna, T.   42, 47, 91
Drizul, A. Y.   16, 39, 66, 123, 126
Drozhzhin, I. V.   28

Egorov, N. V.   31, 47, 83, 151n
Eisenstein, S. M.   110

Filatov, N. A.   16, 22, 47, 62, 63, 108, 111, 117, 151n
Filippov, V. R.   65, 115
Firin, S. G.   112

Gaidul', I. P.   30
Gei, K. V, 31, 47, 79, 88, 93, 148n, 151n
Gende-Rote   118, 120, 121
Guberman, S. E.   34, 56, 57, 94, 109

Gubkin, I. M.   122

Ignatov, E. N.   2
Il'in, I. L.   3, 7
Iofan, B. M.   109, 110
Ivanov, V. F.   79

Kamenev, L. B.   2, 19, 27
Kaganovich, L. M.   x, 5, 11, 16, 17, 27, 28, 29, 30, 31, 33, 35, 37, 42, 43, 44, 48, 56, 73, 74, 75, 76, 78, 79, 81, 82, 87, 90, 93, 96, 98, 100, 105, 107, 110, 118, 119, 120, 121, 122, 123, 124, 125, 132, 141, 144, 149n, 155n, 166n, 170n
  and agriculture   28, 43, 44, 93, 96–105
  and intellectuals   121, 123
  and Kuban   16, 98
  and appointment as Moscow leader   27
  and Politotdel   35, 37, 43, 44, 103, 107, 141
  as Secretary   29, 42, 107
Kaganovich, M. Yu, 75
Kalygina, A. S.   32, 137, 151n
Kaminsky, G. N. , 32, 33, 35, 55 56, 77, 79, 87, 92, 93, 94 100, 109, 110, 132, 150n, 155n
Karavaev, P. N. , 16
Karpov, D. A.   47, 51, 154n
Khoroshilkin, Y. M.   58, 131
Khrushchev, N. I.   20, 31, 35, 47, 49, 56, 62, 63, 108, 110, 113, 119, 120, 122, 123, 126, 127, 140, 144, 146n, 150n, 155n
  and Kaganovich   31
  and Stalin   140
Khvesin, T. S.   57, 109, 110, 113
Kirov, S. M.   16
Kirillov   53
Knorin, V. G.   16, 17, 20, 29

175

Name Index

Kogan, E. S. 32, 150n
Kogan, L. I. 111, 112
Kolchinskii 102
Konstantinopol'skii 114, 117
Korotkov, M. A. 79
Korytnyi, S. Z. 47
Koshelev 96
Kovalev, A. V. 99, 102
Krzhzhanovskii, G. M. 123
Kuchimin, 1 F. 57, 76, 89, 91, 94
Kuibyshev, M. V. V. 88
Kulikov, H. M. 32

Ladovskii 109
Leikand, A. I. 42
Le Corbuisier 109
Lenin, V. I. 2, 65
Liubimov, I. E. 82

Makar, A. G. 42
Makovskii, Y. L. 123
Malenkov, G. H. 25, 37, 40, 42, 87, 88, 91, 128, 144, 150n
Manfred, S. A. 76, 79, 103
Margolin, N. V. 35, 51, 151n
Meierkhol'd, V. E. 110
Mekhlis, L. Z. 26
Mikhailov, M. E. 25, 31, 34, 47, 67, 73, 79, 93, 94, 102, 103, 104, 150n, 151n
Mikoyan, A. I. 102, 112
Mitin, M. B. 29
Molotov, V. M. 3

Nikolaev 100
Nogin, V. P. 2

Obravtsov, V. N. 121
Ordzhonikidze, G. K. 73, 91
Oshinskii, N. 2

Pen'kov, H. A. 47
Perchik, I. M. 53
Peters, Ya. Kh. 16, 17, 48, 67, 93, 94
Popov, G. Kh. 160n
Popov, N. N. 26
Polonsky, V. I. 89

Postyshev, P. P. 24, 47

Redens, S. F. 29, 102
Romanov 157n
Rotert, P. P. 122, 123, 168n
Ruben, R. G. 32, 47, 51, 109, 112
Rudzutak, Y. E. 16, 20, 92, 126
Rykov, A. I. 2, 19, 27
Ryndin, K. V. 29, 31, 34, 47, 56, 67, 73, 77, 79, 85, 88, 89, 90, 91, 92, 93, 94, 126, 128, 151n
and Ural 29, 31
Ryutin, M. N. 3, 19, 27, 47, 149n
and Stalin 19

Sedel'nikov, I. E. 76, 151n
Shamberg 87
Shchuko, V. A. 110
Shternberg, P. K. 57, 165n
Smirnov, A. P. 19, 28
Smirnov 65, 66
Soifer, Y. G. 30
Sol'ts, A. A. 16, 17
Soms, K. P. 19
Stalin, I. V. 2, 3, 4, 19, 26, 27, 29, 96, 110, 111, 122, 135, 142, 168n
Starostin, K. F. 123
Stasova, E. D. 16
Statsevich, G. M. 39, 42, 103
Syrtsov, S. I. 27

Ter 56
Temosyan, I. F. 77
Tosky, M. P. 19
Trainin 127
Trofimov, D. P. 30

Uglanov, N. A. 3, 19, 27, 149n
and Moscow 3, 19, 27, 72, 78
Veklichev, G. I. 28
Voropaev, F. G. 62, 93, 122
Voroshilov, K. E. 87
Voroshilov, T. R. 87
Vyshinsky, A. Y. 92

Zholtovskii, I. V. 35, 143
Zinoviev, G. E. 2, 19, 27

Subject Index

Apparatchik 3, 36, 51, 63, 99, 103, 142
Architecture and planning administration, APU 110 *see also* Arplan
Arplan 35, 109, 110
Automatic rocker 120

Cathedral of Our Saviour ix
 destruction 4
Candidate schools 26
Chapel of the Iberian Virgin 4
Collectivisation 4, 11, 96, 140, 143
 tempo 10, 96; *see also* Kolkhoz
Comintern 2, 24
Communist Academy 24
Communist Party
 X congress 2
 XIV congress 2
 XVI congress 30
 XVII congress 20, 29, 30, 36, 37, 42, 107
 Central Committee 2, 12, 23, 56, 58, 75, 82, 99, 101, 106, 115, 122 123 127, 128, 136, 138, 144
 plenum 106
 June plenum (1931) on Moscow 11, 12, 55, 75, 83, 93, 103, 108, 109, 111, 113, 117, 119, 121, 122
 and Control Commission 103
 and MK, 23
 and Sovnarkom 66, 131, 136
 Orgburo 23
 Politburo 14, 16, 73, 111, 120, 123
 Central Control Commission 16, 19, 21, 22, 23, 32, 126
Control figure of Moscow 61
Correspondence (*opros*) methods 36, 51, 51

Decree on the protection of socialist property 18, 64, 132, 138
 and housing 116
 and rabbit 127
Deep-cut 123; *see also* Open-cut
Democratic centralist 2

Famine 16, 30, 89
 South of USSR 16, 125
Firewood 93, 94, 95
First list 125
Five Year Plan 11, 88, 108, 112, 118
Functional principle, or system 37, 38, 42, 141
 textile industry 81

Genplan 110, 120
Gigantomaniya 11
Gruppartorg 52, 77

Institute for Red Professors 26, 40
Ivanovo-Voznesensk strike 78, 79, 126
 of 1925 160n

Kolkhoz 96, 97, 98, 99, 100, 105, 125, 152n
Kolkhoz market 98, 126, 131, 132, 133, 134, 135, 136, 137
 Sukharevka market 133
Kolkhoz trade 132, 133
Komispol 71, 130
Komvuz 24, 25, 69
Kulak 2, 3, 17, 67, 96, 97, 102, 107, 140
 liquidation of 3, 104,
 and anti-Soviet 105, 106, 135, 139
Kulak sabotage, or saboteurs 16, 28, 97, 98, 105, 126
Kustal' 5, 7, 101

Lenin enrolment 15
Livestock 101

Mikoyan shop 10, 136

Subject Index

Metro ix, 11, 61, 64, 121, 122, 123, 124
  and experts 122, 123
Metrostroi 122, 123, 130
Metro-Vickers 17, 74, 92, 93, 142 158n
Moscow party committee, MK 12, 15, 28, 37, 74
Moscow city party committee, MGK 14, 28, 29, 30, 31, 32, 33, 34, 35, 36, 37, 43, 74
Moscow committee and Moscow city committee departments
  Cadres 17, 20, 37, 39, 40 66 101
  Culture-propaganda 37, 40
  Mass-agitation 37, 40, 41
  Organisation-Instructors, *orginstr* 18, 37, 38, 41, 48, 51, 52, 89, 99
Moscow-Donbass railway 31, 33, 152n, 166n
Moscow-Volga Canal 11, 31, 61
Moscow-White Sea Canal 111
Moskanalstroi 112
Municipal economy 108

NEP 2, 3, 9, 37, 69, 144
Nepman 9, 10, 140
  Bauman on 9
New opposition 2
Nomenklatura 41, 47, 49, 106, 141, 142, 166n
  MK 41, 47
  MGK 41, 60, 136

OGPU 36, 65, 66, 92, 100, 102, 111, 112, 132, 162n
Okrug 45
ORS, Workers supply department 136, 137, 138
Open-cut 123

Passport, internal 8, 64, 66
Passport system 48
People's Commissariat
  Communications 86, 87, 88, 89
  Education 70, 71
  Foreign Affairs 92
  Heavy industry 56, 73, 75, 76, 77, 78, 92, 112

Labour 85, 86, 112
Light Industry 72, 78-85
  for supply 83, 112
  Water transport 111
Pig 102, 103
Plenipotentiary 33, 58, 59, 76, 78, 79, 83, 88, 91, 94, 102, 127, 131
  Mossoviet 58
  Party 59
  People's Commissariat of Heavy Industy 76, 91, 94, 103
  People's Commissariat of Light Industy 78, 79, 83
  Rabbit 127
Podmaster'e 35, 81
Politotdel 17, 39, 43, 104, 105, 106, 110, 141, 148n
  of railways 31, 87
  and Kaganovich 37, 43, 44, 103, 107, 141
Proletarskaya Revolutsiya 26, 52
Promakademiya 31, 151n
Public catering 138
Purge (*chiska*) 13, 16, 17, 18, 19, 20
  Control Commission 21
Pyaterka, five-man sub-committee 56, 57, 141

Rabbit 59, 127
  Institute of 127
Rabkrin 58, 60
Rabochaya Moskva 17, 40, 78
Railway 88
  Mocow-Donbass 36, 86
Rightist 2, 3, 19, 27, 47, 171n
Ryutin affair 3, 19, 27, 47
RZhSKT, 115

Sectionery 59, 120
Shefstvo 41, 73, 87, 99
Shortage 125
Show trial 89, 150n
Siemens-Bau 121
Smolensk 141
  model 32, 33
Sovnarkom 2, 17, 64, 66, 71, 131
Sovpartshkoly 26
Sub-moscow coal mining areas 5, 25, 31, 90, 109 114

Sukharev tower ix, 11, 133, 143, 170n
Supply 125

Technocrat 143
Textile 1, 9, 80, 81, 82, 83, 84, 85, 139, 144
  workers 2, 31, 81, 83, 84, 85

Trade union 2, 32, 76, 138, 139
Tram 119
Trolley bus 120
Trotskyist 19

Urbanism 109, 144